Wisdom for Life

Wisdom for Life

52 Old Testament Meditations

Michael P. V. Barrett

Reformation Heritage Books
Grand Rapids, Michigan

Wisdom for Life
© 2021 by Michael P. V. Barrett

Reformation Heritage Books
3070 29th St. SE
Grand Rapids, MI 49512
616-977-0889
orders@heritagebooks.org
www.heritagebooks.org

Printed in the United States of America
21 22 23 24 25 26/10 9 8 7 6 5 4 3 2 1

Library of Congress Cataloging-in-Publication Data

Names: Barrett, Michael P. V., 1949- author.
Title: Wisdom for life : 52 Old Testament meditations / Michael P. V. Barrett.
Description: Grand Rapids, Michigan : Reformation Heritage Books, [2021]
Identifiers: LCCN 2021038791 (print) | LCCN 2021038792 (ebook) | ISBN 9781601789006 (paperback) | ISBN 9781601789013 (epub)
Subjects: LCSH: Bible. Old Testament—Meditations.
Classification: LCC BS1151.55 .B37 2021 (print) | LCC BS1151.55 (ebook) | DDC 221.071—dc23
LC record available at https://lccn.loc.gov/2021038791
LC ebook record available at https://lccn.loc.gov/2021038792

For additional Reformed literature, request a free book list from Reformation Heritage Books at the above regular or email address.

Contents

Out of the Curse Comes Grace

GENESIS 3:15

Genesis 3:15 is often called the protevangelium, or the first gospel. The Lord said, "I will put enmity between thee and the woman, and between thy seed and her seed; it shall bruise thy head, and thou shalt bruise his heel." This verse certainly highlights the beauty of grace: as soon as man needed it, God announced the gospel. But this grace goes far beyond just answering man's need. Although salvation is certainly good for man, it is ultimately more about God's glory than man's good. The strategic placement of this first gospel message in the threefold-curse pronouncement highlights this truth. Rather than being directed to man, this first declaration of the gospel is part of the curse against the serpent, Satan himself. Man would certainly benefit, but God's glory was the issue. The serpent's defeat and man's salvation were the means of declaring that glory. This short verse suggests three thoughts about the gospel.

God's Idea

The text emphasizes the Lord's sovereign, nonnegotiable resolve in declaring His purpose and means of reversing the curse: "I will put." The almighty God demonstrated His power and resolve to destroy a being who was His inferior but nevertheless His archenemy. Satan stood no chance against God; the devil's doom was sealed from the beginning. God also demonstrated His sovereign grace by promising a Savior for cursed people who deserved wrath and condemnation.

His justice sentenced the race to death; His wondrous grace devised the means whereby the banished might not be expelled (see 2 Sam. 14:14). Even this first general promise of salvation warrants Micah's question of praise and wonder: "Who is a God like unto thee, that pardoneth iniquity?" (Mic. 7:18).

God's Plan

This text declares not only what God's grace will do in reversing the curse but also how God will accomplish it. The first thing the Lord would do was change the relationship between the woman and the serpent. The woman had agreed with Satan against God; now grace would reconcile her to God. In Genesis 3, the woman is specifically Eve. Therefore, the statement testifies to God's grace in saving the very one who had led her husband to disobey the terms of the covenant. This enmity was not an aversion to snakes; it was an awakened conscience that recognized the lie of the serpent and attracted the heart back to God.

The second thing the Lord would do was enlarge the scope of that enmity between the seed of the serpent and the Seed of the woman. Grasping this requires understanding the significance of the word "seed" and identifying the referents to the two seeds.

This gets a little complicated, but thinking it through proves rewarding. Part of the problem is that although the word for "seed" is singular, it can have a collective as well as a purely singular sense. In any given context we have to determine whether the writer has in mind a singular or plural idea. I suggest that Genesis 3:15 includes both a collective sense in regard to the serpent's seed and a singular sense in regard to the woman's Seed. The seed of the serpent would refer to all those who, untouched by grace, retain Eve's preconversion hostility to God and affinity to Satan. It refers to all sinners, who in their natural state are the enemies of God. Obviously they are related to Satan spiritually and not physically. This is an association made in the New Testament. The Lord Jesus said that the Jews were unable to understand Him and refused to believe Him because they were of their father the devil (John 8:44). Similarly, the apostle John declares that those who are given over to the practice of sin are "of the devil; for the devil sinneth from the beginning" (1 John 3:8). The serpent's offspring are the race of unconverted sinners.

The woman's Seed, however, is a singular identity and brings us to the One who is the real enemy of Satan and the only Savior of sinners. The woman's Seed is the promised Christ. That He is identified as the woman's Seed hints of the miraculous virgin birth and most certainly declares that the Savior will be part of the human race. As a real man, He will reverse the curse of sin. There can be little doubt that Paul had this text in mind when he declared that in the fullness of time God sent His Son, "made of a woman" (Gal. 4:4). This first promise of a Savior makes it clear that the Savior must be a man. That Christ came to destroy the works of the devil expresses the open hostility between Him and Satan (see 1 John 3:8). Indeed, Hebrews 2:14 says that Christ became flesh so that He could "through death…destroy him that had the power of death, that is, the devil."

God's Intent

The final statement of Genesis 3:15 reveals God's purpose by predicting the outcome of the hostility: "It shall bruise thy head, and thou shalt bruise his heel." The victory of the woman's Seed over the serpent is absolutely guaranteed. The outcome is that the head of the serpent will be bruised. The word "bruise" literally carries the idea of crushing. *Crushing the head is fatal.* So the Lord Jesus effectively defeated and destroyed the devil. The New Testament identifies this fatal crushing with Christ's work on the cross, with the operation of the church, and with the end times. The Lord Jesus links the casting out of the prince of the world and His being lifted up from the earth (a reference to the cross) in the same context (John 12:31–32). Paul alludes to this verse when he assures the Roman church that "the God of peace shall bruise Satan under your feet shortly" (Rom. 16:20). The final outcome is at the end of time when Satan is bound and ultimately cast into the lake of fire forever (Rev. 20:3, 10).

That the serpent will bruise the heel of the woman's Seed suggests the ineffectiveness of the serpent to frustrate or alter the mission of Christ. *Crushing the heel is futile.* Some interpreters see this as referring to the cross, but I am not so inclined. Genesis 3:15 points to the cross, but not in this part of the verse. It is far better to see the cross in the declaration that the serpent's head will be crushed. Even if the heel crushing does predict the cross, Satan's objective in the death of Christ was hampered and overruled. Ironically, what he intended for his ultimate victory became his ultimate defeat. The cross was not Satan's blow against Christ; it was Christ's ultimate death blow against Satan. Paul said in no uncertain terms that the cross of Christ was the means of disarming and humiliating all powers and authorities, including Satan, and publicly triumphing over them (Col. 2:15). The cross of Christ was not God's making the best of a situation generated by the devil; it was the climax of His eternal plan to redeem fallen and needy sinners.

It may be that the word "crush" in this statement actually derives from another root, a homonym meaning "to snap at." A *homonym* is a word that sounds identical to another but is a completely different word (e.g., there/their). If this is the root, it intensifies the total futility of all Satan's annoying efforts to prevent the inevitable from occurring. If crushing a heel is futile, snapping at the heels is even more so. The evidence of the New Testament is that Satan tried everything he could to kill Christ before He could make the eternally planned atonement. From moving Herod to kill the children in hopes of murdering Jesus, to attempting to discredit Christ during the temptation, to attempting to have the crowds stone Him, to fiercely attacking Him in the garden of Gethsemane on the eve of His crucifixion, Satan was constantly nipping and snapping at Christ's heels. But he could not frustrate God's plan to reverse the curse of sin by the Seed of the woman.

This first gospel message does not reveal all the details about Christ that we know. But it does guarantee the Savior and sets the groundwork for more revealing truths. Every other revelation about Christ fits nicely within the sphere of this first promise. Eve did not know how it would all work out, but her faith in and anticipation of God's promise were so intense that she thought for a slight moment that the birth of her first son, Cain, was the promised Seed. Genesis 4:1 contains some translation difficulties, but it could fairly be rendered, "I have acquired a man, even Jehovah." It was a brief case of mistaken identity, but it suggests that saved Eve was looking for the right one. We want to follow her example in this.

2

Lessons in Saving Faith from Abraham

GENESIS 12–25

"Father knows best." Recognition of the truth of that statement increases with age. Had I always taken the counsel of my father, I would have avoided many of the mistakes that I made. God has given us fathers for us to honor and to obey and from whom we are to learn.

Abraham served many roles in his long life. He was the friend of God; he was faithful Abraham; he was Father Abraham. God, indeed, had chosen him particularly for this purpose. The Lord said that He chose Abraham in order that he would "command his children and his household" that they would "keep the way of the LORD" (Gen. 18:19). He was father to Ishmael and to Isaac, but the New Testament specifically marks him as the father of the faithful—to all those who believe the gospel. Every believer is indeed the seed of Abraham (Rom. 4:11–13; Gal. 3:29). The lessons and the example that Abraham taught and set before Ishmael and Isaac are as relevant for us as they were for them. So as obedient children, we should take our place at the feet of Father Abraham and learn some lessons, particularly about faith.

Father Abraham was faithful Abraham, and he establishes a pattern of faith to follow. He serves as the exemplary recipient of the God-given righteousness that comes by faith. His whole life demonstrates a commitment not to material values—for he was a stranger and a pilgrim—but to the spiritual side of life, for he desired that better, heavenly city (Heb. 11:8–10). He teaches us that faith is necessary both for salvation and for life: "The just shall live by faith." Abraham was not a man of faith because of personal worth or merit; he was what he was by grace. The same is true for all who are his seed. A survey of Father Abraham's inspired biography highlights important lessons about faith.

The first lesson concerns saving faith. Faith marks the beginning of spiritual life. Along with repentance, its counterpart, faith, is the consequence of regeneration, that gracious divine act that imparts life to dead sinners enabling them to believe. When Abraham first heard and responded to God's gracious call, he was living in Ur as much a sinner and idolater as the rest of the population (Josh. 24:2). His faith did not merit favor with God; on the contrary, God's gracious choice of Abraham set him on the whole course of faith. Faith is not the cause of God's saving grace but the evidence of it and the instrument by which it is received.

Although Genesis does not record Abraham's conversion experience, it does declare the fact of his justifying faith in a statement that becomes a proof text for justification by faith alone in New Testament theology (Rom. 4:3). Genesis 15:6 is the key text: "And he believed in the LORD; and he counted it to him for righteousness." Here is a more literal translation that will help put some things in focus: "And he was believing in the LORD, and He regarded it to him—that is, righteousness." The key exegetical question here is to what "it" refers. Resisting every temptation to address the technicalities of Hebrew grammar, I will say simply that the "it" refers to righteousness and not the fact of believing. The word "righteousness" is isolated grammatically from the main clause as a means of special focus. The point is that it is by faith, not because of it, that God regards or imputes righteousness to Abraham. Although faith is the right thing to do, it is not itself the righteousness. Theologically, in justification God imputes the righteousness of Christ, which is received by faith alone. The grammar of this verse expresses the doctrine precisely and highlights three important lessons about saving faith.

Faith Is Objective

Faith is not dreaming or wishing that somehow all will be well. The value of faith is not in its exercise but in its object. Biblical and saving faith is objective. Saving faith saves because of what is believed, not the act of believing. The object of faith determines the value of faith.

This classic text draws attention clearly to the object of Abraham's faith. It was personal and propositional. The personal component is expressly stated: He believed in the Lord. The King James Version's rendering of this name in upper case letters identifies it clearly as the personal name of God. He is Jehovah or Yahweh. This name communicates God's aseity, His eternity, and His absolute sovereignty. But perhaps most significant is the association this name has with the covenant promise; He is the God of grace. He is the Savior of His people. Jeremiah's contrast between the cursed man and the blessed man makes it unequivocally clear that it is the object of faith and not just the exercise of faith that saves. The same word for "trust" characterizes both. He who puts his trust and confidence in the Lord and rejects trust and confidence in self or others is blessed (see Jer. 17:5–8). The object makes all the difference. So Father Abraham teaches his children that Jehovah is the only Savior. Or as Paul said, "Whosoever believeth on him shall not be ashamed" (Rom. 10:11).

Abraham's faith is also propositional; it stands on the promise. Faith is not make-believe; it rests confidently on God's word: "So then faith cometh by hearing, and hearing by the word of God" (Rom. 10:17). What Abraham knew and believed about God was a matter of revelation. The verses immediately preceding this great faith text focus on the promised Seed. The Old Testament's "Seed theology" is richly complex but ultimately Christocentric. Every believer is Abraham's seed; yet at the heart of God's promise to Abraham was the coming of one Seed who would be the source of universal blessing (Gen. 12:3). Paul put it this way: "Now to Abraham and his seed were the promises made. He saith not, And to seeds, as of many; but as of one, And to thy seed, which is Christ" (Gal. 3:16). Abraham received the good news (the gospel) of a promised Christ. That's what he believed to the saving of his soul. That is the lesson about saving faith that we must learn. Abraham rejoiced to see Christ's day (John 8:56), and so do all who are of his seed.

Faith Is Conscious

Saving faith is a deliberate act of the heart, which biblically designates the mind, the affections, and the will. The verb "believed" in Genesis 15:6 is most instructive. The basic meaning of the simple form of the verb means "to be firm or reliable." When we say "amen," we are using this Hebrew word. The particular form of the verb that occurs here is a declarative. To believe the Lord, therefore, means to declare, recognize, acknowledge, or confess that the Lord is firm, reliable, and dependable. To believe is to regard the Lord as trustworthy, and consequently to rest on Him and to take Him at His word. This kind of faith is exclusive. It entails a rejection of anything and everything else as the ground of hope. Saving faith is a receiving and resting on Christ alone as He is offered in the gospel (see Westminster Shorter Catechism 86). It is total dependence on Him for life. Abraham illustrates well the new way of thinking and behaving that marks genuine saving faith. He rejected and turned from his idolatry and old life to trust solely in the Lord and His word. He left Ur not knowing exactly where he was going but convinced that he had no other option but to trust the Lord. This is always the issue of saving faith: to acknowledge that there is no hope or help other than Jesus Christ. To trust Jesus Christ as the only way, hope, and life (see John 14:6) is saving faith. Abraham teaches us to regard Jesus as the Great Amen.

Faith Is Constant

The narrative does not record the moment of Abraham's conversion experience, but it does record the evidence of it. Remembering the crisis moment of initial saving faith in Jesus is not the issue; resting in the present experience and consciousness of it is. The apostle John explains this clearly: "But as many as received him, to them gave he power to become the sons of God, even to them that believe on his name" (John 1:12). The tense sequence is vital. "Received" is a form of verb that simply indicates the fact of the action; "believe" is a form of verb that expresses the habitual exercise of the action. In other words, the evidence of having received Christ is the present, habitual exercise of faith. Believing proves the conversion experience. Abraham's faith illustrates the truth.

Although the translation of Genesis 15:6 says that "he believed," the construction in Hebrew specifically indicates that "he had been and was believing." This verse, therefore, does not refer to Abraham's conversion experience but rather to the ongoing experience of his converted life. Years later, the prophet Habakkuk would say, "The just shall live by his faith" (Hab. 2:4). The New Testament's commentary on that statement makes clear that it refers both to initial faith as the means of justification and to the life of faith as the means of sanctification and all of Christian living. So Father Abraham teaches us that saving faith cannot be relegated to a moment in the past but rather is a persevering faith that never stops believing. There were times when Abraham's faith was weak and sight prevailed (as we will see), but he never reneged on the Lord.

So the first lesson to learn as we sit at the feet of Father Abraham is to set aside all confidence in self and effort and to rely in faith on God's grace for salvation. "Therefore it is of faith, that it might be by grace; to the end the promise might be sure to all the seed; not to that only which is of the law, but to that also which is of the faith of Abraham; who is the father of us all" (Rom. 4:16).

3

Lessons in the Life
of Faith from Abraham

GENESIS 12–25

Abraham is the father of the faithful, and as a good father he is an example to his spiritual offspring of how to live the life of faith. The apostle Paul points to Abraham as an example of saving faith that justifies (Romans 4); the apostle James points to Abraham as an example of living faith that is justified or vindicated by actions (James 2:14–26). Salvation is through faith without works, but that kind of saving faith always works. Faith becomes a way of life that defines behavior. What Abraham believed influenced how he lived. His whole life was a pilgrimage as he wandered through this world looking "for a city…whose builder and maker is God" (Heb. 11:10). Abraham's example teaches lessons about both the ethics and the problems of living by faith.

A Lesson about the Ethics of Faith

In Genesis 17:1 God identified Himself to Abraham as "the Almighty God." This divine self-revelation designates the Lord as the one who is all-sufficient and able to keep every promise. In response to that truth, God commanded Abraham to "walk before me, and be thou perfect." He was to live his faith before God. The form of the word "walk" has the idea of walking around back and forth in constant movement. It refers to the manner, habits, customs, and routines of life. The expression "before me" is literally "to the face of" or "in the presence of God." To be in the presence of God is to walk in the

light as He is in the light (1 John 1:7). This was a place of fellowship and communion but essentially a place that demanded holiness.
Purity is a mark of living faith. To so live in the reality of God was
the exercise of faith. Abraham's life of faith had to be different from
his life of unbelief, and so must it be for his offspring. Justification
initiates sanctification, which in turn evidences justification.

He was also to live with perfection. Being perfect conveys the
thought of that which is whole, complete, and blameless. It does not
refer to sinlessness but rather to wholehearted dedication to pursue
holiness. It is a key Old Testament word for sanctification designating that spiritual maturity in which the whole person is renewed after
God's image and increasingly dies to sin and lives to righteousness.
There were so many instances in Abraham's life that demonstrated
his faith was more than theory. His behavior often made no sense
apart from faith. His generosity to Lot in giving him the first choice
of territory was a selfless decision (Gen. 13:8–9). But in faith he
preferred another above himself, esteeming Lot higher than himself
and submitting to him in the fear of God. Father Abraham teaches
us that how we react to others is a good gauge of how we are with
God. In faith he demonstrated his loyalty to Lot by rescuing him at
his own personal risk from a powerful coalition that far outnumbered
his little band (14:12–14). In so doing, he illustrated James's principle
that true faith meets the needs of the brethren (James 2:14–17). His
intercession for Sodom (Gen. 18:22–32) was an expression of faith
since prayer is a key indication of faith and dependence on God.
Looking at Abraham confirms James's assessment that faith without
works is dead (James 2:20). Father Abraham illustrates the hardest
part about being a father: teaching by example.

A Lesson about the Problem of Faith

The problem with faith is that it requires exercise to increase, to
grow. Testing faith is a key means of strengthening faith. So the
Lord often brings trials into our lives that are designed to increase
our sense of dependence on Him, to reinforce the sensibility of faith.
The whole of Abraham's life was a school of faith with one test after

another. Some tests he passed. Others he failed, but his failures did not jeopardize the divine promise or alter his position before the Lord. If his life was a school of faith, he was never expelled from school because of his failures, but he did have to repeat a few "questions." All of Abraham's children are likewise enrolled in the school of faith, where there are no audits. All will take the tests sooner or later. Four particular tests of Abraham's faith provide a study guide for us regarding the kind of tests we may face.

First, there was the test of the unknown (Gen. 12:1–4). When God called Abraham to leave Ur, He did not specify where to go, just to leave. Abraham had to exchange the known for the unknown, and that is not always easy. There is something comfortable about the known, and not knowing the future can often be fearful. But God wanted Abraham simply to trust Him. He wanted Abraham to take Him at His word. Although He did not provide Abraham a map, the Lord assured him, "I will shew thee," "I will make of thee a great nation," "I will bless thee," "I will bless them that bless thee." All those "I wills" were enough to cause Abraham to rest on God's word and move accordingly. His beginning the journey to the unknown was not a blind leap but a conscious stepping out on the divine promise. Father Abraham passed this test with flying colors; without hesitation he left Ur to follow God wherever He would lead. This test teaches us that God does not always reveal all the details of His will upfront. Obedience to God's call is not a measured response of calculating options; it is rather the confidence of trust.

Second, there was the test of the unexpected (Gen. 12:7, 10). By faith, Abraham left prosperity and comfort to come to famine and desolation. This was, without doubt, contrary to expectation. Here was the all-too-common tension between faith and experience. Faith rested on the promise, but experience seemed to be contrary to the promise. At this point, sight easily prevailed over faith, and Abraham left the promised land, went to Egypt, and further jeopardized the promise with his lie concerning Sarah's true identity (vv. 11–13). When he left Ur, his spiritual eyes were on God. When he left the promised land, his physical eyes were on the famine. This time Abraham failed the test.

At first it appeared that he had made the right move. In Egypt there was plenty of food, and he prospered. There is always the danger that carnal decisions bring seeming success. But apparent success is not the criterion for judging the word of God. God was testing Abraham to teach him to trust and obey regardless of circumstances. But even in Abraham's failure, God was faithful to His promise and protected Abraham from jeopardizing the promise of the Seed, the coming Christ, by restraining Pharaoh from violating Sarah. God graciously addressed Abraham's wrong response with further lessons about the sensibility of trusting Him. But this was a hard lesson for Abraham to learn. Years later, Abraham compromised Sarah in exactly the same way to Abimelech, the king of Gerar (Genesis 20). Again God showed Himself faithful and protected Abraham from himself and his folly. The faith/experience tension is a tough test. Abraham faced it more than once, and so most likely will his offspring.

Third, there was the test of waiting (Genesis 16). At the core of God's initial promise to Abraham was a seed, an offspring. Although Abraham never staggered at the promise through unbelief (Rom. 4:20), the delay in the arrival of the first installment was a great test of faith. Years had passed, and there was no son. The ages of Abraham and Sarah, humanly speaking, made the prospect unlikely. So they took matters into their own hands. Sarah, who received the promise along with Abraham, offered Hagar, her servant girl, to become a surrogate to give birth in her place. Although this arrangement is shocking, it was commonplace in Abraham's world. This in no way justifies the action; indeed, it heightens the transgression. Not only did the union between Abraham and Hagar constitute polygamy but it also reflected his following the way of the world, his walking by sight rather than by faith. The consequences of that union led to a conflict between Ishmael and Isaac that continues to this day. Attempting to accomplish God's purpose through human effort is always deleterious. Waiting is a hard test because we always want God's timing to correspond to ours. But those who wait on the Lord will never be disappointed. Isaac was born in God's timing to show His ability to keep His word, even when it seemed impossible. With God nothing is too hard. That is the lesson to learn.

Fourth, there was the test of the unthinkable (Genesis 22). God's instruction to offer Isaac as a burnt offering on Moriah was the final exam. Notwithstanding how unreasonable this demand seemed to be, Abraham had learned his lessons well. All the other tests had strengthened his faith, and he passed this hardest test of all. Even though God's request was beyond his comprehension, Abraham was convinced that God was faithful and could be trusted regardless of the cost. He believed without doubt that Isaac was the promised seed (21:12) and that one way or another they would return together from the mountain (22:5), even if by resurrection (see Heb. 11:17–19).

Father Abraham knew best, and his lessons about faith remain relevant and important for all his children. He teaches believers that faith is necessary both for salvation and for life. Abraham was not the man of faith he was because of personal merit or worth. He was what he was by grace, and that is true for all his children. If Father Abraham could walk by faith notwithstanding his stumbles, so can his offspring. How great it would be if it could be said of every Christian, "like father, like child."

Lessons from Passover

EXODUS 12

It would be hard to find a major topic of theology that is not expressed in the book of Exodus. Many of the themes that God progressively revealed in Scripture begin in this book. Unquestionably, the greatest single event in Old Testament history was the exodus from Egypt. It was a supreme demonstration of God's grace, faithfulness, and power. It was the paradigm for every other deliverance, whether national or spiritual.

Allusions to the exodus occur in every major section of the Old Testament, and the New Testament refers to it repeatedly as well. When Moses and Elijah appeared on the Mount of Transfiguration to discuss with Jesus His approaching death, Luke deliberately used the Greek word exodus to designate that death. Christ called His death the new covenant sealed by His blood, just like the Passover sacrifice. When the song of the redeemed sounds in heaven, it is the song of Moses and the Lamb. In addition, the New Testament has over thirty explicit references to this epoch event, and over twenty occur in the Passion narratives. If that were not sufficient to confirm the link to the Lord Jesus, Paul explicitly declared, "Christ our passover is sacrificed for us" (1 Cor. 5:7). The Passover is more than history; its message is the everlasting gospel. It has lessons for sinners still in sin's bondage and in jeopardy of the sentence of death and for saints whose memories need to be stirred to think of the grace that rescued them from bondage and death to liberty and life. Three principal lessons stand out from the first Passover.

A Lesson in Sovereign Grace

On that fateful night in Egypt, some were going to die and some were going to live. The death sentence was on all the firstborn in the land of Egypt (Ex. 11:5), but the Lord "put a difference between the Egyptians and Israel" (v. 7). The question is, why? Israel was certainly not delivered because of their righteousness. Scripture is clear that they were guilty of the same sin and idolatry as the Egyptians (Josh. 24:14; Ezek. 23:8, 19). They were not delivered because of their afflictions nor because of any inherent worth or potential, for they deserved their bondage and they had no merit. Israel's bondage pictures the spiritual bondage of every individual—born in sin, held under sin's dominion and power, incapable of freeing self. Later, Moses explained directly that God loved them because He loved them (Deut. 7:7–8). The reason God spared the firstborn in Israel was found within Himself. The first Passover and every following celebration of it was a reminder of grace. It is a reminder to all believers that the only reason they will not die the death of the wicked is because of grace.

A Lesson in Substitutionary Atonement

The exodus teaches that grace, notwithstanding its sovereignty, demands atonement; redemption requires a price (1 Peter 1:18–19). The Passover lamb is a vivid picture prophecy that points directly and unquestionably to the sacrifice of Jesus Christ. Christ fulfilled the prophecy, but the lessons about atonement remain.

The lamb was an obvious substitute. The sentence was clear; all the firstborn were doomed to death (Ex. 12:12). Normally, being the firstborn was a position of honor, but not that night. On that night the firstborn would live only if the substitute died. It had to be the death of the firstborn or the death of the lamb—one or the other. If anyone could ever understand the grace of substitution, the firstborn in Israel could. The Passover lamb provided a vivid demonstration that the basis of life was outside of oneself in the death of another. The Passover declares a fundamental truth of the gospel that Jesus died in behalf of and in the place of those He represented, His people.

The lamb was a perfect substitute. Any imperfections in the lamb disqualified it from being the substitute (Ex. 12:5–6). The value of the death was linked directly to the value of the life, a truth that finds its ultimate reality in Christ. As the Passover lamb was selected from the flock (v. 3), so Christ was the elect or chosen substitute for His people (Isa. 42:1). The eternal Son was set apart to be the only Redeemer of God's elect. As the lamb had to be without defect (Ex. 12:5), so Christ was the Lamb without spot or blemish (1 Peter 1:19); He was impeccably pure. As the Passover lamb was isolated from the tenth day to the fourteenth day (Ex. 12:3, 6) to assure its perfection, so Christ was under scrutiny from His birth until His death. He lived under the law, in view of the world and before the Lord, demonstrating over and again that He was indeed holy and undefiled. His perfect living qualified Him as the perfect substitute to pay for the sins of His people.

The lamb was the slain substitute. The Passover lamb pictured the necessity of death and shedding of blood as essential to atonement (Ex. 12:6–7). Death was the execution of justice (v. 12). Death is the earned end of sin; it is the debt that must be paid. Many in Egypt paid their own debt and received their earned wages, but many others lived by virtue of the death of the substitute. Justice demands the penalty, and the penalty for sin will be paid either in Christ or out of Christ. But one way or the other, it will be paid.

The shedding of blood was the effective cause of deliverance (Ex. 12:7). The Passover demonstrated graphically that without the shedding of blood there is no remission of sin (Heb. 9:22). It was not the corpse or the hide of the lamb that diverted judgment; it was the blood. Death was necessary for the satisfaction of justice; blood was necessary for the satisfaction of divine wrath. One without the other is no atonement. So it is that the sacrificial death of Christ and His precious blood appease the wrath of the rightly angry God, quench the fire of judgment, and wash away the guilty stain.

The lamb was a successful substitute (Ex. 12:13, 23, 27). The sacrifice worked; there was death everywhere except where the blood was applied. The blood was the protective covering between God's people and the curse. The presence of the blood caused the Lord to pass over (to leap over) and block the plague of destruction from entering. As every blood-covered house was spared, so everyone covered with the blood of Christ is safe and secure. There will never be a soul in hell that has been saved by the blood of Jesus Christ. That's the gospel, and it works every time.

A Lesson in Saving Faith

Faith places trust in the blood. There was plenty of bloodshed in Egypt that night, but only where the blood was applied was there life. The blood made the difference. Faith appropriates its benefits and rests in its power. The Passover underscores the objectivity of faith; the object of faith determines its value. Most likely there were some firstborn in blood-covered houses who suffered a restless night wondering if the blood would really work. And there were most likely those who slept well in peace and confidence. The point is that both survived the night; the Lord passed over both houses, and the plague entered neither. Assurance or lack thereof did not affect the outcome. Salvation depended on the Lord seeing the blood, not on how well the inhabitants remembered seeing it. The Lord said, "When I see the blood, I will pass over you" (Ex. 12:13). Whether the faith was strong or faltering, it was of equal value because it rested on the blood. It is not the degree or fervency of faith that saves; it is the object of faith that saves. Saving faith saves because it receives and rests on Christ as He is freely offered in the gospel. The more we grasp that salvation rests on what Christ has done, the more we can come into the blessedness of assurance realizing it doesn't depend on us.

Faith finds sustenance in the lamb (Ex. 12:8–10). The slain lamb became food. Eating was a symbol of peace and fellowship, but it was also an act of nourishment. By eating, the people assimilated the lamb to themselves. What the Passover lamb was to the body, so feasting on Christ is to the soul (John 6:48–56). By feasting on Christ, we receive nourishment and strength for living. Feasting on Christ should not be a one-time meal—the more, the better.

Faith begins a new life. The Passover was the "beginning of months…the first month of the year" (Ex. 12:2). The Passover marked the birthday of the nation, the beginning of a journey that put Egypt behind the people of Israel and the promised land ahead. So faith in Christ is not the end; it is the beginning of a new life. Faith takes the believer on a journey. Faith in Christ marks a new life, with the world and sin behind and eternal glory ahead. Old things are passed away, and all things have become new.

So let us remember that "Christ our passover is sacrificed for us," and "let us keep the feast" (not in fact but in faith in what it teaches) in "sincerity and truth" (1 Cor. 5:7–8).

Lessons at the Sea

EXODUS 14

Christianity is a school of faith with lessons to be learned and tests to evaluate and determine whether those lessons have been learned. In the good providence of God, we often find ourselves in situations where sight must give way to faith. The irony is that the operations of providence pose the biggest spiritual challenge to those who believe in providence the most. This is particularly true when we find ourselves in circumstances that make no sense if God is truly great and good. We feel the tension between what we believe and what we are experiencing. It is the conflict between faith and sight.

In Exodus, the Lord put Israel through a series of tests to teach the newly redeemed people to trust the Lord regardless of circumstances. They usually failed, but God always gave them the right response. In Exodus 14, Israel is camped by the Red Sea, and God is going to teach them how a believer should react when circumstances seem hopeless. The slavery of Egypt was behind; the prospects of the promised land lie ahead. Fresh in memory were the great acts of God. The plagues had demonstrated God's almighty power, and the Passover revealed His sovereign grace. Only a small stretch of desert separated the people from Canaan. God's presence in the daily pillar of cloud and the nightly pillar of fire was there to lead every step of the way (Ex. 13:21–22). Things were going really well, but the Red Sea became a test of faith. There were lessons at the sea for Israel then as well as for us now.

Although there was a direct route east and then north to
Canaan, God instructed the people through Moses to turn south-
ward and to encamp by the sea (Ex. 14:2). It is essential to note
that Israel was not at the Red Sea because they were lost but rather
because of the direct command of God. Sometimes the shortest
route between point A and point B is not the best; sometimes the
journey is more important than the destination. This was the case
for Israel, but nonetheless it was a perplexing command and confusing maneuver. Israel had been enslaved for hundreds of years and
had most likely never been outside the borders of Goshen, but they
had enough sense of direction to realize the land of promise was
the other way. When the Lord led them to one of the most desolate places in the region, it raised the question of how they could
get to the promised land if they turned their back to it. Camping
by the Red Sea seemed to be contrary to the promise. If that were
not bad enough, there was potential danger on top of the uncertainty. They followed God and ended up in worse trouble. Pharaoh
recognized the "wrong" turn as a strategic blunder and mustered
his army, assuming that he could easily retrieve the escaped slaves
(Ex. 14:3, 5–9). Israel was now between the proverbial rock and hard
place; everything seemed to be hopeless. The wilderness hemmed
them in on two sides, the strongest army on earth was pursuing them
from behind, and the impassable sea lay in front of them. Progress
was impossible, and retreat meant surrender or death. Defeat in one
way or another seemed certain. There was no hint of how deliverance
could or would come. In His all-wise providence, God brought His
people to a place where they had to acknowledge they were doomed
without Him. This was a hard test. The Lord let them sit there for a
while to think about the answer.

Not surprisingly, this test generated different responses. The
wrong answer came from the majority and revealed that the people
were walking by sight rather than faith: "The children of Israel *lifted
up their eyes*…and…they were sore afraid" (Ex. 14:10, emphasis
added). Panic and despair were the natural, logical responses to the
situation. From the perspective of sight, they had every reason to

be afraid; the danger was real. Knowing that this life-threatening predicament existed because they had followed Moses and the cloudy and fiery pillars complicated matters. This led to the common complaint leveled against all tests: unfair. Because they did not understand, they misunderstood and misinterpreted what the Lord was doing. They were impatient. Their crying out to God (v. 10) was the right thing to do. But rather than waiting on the Lord, they immediately directed their complaint to Moses, concluding that God had tricked them by bringing them out of Egypt just to let them die in the wilderness (v. 11). Their response also revealed faulty memories of their bondage in Egypt. In Egypt they cried to the Lord for deliverance (2:23), but now they had changed their mind. In comparison to their current circumstance, Egypt, in retrospect, did not seem to be such a bad place after all (14:12). The moment of uncertainty and hopelessness overwhelmed them, obscured their vision of the Lord, and robbed them of faith's serenity.

Although in the minority, Moses had the right answer. He was in the same predicament as everyone else, but his faith enabled him to ignore what appeared to be and to see what really was. Against the people's natural response, Moses outlined the unnatural response of faith: fear not, stand still, and see the Lord's salvation (Ex. 14:13). Not to fear in this scary situation illustrates the essence of faith's opposition to sight. The only way not to be afraid of the pursuing Egyptians and the lapping waves of the Red Sea was to look to the Lord, who is greater than any circumstance. To "stand still" often refers to a military stance of taking and maintaining a position. It is a firm, resolute, and unwavering resistance against all odds. To see the Lord's salvation was the expectation of divine intervention based on confidence in the ability and purpose of God. Humanly speaking there was no way of escape; it was a hopeless situation. Pharaoh was sure of victory. Israel was sure of defeat. But Moses was sure of deliverance. Moses was the only one who was right. In this seemingly hopeless situation, they were to keep still, stay out of the way, and watch God keep His word and fight for them (v. 14). Moses's faith was not the power of positive thinking or blind optimism; it was confidence in the certainty of God's promise. Faith doesn't make things happen; it lays hold of and rests on the word of God that must be true regardless of what is happening. All things are possible to faith because all things are possible to God.

The providence that led the nation to the Red Sea was mysterious, but it was the divinely intended means by which God accomplished His objectives: His glory and His people's good. God's glory is always the cause and aim of providence. The Lord revealed up front that He was going to do something at the Red Sea to achieve honor over Pharaoh and to cause the Egyptians to know that He was Yahweh (Ex. 14:4, 17–18). All of the events and circumstances at the Red Sea happened according to God's plan. He disposed all the events according to His good pleasure. None of the obstacles to His glory would survive. Pharaoh's army was far superior to Israel, but it was nothing before God, who with sovereign ease humiliated them. The Red Sea was a natural force beyond human control, but God with sovereign ease manipulated its raging waves. It did not take long for the Egyptians to recognize that it was Yahweh who fought against them (v. 25). God was glorified among the heathen. It remained for God's ancient people, as it remains for God's people today, to learn that the Lord will not share His glory with another. In His providence He may direct the fearful waves to lap against the feet and dust of Pharaoh's chariots to choke the throat until His people learn to cease from regarding man, whose breath is in his nostrils (Isa. 2:22). God is the only hope when all seems to be hopeless.

If God's glory is the ultimate objective of providence, the good of God's people is the attendant circumstance. The events at the Red Sea were a rebuke to distrust and an encouragement to faith as the Lord taught the people to depend totally on Him. Learning to depend totally on God is good. Israel's crossing the Red Sea on dry ground and the Egyptians' drowning in the same sea reveals some important truths about how God accomplishes His purposes. First, He answers prayer. Although God had planned from the beginning to deliver the nation through the sea, the deliverance followed

Moses's supplication (Ex. 14:15). Moses knew the promise of God, and he prayed. Prayer is a God-ordained means of grace; the more confidence believers have in God's word, the more they will use the means of prayer to entreat the Lord to fulfill His promise. Prayer is a reminder that God has purposed the means to an end as well as the end itself.

Second, the Lord revealed that His protecting presence never leaves His people. The cloud of God's presence and the Angel of God, the preincarnate Christ, positioned themselves between Israel and Pharaoh's army (Ex. 14:19–20). The divine presence was there all along (13:21), but the repositioning was to highlight the consequent safety. The divine presence provided light for Israel while shrouding the enemy in darkness. God's first move in deliverance was to assure the people that He was with them.

Third, He delivered them in fact (Ex. 14:21–23). This deliverance was supernatural and gracious. By dividing the sea and making a dry path, God did something that no human could duplicate or take credit for. In so doing He underscored the folly of unbelief. Ironically for Israel, the sea they dreaded became their ally, their protecting wall. Ironically for Egypt, the sea that they thought was their ally became their deadly enemy, their grave. In this single event God revealed both His goodness and severity (v. 30). Discriminating grace saved Israel as the Egyptian corpses littered the seashore.

Fourth, God revived His people as once again they were confronted with the sensibility of faith. They saw certain defeat turn into a glorious victory. As a result of seeing what the Lord did, they feared the Lord and believed Him (Ex. 14:31). When they saw the danger, they feared the danger (v. 10). When they saw the Lord, they feared the Lord (v. 31). What is seen determines what is feared. That is always true. The sad thing is that it often takes extreme, seemingly hopeless situations to get us to look in the right direction. So God will sometimes take us to our Red Sea to teach us again to trust Him.

6

God's Way of Worship

EXODUS 25–40

My ineptness regarding mechanical things is no secret. The only thing that excels my ineptness is my impatience. Occasionally over the years we have had to purchase items that require assembly. Included in the boxes with the unassembled products are all the necessary components and detailed instructions—often in multiple languages—that explain step-by-step how everything is supposed to fit together. Sometimes there are even "helpful" diagrams. In theory, everything necessary for the job is there; it is supposed to be as easy as one, two, three. But notwithstanding the advertised simplicity designed to make the task look enjoyable, my wife learned long ago that rather than making these projects occasions for family bonding, it would be best for me to leave until the job is done. She possesses skills that I do not have. Sometimes I will just watch her while she puts the pieces together, and she makes it look easy. Watching her sheds light on the instructions. It often helps to see somebody do something in order to see how something should be done.

God's Word, as our only guide and rule for faith and practice, sets down clear instructions as to what worshiping God means and how we are to worship Him. But in addition to the commands and precepts of His law, the Lord has given us many examples to look at to help us actually see what worshiping Him looks like.

The Mosaic administration of the covenant of grace was marked by patterns and blueprints designed to teach, illustrate, and predict important principles of spiritual worship. Before Moses, the essential components of worship were operative. But beginning with Moses, for the pedagogic benefit of the covenant nation in its infancy, God provided precisely defined pictures to portray how a redeemed people were to worship and serve Him. The complex and external symbols have given way to simplicity, but the lessons about worship illustrated in the old dispensation's ritual structures are valid still. The manner and attendant circumstances have changed, but the essence has not. So we should look and learn.

The Lord used people, times, things, and places to teach about both the mechanics and themes of worship. The priesthood, for instance, taught that man's access to the holy God was only through a mediator. And all the problems and imperfections plaguing those priests pointed to the necessity of the ideal Priest, the Messiah, the Christ, who could and would perform the mediation perfectly. That was a vital lesson, the truth of which still governs true worship: it is only through the Lord Jesus Christ that man can dare approach God in worship. It was fearfully clear in the Mosaic economy that people, including priests, could die for trying to worship in a way not prescribed, as was the case with Korah in Numbers 16 and Nadab and Abihu in Leviticus 10.

The designated times for special services, for another instance, identified significant themes for worship. In addition to the weekly Sabbath mandated by God's unchanging moral code, the Lord marked other times for His people to observe and to reflect on some of the particulars of His redeeming activities. In one way or another, each of the feasts (the Passover and Feast of Unleavened Bread, the Feast of Weeks, the Feast of Tabernacles, the Feast of Trumpets) and the single day of fasting (the Day of Atonement) highlighted special and paradigmatic demonstrations of God's grace, goodness, and greatness in all His works of salvation and providence. Each occasion focused on reasons to worship. The ceremonies of the special times are no longer appropriate for this dispensation, but the reasons for the ancient holidays remain for us reasons to worship. So we should look and learn.

If any one thing more than anything else was a showcase for worship, it would be the place for worship that God ordained for the covenant nation. Through Moses the Lord revealed that He would govern the place for corporate worship, the place where He would cause His name to dwell, thus signifying His unique ownership and presence in the place worship occurred (see Ex. 20:24; Deut. 12). In the visually oriented Old Testament, that centralized place of worship moved with the wanderings in the wilderness; settled temporarily in Gilgal, Shiloh, and Gibeon; and finally rested in Jerusalem where tent gave way to temple.

If any one thing was central to the ceremonial laws defined in the Mosaic covenant, it was the tabernacle. It was a simple yet complex structure that foreshadowed Christ and the gospel from every angle and from every action associated with it. The tabernacle, with its constituent parts, was a picture prophecy that found fulfillment not only in the person and work of Christ but also in the benefits, blessings, and obligations attendant to and flowing from Him. The tabernacle with its rituals taught by object lesson how to worship the holy God and how to experience the covenant promise of life and fellowship with Him.

As we try to figure out all the salient points about worship from the tabernacle, it is easy for us to get lost, bogged down, overly imaginative, or discouraged in all the details. Notwithstanding the details, there are some key lessons from the tabernacle that picture gospel truths, point to Christ, and instruct us about spiritual worship. Volumes have been written and long series of sermons have been preached on the tabernacle, so obviously I can touch only on the surface in this first of a series of meditations.

Exodus 25:8 provides the main clue for ascertaining the primary message of the tabernacle in God's statement of His intent: "Let them make me a sanctuary; that I may dwell among them" (Ex. 25:8). Leviticus 26:11–12 expands on that statement of divine purpose in terms of covenant relationship and fellowship: "And I set my tabernacle among you.... And I will walk among you, and will be your God, and ye shall be my people." The New Testament identifies the ultimate message by drawing four lines from the tabernacle's rich symbolism to its richer realities.

First, it draws a line to the *incarnation of Christ*. John unquestionably plays on tabernacle prophecy when he declares, "The Word was made flesh, and dwelt among us" (John 1:14). The word "dwell" could well be translated "tabernacled." It teaches, therefore, that Christ is at the heart of all true worship.

Second, it draws a line to *heaven*, the principal dwelling place and throne of God. Hebrews settles this: "It was therefore necessary that the patterns of things in the heavens should be purified.... For Christ is not entered into the holy places made with hands, which are the figures of the true; but into heaven itself, now to appear in the presence of God for us" (9:23–24). Not only does the tabernacle proclaim that God is present with His people on earth but it also pictures the final destination of His people who will dwell with Him in heaven. It teaches, therefore, that worship on earth is to mirror that in heaven.

Third, the tabernacle draws a line to *the church corporately*. Paul reminded the Corinthian church that they were indeed the temple in which the Holy Spirit dwells and then warned ministers to guard their ministry lest they defile the temple of God (1 Cor. 3:16–17). Using tabernacle language, John identified the seven churches as golden candlesticks and declared that Christ was walking in the midst of them (Rev. 1:13, 20; 2:1). It teaches, therefore, that worship is to be a spiritual exercise in the Lord's immediate presence.

Fourth, it draws a line to *believers individually*. Paul's argument for individual purity and separation included that God regarded believers as His temple: "Ye are the temple of the living God; as God hath said, I will dwell in them, and walk in them; and I will be their God, and they shall be my people" (2 Cor. 6:16). It teaches that corporate worship consists of individual participation. So the tabernacle declares both God's purpose to dwell with His people and His plan whereby that goal of fellowship is achieved.

The divine intent of the tabernacle as an object lesson of truth is clear from all the specific instructions that God gave to guide its erection (Exodus 25–31) and from the detailed record of those instructions being carried out (Exodus 35–40). Page after page of Exodus records the minutiae of the heavenly blueprint for the tabernacle and then the execution of that plan by Moses and his construction crew. The tabernacle section begins with God's command to Moses to follow the pattern that was revealed to him on the mount (25:9, 40). The book ends with frequent testimony that Israel had followed the divinely given blueprints: they made it "according to all that the LORD commanded Moses" (39:42; note that at least eight times in chapter 40 Moses did as the Lord commanded). The details were obviously important.

Nevertheless, this plethora of detail makes for considerable repetition and causes some to skim hurriedly through the section. Others tend to squeeze out from every detail a latent gospel truth. I am not inclined to find a gospel sermon in every thread or socket, but I am equally disinclined to regard the details as insignificant. God did reveal all the details on purpose—some for beauty, some for utility, some for sermons. Together the details underscore the important truth that God orders the way of worship, and man cannot and must not alter that way. His instructions to make the tabernacle so long and no longer, so wide and no wider, with this material and no other warn that He is concerned and takes notice of every facet and dynamic of worship. It is important not only that we worship the right God but that we worship Him in the right way. The tabernacle stood as a constant, visible witness that worship was God's way or no way. Or to use theological jargon, the details of the tabernacle illustrate the regulative principle of worship.

7

God's Presence in Worship

EXODUS 25–40

Acceptable worship flows from a true knowledge of God and follows His revealed will. Worship is holy service rendered to the Lord, not an occasion adapted to the likes or dislikes of would-be worshipers. To recognize the Lord's infinitely august person, His infinitely attractive perfections, and His infinitely awesome works demands that the finite creature bow submissively before His presence. How we act in God's presence is important. God is in heaven, and we are on earth. But amazingly, while we are on earth, the Lord invites us into His presence. Being in the presence of God is a privilege that ought to overwhelm us and create within us a sense of caution and reverence. As we become increasingly conscious that biblical worship brings us into the holy presence of God, we must be increasingly cautious that we do nothing to offend that holy presence.

If we truly desire God's presence, it is imperative that we get to the places God has promised to meet with His people. At the tabernacle, the Lord was saying to His people, "Here I am." The tabernacle was a visible means whereby God taught His people how to approach Him. It provides a theology of worship. It was designed to develop covenant fellowship, to show what holiness looks like, and to show the meaning and manner of worship. Although the tabernacle in the wilderness long ago disappeared, its lessons in worship remain relevant for us today. Even the designations of the tabernacle and its

architecture teach important lessons about meeting with God and
worshiping Him the way He wants us to worship Him.

Lessons from the Nomenclature

Many lessons are derived from the names of the tabernacle. The
word translated "tabernacle" simply means "the place of dwelling"
(*mishkan*). Although shekinah isn't a biblical word, we often speak
of the shekinah glory to designate the manifest demonstrations of
God's presence, the theophanies associated with both tabernacle and
temple. For instance, at the end of Exodus the cloud covers the tent
and the "glory of the LORD" fills the tabernacle (Ex. 40:34; see also
vv. 35–38). To label that manifestation the shekinah glory is appropriate because *shekinah* means "dwelling." *Shekinah* and *mishkan* are
derived from the same verbal root that means "to dwell or to inhabit."
The word *tabernacle*, then, declares that God takes up residence with
His people. He does not simply drop in from time to time; He lives
with them. The tabernacle pictured the constant abiding presence
of God with His people. Certainly God, being omnipresent, fills all
space immediately, but He dwells with His people in a most special
and intimate way. That truth has never changed, and it never will
change. Let's remember not to confuse the object lesson with the
reality. God's presence with His people was not literally confined to
the tabernacle; it was a visible reminder and declaration that God
was with them. What the name Immanuel declares, the tabernacle
illustrated and Christ fulfilled. The key lesson here is that God's
special presence is in the place of worship. That knowledge ought to
dictate what happens in that special place.

Sometimes the tabernacle is called the "tent" (*'ohel*). As a port-
able structure, it testified to the Lord's identification with His people
in their circumstances. They were living in tents; He dwelt in a tent.
Again, it would be theologically ludicrous to conclude that the tent
localized or limited His presence and ministry to the people. The tent
illustrated what Isaiah later said concerning the Lord during Israel's
wanderings: "In all their affliction he was afflicted, and the angel of
his presence saved them" (Isa. 63:9). Christ most vividly fulfilled the

tent prophecy as He came in the likeness of sinful flesh (Rom. 8:3); He is able, therefore, because of His personal experience, to "be touched with the feeling of our infirmities" (Heb. 4:15). That the temple ultimately replaced the tent testifies to the same truth. The people were living in houses; He dwelt in a house. This suggests that some aspects of worship are temporally and culturally elastic. That is not to say, however, that time, culture, or personal preference dictate worship practice; rather, it says that God is sensitive to our circumstances, and His truth is pragmatically relevant and applicable to every circumstance. In other words, the regulative principle is intact. Two other names of the tabernacle build on the tent idea: the tent of testimony (*'ohel ha'eduth*) and the tent of meeting (*'ohel mo'ed*). These underscore particular benefits and blessings that derive from God dwelling so intimately with the people. The tent of testimony identifies the tabernacle as a place of revelation. God would communicate, explain, and reveal Himself at this designated place. All the rituals that occurred at the tabernacle were points that the Lord made in this visible sermon. It prophesies Christ, who dwelled among men as the perfect and ideal Prophet, revealing God in person. The tent of meeting certainly suggests meeting together in communion and fellowship, but it also includes the important idea of meeting by appointment. Meeting with God is not haphazard, casual, or accidental. God sets the terms of meeting; He makes the appointment and guarantees His presence at those meetings. Follow the statements in Exodus 25–30 where the Lord says, "There I will meet with thee" (25:22; see also 29:42; 30:6), and you will learn three important truths concerning where God meets His people. At the ark, God meets His people at the place of propitiation. At the altar of burnt offering, God meets His people at the place of consecration. At the altar of incense, God meets His people at the place of prayer. Each of these places finds ultimate significance in Christ, the only place sinners can ever meet God in peace. These names highlight the function of Scripture, prayer, preaching, and spiritual communion in the place of worship.

The final common designation of the tabernacle is sanctuary (*miqdash*)—literally, "the place of holiness." The core component of holiness is separateness or otherness. Although including the notion of separation from sin, the concept of holiness goes far beyond that. Interestingly, the antonym to holiness in the Old Testament is not that which is sinful but that which is common, mundane, or ordinary. The tabernacle was no ordinary tent; it announced its distinction from every other place. The sanctuary declared that being in God's presence is special and therefore requires reverent caution. There is no barging into God's presence. The sanctuary stood as witness to the truth that although He was near, access to Him was restricted. Approaching God requires clean hands and a pure heart (Ps. 24:3–4). The sanctuary declared loudly the need for an absolutely clean and pure mediator who could approach the most holy God, taking those He represented with Him. That is exactly what Christ did and does. Although the tent transitioned to the temple, suggesting temporal adjustments, the designation *sanctuary* refers to both structures. The fact that the place of worship is a holy place overshadows every other notion and precludes any attempt to introduce worldly and mundane elements into worship. That fact is a key lesson about worship.

Lessons from the Configuration

The structure and floor plan of the tabernacle impart some lessons also. The tabernacle was divided into three distinct sections: the outer court, the holy place, and the most holy place. The outer court was under the open sky and accessible to the covenant community. The holy place was veiled but lighted and accessible only to the priests. The holy of holies (a superlative statement meaning "the most holy place") was completely veiled, dark, and accessible only to the high priest only once a year and never without blood. One of the most important lessons conveyed by the floor plan was the safeguard it provided against confusing the object lesson with the reality above and beyond it. Hebrews says that by these increasing restrictions, the Holy Spirit was "signifying...that the way into the holiest of all was not yet made manifest, while as the first tabernacle was yet standing: which was a figure for the time then present" (9:8–9). Any Israelite with the slightest spiritual perception would conclude that the tabernacle economy was not working if it was meant to bring people personally into the presence of God. But it was not supposed to. This was the built-in obsolescence that demanded and increased the hope for Christ, who by His own blood would enter once into the holy place, having obtained eternal redemption (v. 12).

But apart from the important dispensational lesson, the structure conveyed a vital lesson about worship. Vividly, the floor plan declared that the closer to God one approaches, the greater the restrictions or requirements for holiness. The greater the awareness of God's holiness, the greater will be the consciousness of personal unholiness and of the need for a perfect mediator. The greater that awareness, the greater will be fearful reverence as worship unfolds.

8

God's Order in Worship

EXODUS 25–40

The tabernacle was a visible sermon declaring truths about God and how to worship Him, and the items of furniture in the tabernacle were key points in that visible sermon. Each of these items, rich with spiritual symbolism, deserves much more attention than I can give here. But let's note some of the more salient lessons.

The Altar

Just inside the outer court was the *altar*. The first point in the sermon was that the only way to get to the Lord was through the blood of the sacrifice. The altar, the foundation of which was constructed of the raw materials of earth and of stones not hewn, testified to the inability of man to contribute any part or effort toward the work of salvation (Ex. 20:24–25). The altar itself, made of hard acacia wood overlaid with brass, suggests that it was the place of righteous judgment. It points to the place of sacrifice and shedding of blood, without which there can be no forgiveness of sin. At the place of sacrifice, justice was served and pardon was won. There can be no genuine worship without the consciousness that Christ's sacrifice has opened the way for the believer to come into God's holy presence.

The Laver

Also in the outer court just past the altar was the *laver*, the wash basin. On the other side of the altar, the laver symbolized the purity and cleanness required for fellowship with and service of God and the means whereby the sanctifying cleansing was achieved. Sinners did not clean themselves up before approaching the altar; they came to the place of sacrifice with their sins. Then, as the sinner's representative, the priest ritually washed. That the laver was made from donated mirrors (Ex. 38:8) helps to identify the antitype. The New Testament more than once compares the word of God to a glass that reveals blemishes and guides in the cleansing process (John 15:3; 2 Cor. 3:18; James 1:23–25). Paul seemed to have laver theology in mind when he said that Christ gave Himself for His church "that he might sanctify and cleanse it with the washing of water by the word, that he might present it to himself a glorious church…holy and without blemish" (Eph. 5:26–27). The laver represents the word as an essential means of grace and the necessity of approaching God with clean hands and a pure heart.

The Shewbread

There were three items inside the holy place. On one side was a table with the *shewbread*—literally, the "bread of faces" or "presentation." Leviticus 24:8 indicates that Israel presented this as a pledge of the covenant. The bread was something they had made from the grain God had supplied. The regular presentation of the bread acknowledged that they owed everything to the goodness of the Lord. It stood as a testimony to their pledged consecration and dedication to the Lord and taught that praise and thanksgiving were an essential part of worship. Presenting oneself to the Lord for His praise is always the necessary corollary to and consequence of having been saved by the blood (see Rom. 12:1). It certainly points to Christ, who in every way dedicated Himself completely to the glory of the Father, presenting His work as a perfect fulfillment of the covenant.

The Lampstand

On the other side stood the *lampstand*, constructed of a single piece of gold with a predominant center shaft having six branches, three on each side. A regular supply of oil fueled the lamps. The light represents the spiritual enlightenment God gives His people through His revelation. David noted the link between light and life: "In thy light shall we see light" (Ps. 36:9). The New Testament suggests the same when it speaks of the light of the gospel (2 Cor. 4:4). If the light represents the gospel, the lampstand is a prophecy of both Christ and the church, corporately and individually. The Lord Jesus identified Himself and believers as the light of the world (Matt. 5:14; John 8:12). That the seven churches in the book of Revelation are designated as seven lampstands confirms the corporate relevance. All of this is wonderfully suggestive. The predominantly higher center shaft points to Christ, who as the ideal Prophet reveals God and truth. The branches with their lamps directing light to the center shaft picture the function of the church to bear witness to Christ, "the true Light, which lighteth every man that cometh into the world" (John 1:9; see also v. 7). Because the lampstand was a single piece of gold, the branches could not be separated from the center shaft. Just so are believers inseparably united to Christ. As the oil was the energy source for the lamps, so the Holy Spirit empowered Christ and continues to empower and enable believers for their service. Christ had the Spirit without measure; we have the Spirit not only dwelling within us but enabling us every time we ask for His gracious power (Luke 11:13). The light cannot shine without the oil.

The Altar of Incense

The last item in the holy place was the *altar of incense*, right up against the veil separating the holy place from the most holy place. Significantly, this altar was fueled by coals from the altar of sacrifice in the outer court, and the priests would offer incense every morning and evening. As the smoke ascended from the altar, its fragrance would waft over the veil into the most holy place. The incense was a symbol of prayer, an integral component of worship. David obviously alluded to this altar when he prayed, "Let my prayer be set forth before thee as incense; and the lifting up of my hands as the evening sacrifice" (Ps. 141:2). Two significant truths stand out: prayer takes us as close as possible to the holy presence of God without our actually being there in person, and prayer works only because of the blood of Christ's sacrifice, which opened up the way to God.

The Ark of the Covenant

The holy of holies had one item: the *ark of the covenant*. Without question, the ark was the climactic and central piece of all the tabernacle furniture. The ark was simply a box that symbolized the presence of the Lord with His people. Although the ark was just an object lesson, the restrictions guiding its construction, content, location, and transportation were rigid and inflexible. By the box, God was declaring that there is something wonderfully fearful about His presence. Although manifold spiritual lessons are taught by the ark, five key lessons are on the surface.

First, its being overlaid with gold declares the sovereign majesty of God. To be in the presence of God is to be in the presence of the King, and consequently it requires humble submission to His authority. This element of ark theology was prominent in later inspired writers who referred to the ark as the throne and footstool of God (1 Chron. 28:2; Pss. 99:1–5; 132:7–8; Jer. 3:16–17).

Second, its being overshadowed by the cherubim declares the holiness of God. The cherubim are the guardians and heralds of divine holiness and glory. Their first appearance was at the gate of Eden, wielding swords to prevent fallen man from entering Paradise and reaching the tree of life (Gen. 3:24). Years later, Ezekiel identified the four living creatures that attended the majestic and holy throne of God as the cherubim (Ezek. 1:5–14; 10:20–22). Stationed over the ark, they silently proclaimed to unholy sinners that to approach the holy God was prohibited so long as they were unholy. Worship and fellowship with God demand purity. At first sight, the cherubim do not extend much hope.

Third, its containing a pot of manna (Ex. 16:33–34) and Aaron's rod (Num. 17:10) testifies to God's gracious provision for His people. The manna was evidence of the Lord's faithfulness in sustaining His people and a reminder that man does not live by bread alone but by every word that proceeds from the mouth of the Lord. As they trusted God's promise for a new supply of the daily bread, so God's people of every generation can and should trust His every promise. Aaron's rod that budded confirmed that human beings could approach God only through mediation and only through the mediator of His choice. God set the terms: the way to His presence is His way or no way.

Fourth, its containing the tablets of the law speaks of God's righteousness and His inflexible demand for righteousness. The law testified to God's covenant will toward His people yet stood as witness against them. To be righteous in terms of the law required absolute obedience both to the letter and to the spirit. From the open box, the law cried for righteousness and demanded condemnation for unrighteousness. If the box were left open, humankind had no hope.

Finally, its being covered with the mercy seat proclaims hope. The mercy seat symbolized the essence of the gospel: there is a way into the presence of the sovereign, holy, and righteous God. The mercy seat is literally the "atoning lid." If the open box demanded the sinner's condemnation, the closed box declared the sinner's salvation. The mercy seat was God's visible pledge that He will be satisfied with the atonement and will by virtue of that atonement dwell with men. When the blood was sprinkled on the atoning lid, the impediments to fellowship with God were removed. The blood was a propitiation of God's just wrath against the sinner. The blood was placed over the demands of the law, and all was well. As clear a picture of the gospel that the ark was, it was only a picture. All that the ancient box pictured, Jesus Christ is.

Jeremiah evidenced his understanding of the messianic reality conveyed by the ark when he prophesied that the day would come when no ark of the covenant of the Lord would be necessary (Jer. 3:16). There would be no need for the shadow when the reality was present. The apostle Paul in one of his great expositions on justification explained that we are "justified freely by his grace through the redemption that is in Christ Jesus: whom God hath set forth to be a propitiation through faith in his blood" (Rom. 3:24–25).

Significantly, the word translated "propitiation" is the same word that the Septuagint, the Greek translation of the Old Testament, used to translate "mercy seat." Paul knew that and made an intentional link between Christ and the ark, between antitype and type. Although the prophecy of the ark has been fulfilled, its message is still the glorious gospel and the only hope for sinners. The old hymn says it well:

> There is a place where mercy sheds
> The oil of gladness on our heads,
> A place than all beside more sweet:
> It is the bloodstained mercy seat.

God's Pictures of Worship

EXODUS 25–40

The tabernacle pictures gospel lessons not only from its structure and furniture but also from the rituals that occurred there. Preeminently, the tabernacle was the place where the rituals and ceremonies of worship occurred. The sacrificial system that was so specifically defined under the Mosaic administration was a graphic but intentionally imperfect picture of the work of Christ. In part, the sacrifices were typical events, but they were such an integral part of the tabernacle economy that any consideration of tabernacle theology necessitates an explication of them. In every way these sacrifices were types that prophesied of Christ, "the Lamb slain from the foundation of the world" (Rev. 13:8). Since these sacrifices had no independent significance apart from what they pictured about Christ, to obey the ritual—in faith, looking beyond the visible—was tantamount to obeying the gospel. The sacrifices were picture sermons of the gospel. The general and regular sacrifices fell into two broad categories: sweet savor offerings and guilt offerings. Leviticus 1–7 records the most detailed instructions about the sacrifices.

The Sweet Savor Offerings
The *burnt offering*, the most general of the sacrifices, was a sweet savor offering. It shared some common features with the other sacrifices and taught five key lessons about the atonement.

1. The animal selected for this offering had to be a "male without blemish" (Lev. 1:3, 10). Symbolically, this taught that the only acceptable sacrifice had to be pure, perfect, and blameless. Since the offerer was guilty of sin, this strict requirement made it clear that atonement had to come from a source outside the self. Typically, this pure victim was a picture of Christ, the "lamb without blemish and without spot" (1 Peter 1:19). The lamb without blemish points to the whole active obedience of Christ, which offered to God a perfect righteousness and demonstrated to the world His absolute perfection and sinlessness.

2. The offerer leaned on the animal (Lev. 1:4). The forcible laying on of hands symbolically represented the transfer of guilt from the sinner to the perfect animal—the otherwise innocent animal becoming the substitute for the guilty party. Leaning one's weight on the sacrifice suggested something as well of the nature of faith that rests on the object of sacrifice. The result of this transfer and substitution was that "it shall be accepted for him to make atonement for him" (v. 4). Peace with God was the goal, and propitiation (atonement) of God's wrath was the means to achieve that goal. This detail proclaimed vividly the gospel truth of vicarious atonement. Typically, it declared that Christ, who knew no sin, was made sin for us "that we might be made the righteousness of God in him" (2 Cor. 5:21).

3. The offerer had to kill the animal (Lev. 1:5). The death of the substitutionary sacrifice symbolically taught the terrible penalty of sin. The demand of God's holy law was absolute, and its penalty was severe. God's gracious mercy provided a substitute, but His holy justice could not overlook the broken law. Wages were earned, and wages had to be received (Rom. 6:23). That the offerer had to slay the animal impressed on him the solemn reality that it was his sin that required the penalty; he was personally responsible for the death of the sacrifice. Typically, the slaying points to Christ, "who was delivered for our offences" and who "died for the ungodly" (4:25; 5:6). Christ's dying as the perfect sacrifice was the only way that God could be both just and the justifier (3:26).

4. The priests sprinkled the blood of the victim on the altar (Lev. 1:5). This use of blood shed through death achieved something positive. Whereas death was the necessary penalty of sin, the blood shed through death was the specific means of propitiation, satisfying the wrath of God. Sprinkling the blood on the altar, the first piece of tabernacle furniture, symbolically showed that there was no approach to God apart from blood. Typically, it pictures Christ's presentation of the blood of His atonement (Heb. 9:12) whereby the believer has access into the holy place (10:19). This is the gospel: approach to God is only through the blood of Jesus Christ.

5. The priests burned the entire sacrifice on the altar (Lev. 1:9). Whereas each of the bloody sacrifices shared the first four steps, burning the whole victim was unique to the burnt offering. It was this burning that was a "sweet savour" to the Lord (v. 9). This smell that placates represented what was pleasing and acceptable to God; it put His wrath to rest. Atonement having been accomplished by the death and application of blood, the burning was a sign of reconciliation, satisfaction, and consecration. Typically, this is a clear prophecy of Christ, who gave "himself for us an offering and a sacrifice to God for a sweetsmelling savour" (Eph. 5:2).

The *meat offering* had nothing to do with meat as we understand the word today. Rather, it was a non-bloody cereal, or grain, offering that was presented to the Lord in association with one of the bloody sacrifices—usually the burnt offering. This offering of grain could be in the form of whole grains, fine flour, or baked loaves roasted in fire. Oil, incense, and salt were required for every offering, but honey and leaven could never be used. The materials for these offerings were produced by man's labor. By presenting the fruit of his labor, the offerer demonstrated his devotion of life, possessions, and occupation to the Lord. Of all the details specified for the cereal offering (Leviticus 2), the prohibition of honey and leaven and the requirement of salt were the most significant for the symbolic and typical truths about the gospel. Whereas the leaven and honey would cause the offering to spoil, the salt would preserve it. It is specifically called "the salt of the covenant of thy God" (v. 13). The association of this preservative with the covenant symbolically declared that God's contract with the people was eternal and inviolable. God would not refuse any who came in faith by way of the sacrifice that He had prescribed. Typically, the cereal offering points to Christ, the surety of the covenant, who is completely devoted and consecrated to God and His divine commission.

The *peace offering* was the last of the sweet savor offerings, and its restrictions were not as rigid as those of the other offerings (Lev. 3:1–17; 7:11–34). The animal could be a male or a female of any age. The ritual was like the other sacrifices except that it was offered at the entrance to the outer court. The choice inward parts were burned, and the breast and the shoulder were given to the priest. The priest could share them with his family, something he could not do with the other sacrifices. The rest of the animal was returned to the offerer for a communal meal with his family, his friends, and the Levites. This was a time of fellowship between God and man. The peace offering was an object lesson showing that man was reconciled to God; there was peace between them because of the atonement. Typically, the peace offering points to Christ, who reconciles believers to God, having made peace through His blood (Rom. 5:1, 10). Christ's blood satisfies all the parties concerned: the offended God, the mediating Christ, and the offending sinner.

Guilt Offerings

The *sin offering* (Lev. 4–5:13; 6:24–30) and the *trespass offering* (5:14–6:7) were the guilt offerings that pictured both the satisfaction of God's wrath against sin (propitiation) and the removal of sin's guilt (expiation). Both of these sacrifices were for specific sins to teach that every sin is intolerable to God and that confession should be as specific as the sin. Although the initial steps of these sacrifices paralleled those of the burnt offering and declared the same general lessons, certain specific emphases were especially apparent. The main objective was to put an end to the separation between God and man caused by sin. Sin pollutes and prevents fellowship with God. In each of these sacrifices, blood was shed, a reminder that blood is the only means whereby God will forgive sin. These sacrifices particularly pictured expiation, the effect of the atonement toward man, made possible because of propitiation, and the effect of the atonement toward God. Because divine wrath is satisfied, a sinner can be cleansed from the defilement that offends God. This aspect is a vivid object lesson of 1 John 1:7, 9 and 2:1–2, which explicitly state the importance of both confessing sin and the relationship of Christ's blood to receiving forgiveness.

Perhaps the most distinctive feature of the guilt offerings was the disposal of the sacrificial victims; they were burned outside the camp. This feature finds ultimate significance in Christ's suffering "without the gate" (Heb. 13:12), the place of shame and uncleanness. In addition, the trespass offering required compensation to the offended party as an evidence of genuine repentance. This act of compensation points directly to Christ, who positively rendered to God everything that the law required and then paid the penalty of the broken law on behalf of His people. The trespass offering combined both the active and the passive obedience of Christ. Significantly, Isaiah refers to the Suffering Servant as the trespass offering (Isa. 53:10) who offered to God everything necessary for the salvation of the promised seed. That Isaiah rightly saw Christ as the reality and the fulfillment of this picture prophecy demonstrates how every Old Testament saint saw the sacrifices.

The bottom line is that the ritual ceremonies told the story of redemption. The message they preached in picture is the same message that we must preach in plainness of speech. To repeat the rituals of the tabernacle would violate the finished work of Jesus, but we can still look at the old pictures and learn lessons about worship and the good news of the gospel.

10

Dressed for Work

EXODUS 28

For many Christians, prayer has become a series of personal petitions punctuated by multiple vocatives with an "amen" preceded by
"in Jesus's name." The vocabulary of prayer has degenerated to verbal pauses and thoughtless expressions. Hebrews 4:14 explains the
logic of prayer, specifically the logic of praying in Jesus's name. We
have access to the gracious throne because we have a Great High
Priest who knows us intimately, has passed through the heavens, and
sits exalted as our intercessor and Mediator. Under His guidance
we may approach God boldly, knowing that because Christ is who
He is, nothing we ask in His name according to His will can be
denied because there is nothing the Father will deny the Son. As our
Great High Priest, Christ bears us so that the throne of judgment is
for us a throne of grace.

Much of what we know about Christ's priestly ministry we learn
from the object lessons, the picture prophecies, in the Old Testament. Exodus 28 describes the garments of the high priest that were
for glory and beauty. Each of the seven specific garments or acces-
sories worn by Aaron, the first high priest, illustrates some aspect of
the priestly work and points to Christ the ideal High Priest, who
fulfilled that ministry perfectly and finally. Of the seven items, three
stand out especially: the ephod, the breastplate, and the crown. The
word "bear" occurs in connection with these garments and suggests
some remarkable truths about Christ's priestly work that justifies

our boldness before God's throne (vv. 12, 29, 38). Every day when Aaron dressed for work, he was a walking sermon, a living prophecy of what Christ does. When the people looked at Aaron all dressed up, they were to reflect on the visible message and learn the spiritual truth that corresponded and pointed to the ideal High Priest. In ideal reality, Christ is dressed for the work He does for His people.

Ephod: Christ Has the Might to Uphold Us

The ephod was a short garment of two pieces joined together that hung from the shoulders to the waist. Made of fine linen colored with blue, purple, and scarlet, it symbolized purity, royalty, and sacrifice. But most significant were the two onyx stones set in the gold sockets on the shoulders. On the two stones were engraved the names of the tribes of Israel, six listed on each stone. Aaron was to bear these names on his shoulders as a memorial before the Lord (Ex. 28:12). Everywhere that Aaron went doing his priestly tasks, he carried the covenant people he represented with him. The lesson of the picture points wonderfully to Christ. The shoulders are the place of power and strength; Christ has sufficient strength, power, and ability to uphold us and all of our concerns in the very presence of God, where He ever lives to intercede for us. On His omnipotent shoulders, He bears us and carries us to the holy place. When Christ, our High Priest, passed through the heavens, He triumphantly carried His people with Him. We have burdens that so often weigh us down, but we should without hesitation cast our burdens on Him. By virtue of His bearing us on His shoulders, He is already bearing the load of our burden. It is foolish for us to hang on to the burden when He already bears it. He has the might, and He will never let us down.

Breastplate: Christ Has the Mercy to Plead for Us

The breastplate was made of fine linen doubled over to make a pouch and was held in position by gold chains and blue lace hanging over the ephod. Most significant were the four rows of twelve precious jewels, each inscribed with a tribe's name. Wearing the breastplate,

Aaron bore the names of the people over his heart when he ministered in the holy place (Ex. 28:29). The picture is clear since the heart is the place of love, mercy, pity, compassion, and sympathy. The point of the picture is amazing as it directs our gaze to Christ. As our High Priest, He is touched with the feeling of our infirmity. He knows us, loves us, feels for us, and pleads mercy for us. He purchased us, and we are precious to Him. Christ bears our names on His heart, and with tender thoughts toward us, He is in God's presence to intercede for us. His heart for us turns the judgment throne into the mercy throne where we find all the help and grace we need. There are times when we feel so alone with our problems and trials that we convince ourselves that nobody cares. Does Jesus care? O yes, He cares because He holds us near His heart.

The Holy Crown: Christ Has the Merit to Present Us

The miter was a turban-like headdress, the most noticeable feature being the plate of pure gold on the front with the inscription "HOLINESS TO THE LORD" (Ex. 28:36). With this blazing message on his forehead, Aaron would bear the iniquity of the holy things so that the people would be accepted before the Lord (v. 38). Sin makes man unworthy and incapable of approaching God, for without holiness no man can see God or have any communion with Him. But God saw holiness flashing from the high priest's brow and therefore accepted Aaron and those he bore on his shoulders and over his heart. The picture was vivid and points to our salvation. By ourselves, we have no merit to stand before the holy God. But as our High Priest, Christ bore the guilt of our iniquity in His propitiatory sacrifice. In union with Him, God accepts us on the merits of Christ's righteousness imputed to us. As we rest on Christ's mighty shoulders and repose over His tender heart, God sees us only through the flashing glory of Christ's holiness. Our acceptance before the heavenly throne is perfect and complete in Christ. We are accepted in the Beloved. His merit is our only worth.

How a person dresses is often an indication of his or her occupation. Many jobs require distinctive wardrobes appropriate for the tasks. Clothes do say something. That was dramatically so with the work clothes God designed for the high priest for his service in the tabernacle. Every day he dressed in these beautiful, glorious garments, and everyone who saw him knew what he was going to do that day. But as beautiful as Aaron's work clothes were, they pale before the heavenly pattern they were designed to picture. So as we look at Aaron, with the eye of faith we are to see Jesus and consider what He has done and continues to do for us as our Great High Priest. If we believe that He bears us on His shoulders and over His heart and carries us into God's presence in the light of His perfect holiness, then we will appeal to His precious and powerful name every time we seek to draw near to God in prayer or to engage in any other means of worship. Approaching God in Jesus's name is not just empty formula; it is the only way to come.

11

Two Fiery Sermons

LEVITICUS 9–10

The narratives of Leviticus 9 and 10 draw attention to two different manifestations of God's fire: one of grace and one of wrath.
These chapters illustrate the age-old contrast between God-revealed
religion and man-imagined religion. Chapter 9 records Aaron's obedience in following God's detailed instructions for proper worship.
God demonstrated His acceptance by revealing His glory and sending a fire to consume the sacrifice (vv. 23–24). That was a fire of
blessing. Chapter 10 records the disobedience of Nadab and Abihu
in their attempt to worship in a way that God did not command.
God demonstrated His rejection by revealing His glory and sending
a fire to consume the offenders (vv. 2–3). That was a fire of judgment.
These two fires are sermons preaching vital lessons about God's
inflexible standards for approaching Him. Triumph and tragedy are
side by side. Nadab and Abihu stand as memorials to the narrowness of true religion and God's just intolerance of sin. Unfortunately,
the contrast between God's way and man's way is as great today as
it was during the days of Moses and Aaron and Nadab and Abihu.
The proposition of the two sermons is clear: the acceptable way to
approach God and enjoy His glorious presence is through the atonement, and any substitution earns the curse of God. But whether in
grace or in wrath, the two fires reveal God's glory.

The Fire of Grace

The fire of Leviticus 9:24 was the ultimate proof of God's acceptance of the worship offered to Him through the sacrifices. Three truths stand out from the narrative about this fire.

Preceded by Obedience

Leviticus 9 has four references to the Lord's direct commands or to His commands through Moses (vv. 5, 7, 10, 21). In each instance, the command directed some detail for the sacrifices that were to be offered. In each instance, Aaron, the high priest, explicitly obeyed as he performed the rituals on behalf of the people he represented. These sacrifices were divinely revealed object lessons to teach key truths about God's way for man to approach Him. In every way, these sacrifices represented and pointed to Christ, "the Lamb slain from the foundation of the world" (Rev. 13:8). Since these Old Testament sacrifices had no significance apart from what they taught about Christ, the ultimate Lamb of God, to obey the ritual with faith looking beyond the visible was tantamount to obeying the gospel. God's blessing is impossible apart from obedience to the gospel. Each of the sacrifices offered combined to teach specific aspects about both Christ's active and His passive obedience. Christ was, is, and will always be the unique and necessary substitute for believing sinners.

Revealed the Glory of God

After Moses and Aaron had finished the divinely prescribed sacrifices, they came out of the tabernacle and blessed the people. Accompanying the appearance of Moses and Aaron was the glory of the Lord to all the people (Lev. 9:23). God revealed His splendid glory with the fire coming out from His presence to consume the sacrifice on the altar (v. 24). This fire of blessing was unmistakable evidence that God had accepted the way of worship. The fire that fed on the sacrifice pictured the appeasement of divine holiness and proclaimed that man could now approach in peace. Because of propitiation, the tabernacle became a place of peace, the meeting place between God and men. God is most glorious in salvation.

As the brightness of fire revealed God's glory to ancient Israel, so the light of Christ reveals God's glory to the present church. Indeed, Christ is the "Light" whose glory was "of the only begotten of the Father...full of grace and truth" (John 1:9, 14). Paul compared the power of the gospel to God's creating word. Just as God commanded light to shine in darkness, so He commands the light to shine in the Christian's heart, revealing "the light of the knowledge of the glory of God in the face of Jesus Christ" (2 Cor. 4:6).

Received with Reverence
The revelation of God's fire of grace produced two immediate responses (Lev. 9:24). First, the people yelled. The yelling expressed their enthusiastic excitement over the evidence of God's favor. This word most often has the idea of shouting for joy and occurs frequently in contexts of salvation (see Isa. 12:6). Praise and thanksgiving must fill the heart and find expression in every life that has experienced the saving grace of the gospel.

Second, the people fell on their faces. Awe filled their hearts, and they prostrated themselves before the Lord. This was an act of worship, which is the inevitable consequence of seeing the glory and grace of God. When Ezekiel saw God's glory, he fell on his face (Ezek. 1:28). When John saw Christ's glory, he fell on his face (Rev. 1:17). Seeing God as He reveals Himself in Christ demands that those who see in faith worship in spirit and in truth (John 4:24). Although a necessity, worship is the joy and desire of all who have acceptance with God through the atonement of Christ.

The Fire of Wrath
This was the very first day of Levitical sacrifices in the tabernacle, and the fire of grace had no sooner fallen than Aaron's two sons had to die for infringing God's law. The fire that had just revealed grace became the instrument of judgment. Nadab and Abihu stand as warning to all who think that pedigree and religion are viable alternatives to God's exclusive way. As the sons of Aaron and nephews of Moses, they had a great heritage. They had accompanied

Moses to Sinai when God gave the law (Ex. 24:1). They had just been ordained to the priesthood (Leviticus 8). But godly heritage and religious experience alone are not guarantees of spiritual life. Three truths stand out in the narrative.

Preceded by Disobedience

Rather than following God's way, Nadab and Abihu charted their own course. Leviticus 10:1 identifies their disobedience as offering "strange fire"—something foreign and unauthorized that the Lord did not command. It was a fire of their own kindling, a fire that had not fed on the sacrifice. Where they got the fire is unknown, but the text implies it was not from the altar. By using their own fire, they altered the symbol God had given; they changed the gospel. The fire of judgment that devoured them (v. 2) is vivid witness to the narrowness of true religion. To replace God's way is nothing but will worship, which is an abomination to God. Those who attempt to approach God on their own, apart from atonement, repeat the sin of Aaron's sons and will share their jeopardy. God's way of blessing is always through the blood of the one great sacrifice, Jesus Christ.

Revealed the Glory of God

God declared, "I will be sanctified.... I will be glorified" (Lev. 10:3). God's holiness and glory are inseparable. Nadab and Abihu are unwitting testimonies that God is as glorious in judgment as He is in salvation. It is impossible even for man's sin and rejection of the gospel to distract from God's glory (Ps. 76:10). The execution of these two priests for their irreverent disobedience taught lessons important to understanding the gospel. First, their death evidenced the inflexible justice of God. God had declared the blood sacrifice as the only way to satisfy justice, and thus every attempt to bypass the blood leads to destruction. Second, their death demonstrates the irresistible power of God. The fire came from heaven, and there was no escape (see Nahum 1:6). Third, their death testifies to the immeasurable goodness of God. That God destroyed them but not those who faithfully obeyed God's terms assures true believers that "the LORD is good…and he knoweth them that trust in him" (v. 7). God's judgment is infallible.

Received with Reverence

Whereas the fire of grace generated a jubilant worship, the fire of wrath resulted in the worship of silence. After witnessing the destruction of his sons, Aaron "held his peace" (Lev. 10:3). The priests were to forego the common mourning rites (v. 6). Although these were not normal reactions for those who lost relatives, it was imperative that the people who ministered before the Lord did not grieve over the unmistakable display of God's justice. The acknowledgment of God's glory is more important than personal feelings.

God's fire consumes either the sacrifice or the sinner. The gospel, pictured in the Old Testament sacrifices and accomplished by Jesus Christ, is the only way whereby condemned sinners can escape the fire of judgment. Because Christ received the burning wrath of God on Calvary, every sinner who comes to God through Christ is forever exempt from divine wrath. The same divine justice that demands the full payment of sin will not demand a double payment; judgment cannot fall on those who are in Christ by faith in His shed blood.

The Heart of True Religion

DEUTERONOMY 10:12–22

Moses had an advantage that most preachers don't have. In Deuteronomy, when he preached to the church in the wilderness, he knew it would be his last sermon before they entered into the promised land and he into glory. Since Deuteronomy was his last sermon, the message is sobering. What could be so important that this unique preacher would make them his dying words? His dying desire was that the people he had poured his life into would know God spiritually, inwardly, externally, and eternally. Moses was concerned that these people who were so immersed in religion might not substitute their rituals and routines for true heart devotion to the Lord. Significantly, this is a theme that the prophets following Moses reiterated over and again, and none less than Christ, the ideal Prophet, who denounced those in His day who had perverted Moses by ignoring the spirit of the law. True religion is internal and experiential. Not in the days of Moses or of Christ or today has God ever been satisfied with the perfunctory performance of religion without heart. This point from Moses's last sermon is the focus of this section from Deuteronomy 10. It is a classic exposition of true religion that can be summed up under three heads: the basis, the beginning, and the business of true religion.

The Basis Is the Person of God

Knowing God and establishing a relationship with Him is what true religion is all about. The text suggests two significant propositions about God. First, His person is worth knowing. Deuteronomy 10:17 highlights three truths that explain Moses's conclusion in verse 21 that God is the praise of His people. *He is supreme*: "God of gods, and Lord of lords." The titles of God are always important, and here the grammatical structure is as well. The title God refers to His creative power, transcendence, and majesty, whereas Lord refers to His ownership and sovereignty over all His creation. The linking of the word with its own plural is a means of expressing a superlative idea. Moses thus identifies God as the infinitely unique and supreme One who exercises absolute dominion and power over the entire universe. *He is awesome*: a great God, a mighty, and a terrible (fearful or awe-inspiring). These descriptions, heaped one on the other, emphasize that God is worthy of all praise and deserves our worship and service. *He is consistent*: no respecter of persons. Literally, He is not "a lifter up of face," an idiom meaning "to show partiality." God deals with all people the same way in terms of what is required for knowing and experiencing fellowship with Him. Knowing God is on His terms, and His terms are expressed in the gospel. Christ said, "And this is life eternal, that they might know thee the only true God, and Jesus Christ" (John 17:3). Knowing Christ is knowing God; there is no other way. That was as true in Moses's day as it is now.

Second, His grace makes knowing Him possible. In Deuteronomy 10:17 Moses refers to the "LORD" their God. The reference is to Jehovah, the personal name of God that is directly associated with His covenant grace and salvation. Verses 14–15 explain the wonder of this covenant grace. All the earth belongs to the Lord by virtue of His being the Creator, but He has a restrictive delight for His people based in His gracious choice. In loving their fathers, He loved what was unlovely. In choosing their seed, He chose what had no merit. But herein is the mystery of grace: God, who is so infinitely high, delights in a people so low. Were it not for gracious, electing love flowing from covenant promise, there would be no possibility of knowing Him in truth. True religion recognizes and relies on God's grace.

The Beginning Is Inward

True religion is a matter of the heart, and verse 16 expresses the heart
of the matter: circumcise the heart. Although circumcision as the
sign of the covenant had not been practiced during the wilderness
wanderings, in his last sermon Moses says nothing about the circumcision of the flesh. As important as it was, there was something
of greater concern. With emphatic language he commanded, "Circumcise therefore the foreskin of your heart." To *circumcise* means
"to cut off." In the theology of circumcision, the foreskin represented
the filth of the flesh—the defilement, depravity, and impurity of man
from his birth. Since sin separates from God, it must be addressed if
there is to be any hope of fellowship with God. In our flesh dwells
no good thing; true religion requires the removing of that obstacle.
Biblical religion is the only one that offers and provides the full pardon and forgiveness of sin. That is amazing!

Significantly, this circumcision must take place in the heart. The
heart represents the entirety of the inner person: the mind, emo-
tions, and will. Something that is uncircumcised does not function
properly. "Uncircumcised lips" refers to some sort of speech impediment; "uncircumcised ears" refers to deafness. An uncircumcised
heart is one that spiritually malfunctions. It does not think right,
feel right, or do right in terms of God. Therefore, to circumcise the
heart involves a change of thought, feeling, and decisions; it involves
a new nature. Christ expressed this necessity in terms of a new birth.
Moses said, "You must circumcise the heart." Christ said, "Ye must
be born again" (John 3:7). With different imagery, they said the same
thing. Just as Christ explained to Nicodemus that He was talking
about a spiritual birth, so Moses is talking about a spiritual circumcision. Paul referred to heart circumcision this way: "In whom also
ye are circumcised with the circumcision made without hands, in
putting off the body of the sins of the flesh by the circumcision of
Christ" (Col. 2:11). This is where true religion begins, not with a reformation of behavior but with a transformation on the inside.

The Business Is Pervasive

True religion starts on the inside, but it lets loose in life. Ultimately, there is no part of life not affected by biblical religion. Moses begins this section by informing Israel about what God requires or, more literally, asks of them (Deut. 10:12–13). A series of five infinitives, arranged in a chiastic pattern (an inverted structure in which the first and last units are parallel and the principal thought occurs in the middle of the list), delineates God's expectations of those with whom He has entered into covenant, putting loving Him at the center. Interestingly, the list begins with fearing God and ends with keeping His commandments, which according to Ecclesiastes 12:13 is "the whole duty of man." But let's consider them in order.

To fear God is to know Him as He reveals Himself. Fearing God quite simply is living in the awareness of God, factoring Him into every circumstance and situation of life. The fear of God will affect worship and ethics in reverence for Him and dread to displease Him. Fearing God is the essence of piety.

To walk in His ways is to adhere to a manner of life that imitates Him. We are to be holy because He is holy; we are to walk in the light as He is in the light. Moses illustrates by linking God's care for orphans, widows, and strangers to the command for God's people to love strangers as well (Deut. 10:18–19). This parallels James's definition of pure, undefiled religion as visiting the orphans and widows (James 1:27), the keeping of the second great commandment.

To love God is evidence of being loved by God since we love Him because He first loved us (1 John 4:19). Genuine love for God from the heart is a mark of saving grace and the fulfillment of the greatest of all the commandments, to love Him totally (Deut. 6:5).

To serve Him diligently is a labor of love that directs and dedicates all activity, whether secular or sacred, to His glory. Whatever our hands find to do, we are to do it heartily to the Lord (see Col. 3:23).

All of life should be with a view to Him who loved us and gave
Himself for us.

To keep His commandments is to guard, to pay close attention
to, and to give diligent care to obey Him. His law should be the
delight of life, and obeying His commands is a manifestation of love.
Christ Himself linked loving Him to keeping His commandments
(John 14:15).

Together, these infinitives make it clear that true religion, Christianity, is more than rituals or creeds. It is a way of life that flows
from a regenerated, or circumcised, heart that knows the person of
God personally.

13

Manasseh, the Real-Life Prodigal

2 CHRONICLES 33:1–17

Luke 15 records the parable of the prodigal son. The story is an expression of the depths of depravity in the human soul, the awakening of the soul to the terrors of evil, and the gracious mercy of God. It is a warning to every sinner; it is hope to every sinner who repents and comes to Christ. The story affirms that God never refuses those who come to Him by the gospel.

The life of Manasseh verifies that this is not just a story. The adage "like father, like son" is not always true. Hezekiah was one of Judah's most godly kings, yet he was the offspring of Ahaz, one of the most ungodly. Tragically, Manasseh, whose name means "forgetting," forgot the godly influence and legacy of his father's spiritual reformation and led an ungodly counterreformation that brought the nation across the line of God's longsuffering. His reign epitomizes the worst of Judah's history. To add to the evil, Manasseh reigned for fifty-five years, longer than any other king. The Bible is explicit concerning the wickedness of his rule and his corrupting influence on the nation. Indeed, when God pronounced judgment on the nation, He put the blame squarely on Manasseh.

Notwithstanding the depths and extent of his depravity, Manasseh repented and received mercy from the Lord. He is a classic example of Ezekiel's man who does wickedly all of his life only to repent and be saved (Ezek. 18:21–22). He stands as a warning to every young person who desires the ways of the world before taking religion seriously. There are temporal consequences of sin that conversion cannot erase. He also testifies to the marvelous grace of God that is greater than all our sin. Since grace super-abounds where sin abounds, no sinner, regardless of how deep in sin, should ever despair of coming to the Lord in true faith and repentance. Manasseh's sin and conversion teach vital lessons about both sin and salvation.

Lessons in Sin

First, *the existence of sin is innate.* Manasseh was the son of a great saint, but his being a son of Adam was more significant than his being a son of Hezekiah. What a privileged child Manasseh was, as he was able to witness firsthand all the policies and spiritual accomplishments of his godly father! He enjoyed the privilege of being a covenant child but rebelled against the godly influence of his home. He reversed his father's reforms, razed all that his father had built, and rejected his father's God. He personified the prodigal, who abandoned the sanctifying influences of a godly home for the ways of the heathen. His problem was not his environment but his heart, for he was born in sin and shaped in iniquity (Ps. 51:5). Here is a stark warning to every young heart not to despise or take lightly the privileges of a Christian home.

Second, *the extent of sin is total.* The natural heart is bent to evil and has within it the ability to commit any conceivable wickedness (Rom. 3:10–20). Manasseh gave evidence to the total depravity of his heart; he followed all the disgusting ways of the heathen (2 Chron. 33:2). Verses 3–7 detail some of the perversions. He erected the high places, a circumvention of God's rigid requirements for the central sanctuary. He reestablished Baal worship by setting up the "groves," wooden poles around which all sorts of promiscuous behavior occurred in the name of religion. He introduced the astral worship associated with Babylon, worshiping the host of heaven, deifying the planets, and burning incense to the zodiac signs—all in direct violation of God's law (Deut. 4:19; 17:3). He practiced the occult, which included child sacrifices, wizardry, and demonism. It seemed that there was no dirty thing he did not do, no error he did not embrace, no sin of which he was not guilty. Not every sinner commits every sin possible, but Manasseh came close.

Third, *the essence of sin is defiance against God.* Every sin is a violation of God's word and will and is ultimately against God Himself. Manasseh bears witness to this fact. He did "evil in the sight of the LORD" (2 Chron. 33:2). He profaned the house of God in an exhibition of blasphemy, irreligion, and apostasy by erecting altars and cult objects in the temple, even in the most holy place (vv. 4, 5, 7). The account in 2 Kings includes his shedding of innocent blood, most likely a reference to his persecution of the righteous who withstood his apostasy. In his *Antiquities* Josephus says, "He barbarously slew all the righteous men that were among the Hebrews; nor would he spare the prophets, for he every day slew some of them, til Jerusalem was overflown with blood" (10.3.1). Tradition places Isaiah's martyrdom during his administration. The bottom line is that he rejected the word of God (2 Chron. 33:10) and thus provoked the Lord to anger (v. 6).

Fourth, *the influence of sin is tragically irreversible.* Second Chronicles 33:9 says, "So Manasseh made Judah and the inhabitants of Jerusalem to err." Literally, he "seduced them or tempted them" to sin (see the translation of the same word in 2 Kings 21:9). It is the deception of sin that its effects are self-contained. There is no such thing as a private sin. One way or another—either by example or by consequence—sin touches others. Tragically, even after Manasseh's conversion, he could not reverse his bad example and influence: "Nevertheless the people did sacrifice still in the high places" (2 Chron. 33:17). How sad is the word "nevertheless"! Even sadder is that he put the nation on a course straight to judgment. Notwithstanding the sins of Amon, Jehoahaz, and Jehoakim that followed his reign, Manasseh was directly blamed for the Babylonian invasion during the reign of Jehoakim: "Surely at the commandment of the LORD came this upon Judah, to remove them out of his sight, for the sins of Manasseh" (2 Kings 24:3). Not even the revival during the reign of Josiah could reverse what Manasseh did. The consequences of sin are terrible. That is a key lesson to learn.

Lessons in Salvation

If the account in 2 Kings was all we had, we would assume that Manasseh perished in his sins; if anyone deserved damnation, he did. But 2 Chronicles records the whole story. If sin goes deep, grace goes deeper still. No one can go so far from God or live so long in sin that God will not abundantly pardon if he or she truly repents and comes humbly to the Lord. Manasseh's conversion highlights three lessons about salvation.

First, *the Lord awakens the sinner*. The way of the transgressor is hard, and the Lord showed Manasseh how hard that way was. In His providential judgment, "the LORD brought upon them the captains of the host of the king of Assyria, which took Manasseh among the thorns, and bound him with fetters, and carried him to Babylon" (2 Chron. 33:11). This Assyrian captivity was humiliating. Old Assyrian records depict captured dignitaries being led with chains fastened to rings piercing the lips. There is a tradition that says Manasseh was fed a diet of water, vinegar, and bran—even less nourishing than the meager fare of the prodigal. But this humbling was the moving of grace. Sometimes grace is severe in awakening the sinner. Manasseh suffered the destruction of his world, the sweeping away of every prop to bring him to the end of himself. He lost his wealth, honor, power, kingdom, and freedom. Convicting and compelling grace does not always move the same way, but it moves to the same end. The sinner will be forever dead until God intervenes and interrupts to bring him to his spiritual senses. This was the divine objective in Manasseh's humiliation; God was bringing him to his spiritual senses.

Second, *the awakened sinner responds*. Responding to grace is evidence of grace. Manasseh illustrates Psalm 119:71: "It is good for me that I have been afflicted; that I might learn thy statutes" (see also v. 67).

He responded to God's intervention in two ways. God had used the Assyrians as the means of humiliating Manasseh, and he answered the external humiliation with self-humbling (2 Chron. 33:12). Like the prodigal in Christ's story, he came to his senses as he saw himself as helpless and hopeless. A broken and contrite heart is a key component in evangelical repentance. This self-humbling evidenced a sense of guilt that could not be resolved by self-effort. This led to his expression of total dependence on the Lord: Manasseh sought the Lord with the desire to assuage His anger, and he prayed, acknowledging that God was His only hope (vv. 12–13). Saving repentance apprehends God's mercy and lays hold of grace as the only solution to sin. All his life, Manasseh was alienated from God, but now he turns in confession, submission, and faith. If salvation was to come to him, it had to come from the Lord who saves. The Lord Himself declared, "I dwell…with him also that is of a contrite and humble spirit, to revive [make alive] the spirit of the humble, and to revive [make alive] the heart of the contrite ones" (Isa. 57:15; see Ps. 51:17).

Third, *salvation makes a difference*. Grace resulted in a new relationship with God. Manasseh experienced acceptance with God, who heard and answered his prayers (2 Chron. 33:13). God hears the prayers of His people, and now Manasseh experienced the same approach to God as did Moses, David, and Hezekiah, his father. Grace is amazing indeed! Grace also resulted in a new knowledge of God: "Then Manasseh knew that the LORD he was God" (v. 13). This was an experiential knowledge of personal communion, not just a mental recognition. This knowledge of God is inseparably connected to the fear of God that affects all of life: "The fear of the LORD is the beginning of wisdom: and the knowledge of the holy is understanding" (Prov. 9:10). His creedal and experiential knowledge of God resulted in a new life. Grace transformed him into a new creature with old things behind him and all things new before him. He endeavored to reverse all the wickedness he had done and exhorted the nation that he had led astray to do the same

(2 Chron. 33:14–16). Grace on the inside always shows itself on the outside; true conversion puts away every known sin and seeks to perform every known duty.

If any character in the Bible illustrates the transition from misery to deliverance to praise, Manasseh does. How great and powerful is grace that reaches into the pit of sin and rescues sinners!

A Paradigm for Worship

THE PSALMS

Imperatives, instructions, and illustrations concerning worship occur throughout the Bible, but nowhere are the theme and theology of worship more noticeable, central, and pervasive than in the book of Psalms. The Hebrew title for this book that we call Psalms—thanks to the Septuagint—is Praises. That hints at the book's prime purpose. The book of Psalms was written by multiple inspired poets over a span of centuries. Although many psalms are anonymous, the superscriptions specify the names of David (seventy-three times), Asaph (twelve times), the sons of Korah (eleven times), Jeduthun (four times), Solomon (two times), Moses (one time), Heman (one time), and Ethan (one time) as being either authors or dedicatees of particular psalms.

Interestingly, the same preposition governing the names can indicate either "by" or "for," so we are not always certain how to understand the status of the person named. For instance, the superscription of Psalm 72 could be translated either "by Solomon" or "for Solomon." At any rate, the inclusion of Moses in the list shows the composition of the Psalms started long before David, and Psalms 126 and 137 with their exilic or postexilic themes indicate that inspired psalms were being composed long after David as well.

Since the Psalms were written by so many poets over so many years, there had to be a process of collecting and collating all the individual songs that was independent from the compositions. The Bible does not reveal the process, but there is evidence that at least two collections—one associated with David and one with Asaph—were in place during the days of Hezekiah (2 Chron. 29:30). Since some of the inspired psalms were not yet written, and since the canonical order does not place all of David's psalms together, it is obvious that Hezekiah's collection neither substantially nor sequentially would have matched our current collection. My guess is that the canonical form took shape in the postexilic period, most likely under the direction of Ezra. That Paul identifies the statement "Thou art my Son, this day have I begotten thee" as coming from the second psalm (Acts 13:33) suggests that by the New Testament era the order of the Psalms corresponded to what we know in our Bibles today.

Interestingly, the canonical order framed by doxologies sets the collection in five units—according to both Jewish and Christian traditions, a miniature Pentateuch. A frequently quoted Jewish midrash, or commentary, on Psalm 1:1 says, "Moses gave the Israelites the five books of the Law, and to correspond to these David gave them the Book of Psalms containing five books." This dates around the tenth century AD but reflects what seems to be an earlier tradition. Similar statements from Ambrose, Hippolytus, and Jerome reveal that the same tradition existed in the early church. Here are the divisions with the doxologies that mark them:

Book 1 (Psalms 1–41): "Blessed be the LORD God of Israel from everlasting, and to everlasting. Amen, and Amen" (41:13).

Book 2 (Psalms 42–72): "Blessed be the LORD God, the God of Israel, who only doeth wondrous things. And blessed be his glorious name for ever: and let the whole earth be filled with his glory; Amen, and Amen" (72:18–19).

Book 3 (Psalms 73–89): "Blessed be the LORD for evermore. Amen, and Amen" (89:52).

Book 4 (Psalms 90–106): "Blessed be the LORD God of Israel from everlasting to everlasting: and let all the people say, Amen. Praise ye the LORD" (106:48).

Book 5 (Psalms 107–150): A series of doxologies beginning with Psalm 146 and ending with 150 that is a climactic finale not only to the section but to the entire Psalter.

I hesitate, however, to draw forced lines between the five books of Psalms and the five books of Moses since there is no strict correspondence in the order of themes as they appear in the Pentateuch and the Psalms. It seems artificial to identify books 1 to 5 with Genesis to Deuteronomy specifically or respectively since the "books" were not written in that order and since the authority of inspiration rests in the composition, not the collection procedure. Nonetheless, the five divisions are an intentional canonical marker to suggest that this worship manual does mirror the Mosaic corpus, which reveals the essence and foundation of God's covenant purpose and the inception of God's redemptive program. There is hardly a covenant theme introduced in the Pentateuch that does not find poetic and worshipful expression in the Psalms. "Let the redeemed of the LORD say so" (Ps. 107:2) could well sum up the function of the Psalter in its totality and in each of its constituent parts.

This book of praises is a divinely inspired handbook of worship—God's "how to" book of worship. Only the supernatural operation of inspiration can explain the book's remarkable unity in spite of the inevitable diversity resulting from its multiple authors. Since the writers of Scripture did not originate what they said but rather were moved by the Holy Spirit to say what they said (2 Peter 1:20–21), the only legitimately logical conclusion is that the personal and sundry ways that each expressed his feelings, fears, doubts, joys, sorrows, and desires are paradigms illustrating how God expects worshipers to express themselves. The Psalms give patterns for both individual and corporate worship, guiding worshipers in how best to communicate to God in response to His gracious communication. Worship entails meeting with God with ears attentive to His word, and while worshipers are to be more ready to hear than to speak (Eccl. 5:1–2), they are not to be silent. The Psalms teach us how to give voice to praise and to prayer, the suitable expressions of worship.

I love the Psalms. I love to read them, pray them, teach them, preach them, and sing them. I love the elegant yet simple beauty of the poetry with all of its rich imagery, the essence of which is transferable and retainable in translation—most unusual for poetry. Whereas so much of English poetry depends on the rhyme or cadence, Hebrew poetry tends to rhyme meaning. One line in some way or another relates to the other—either synonymously, antithetically, climactically, emblematically, or complementally. Sounds between languages typically do not correspond, and thus translating poetry from one language to another inevitably loses something, but because Hebrew poetry is more oriented in meaning than sound, the essence of its beauty can be experienced in translation.

The book of Psalms is an inspired hymnbook. Although the ancient melodies were neither inspired nor preserved, the inspired words of the Psalter transcend any tune and serve a vital function for both public and private meditation and prayer, even if not sung at all. The Psalms constitute a blueprint for worship. They identify the themes for worship as well as address the obstacles and hindrances to spiritual praise. They teach us to pray, whether in confessing our sins, praying our way out of trouble or depression, or praising the Lord for all His perfections and works. Although they deal with the issues of personal experience and testimony, they predominantly set forth essential objective truths of doctrine and the gospel. If there is any surface lesson from the Psalms, it is that worship is all about God and not about man. The Psalms reveal a theology of worship.

In the next few meditations, I will consider the focus, formula, and function of the Psalms. It is my prayer that this will be a means of providing instruction regarding how and why to worship the Lord in the beauty of holiness.

The Focus of Worship

THE PSALMS

The principal focus of the Psalms is God. Given that God is the sole object of true worship, it should not be surprising that He would be the focal point of a worship manual. One of the preeminent precepts of true and spiritual worship is that it must be theocentric (God centered) and not anthropocentric (man centered). The Psalter highlights this precept both by what it says and by what it doesn't say. It says volumes about God, but conspicuous by comparison, absent are references to people and their achievements—even of those who rendered great and notable service to the Lord. Indeed, references to specific individuals are incidental, and none celebrate what these individuals did for God but rather what God had done for them. For instance, Abraham is mentioned only three times (Psalm 47 and twice in Psalm 105), Moses only eight times (Psalms 77, 90, 99, 103, 105, and three times in Psalm 106), and David only thirteen times apart from the superscriptions. That itself gives a clear directive for worship: worship is about God and not about man. Far too frequently, modern "worship" directs attention to people's accomplishments, motivating the congregation to imitate some biblical character's traits or behavior, and attempts to make people either feel good or, sometimes, even bad (the old guilt motivation) about themselves. God receives only the incidental reference.

The divinely inspired paradigms elevate the Lord to His rightful place, ascribing to Him the infinite worth of His person and the glory of His works (praise) and appealing to Him for His necessary mercies (prayer). Even a cursory reading of the Psalms reveals how consistently the Lord is in view. It is impossible not to notice how frequently the name and various appellations of God occur throughout the collection, directing attention, praise, and prayer to His person. For instance, the covenant name of God that is so wonderfully linked to His gracious redemption and faithfulness, Jehovah (usually LORD in several translations), occurs almost seven hundred times scattered throughout the 150 psalms. In addition, the hundreds of other direct references to God by His many other titles, each of which declares some self-revealed truth about Him, support the claim that God is central in biblical worship. He is the Most High (Pss. 7:17; 46:4; 78:35), the Holy One of Israel (Ps. 78:41), the mighty God of Jacob (Ps. 132:5), the God of my righteousness (Ps. 4:1), and the list goes on. There is little wonder that David declares, "O LORD our Lord, how excellent is thy name in all the earth!" (Ps. 8:1, 9).

Praise, however, is to be offered not only because God is who He is but also because He is like He is and because He does what He does. Therefore, following the inspired paradigm for worship requires giving attention to the divine perfections and works. In regard to His perfections, the bottom line is that there is no God like our God, and a whole lot of worship can occur just by reflecting on and recounting His infinite, eternal, and unchangeable virtues. The greatness of God and His glory are indisputable facts (see Pss. 135:5 and 138:5 for forthright declarations).

Here is the description of God in the Westminster Larger Catechism 7: "God is a Spirit, in and of himself infinite in being, glory, blessedness, and perfection; all-sufficient, eternal, unchangeable, incomprehensible, every where present, almighty, knowing all things, most wise, most holy, most just, most merciful and gracious, long-suffering, and abundant in goodness and truth." Let me suggest a little exercise. As you read through the Psalms, mark the biblical support or proof that you find of each of the catechism's statements. I daresay that it will be virtually impossible to select any psalm without finding some reference to or evidence of one or more of God's attributes.

Similarly, in regard to God's works, there is plenty to worship about. In one place David announced his worship agenda in terms of God's acts: "I will praise thee, O LORD, with my whole heart; I will shew forth all thy marvellous works" (Ps. 9:1). A key exercise of worship is to reflect on what God has done, is doing, and will do. The Psalms address each of these perspectives—particularly in terms of creation (for example, Psalm 104), providence (for example, Psalms 65; 78), and redemption (for example, Psalm 68)—with all the respective implications and applications for both the righteous and the wicked. The association of creation and redemption is a thoroughly biblical link. Read these passages for illustrations of this theological connection: Isaiah 42:5–9; 43:1–7; 45:12–17; John 1:1–18; 2 Corinthians 4:6; Colossians 1:13–20. Significantly, the fourth commandment that defines the Sabbath mandate connects the two as necessary themes for worship. Note that Exodus 20 links the Sabbath day to creation, whereas Deuteronomy 5 links it to redemption. Throughout the Psalms, the psalmists illustrate how these uniquely divine works are reasons for praise and motives for prayer.

I cannot finish this section concerning the focus of the Psalms without reference to Christ. No true worship is possible apart from Jesus Christ, the only way, truth, and life. He is the only Mediator between God and men. It should not be surprising, then, that the inspired "how to" book of worship includes so much about Christ. In His postresurrection, heart-enflaming conversation with the two disciples on the way to Emmaus, the Lord started with Moses and expounded the whole of what the Old Testament Scriptures said about Him (Luke 24:27). And then to the gathered disciples He said specifically, "These are the words which I spake unto you, while I was yet with you, that all things must be fulfilled, which were written in the law of Moses, and in the prophets, and in the psalms, concerning me" (v. 44). Therefore, to miss finding Christ in the Old Testament is to miss the essential message of that book, including the Psalms. Indeed, finding Christ in the Psalms is a sure thing. It follows that if Christ is in the Psalms and the Psalms are about worship, then worship is in some way about Christ. The Psalms were an effective means of keeping the messianic hope before a worshiping people. Not every psalm is specifically messianic, but the messianic theme runs through the entire Psalter and is not difficult to discover. Messianic clues include four key principles: (1) The analogy of Scripture involves comparing Scripture with Scripture. If the psalm parallels other texts that are clearly messianic, the psalm will be messianic. (2) The uniqueness principle consists of statements that could not refer to anyone other than Christ. (3) The type-antitype connection refers to historical figures who prophetically point to Christ. (4) The authority of New Testament confirmations removes any doubt. When the New Testament applies or interprets a psalm as referring to Christ, that settles it. Although the Psalms do not speak of Christ in historical terms since the eternal Son had not yet become man, there is hardly a truth about Christ's person, nature, or work that does not find expression—all of which have implications for worship. His humanity and deity, His death and resurrection, His mediatorial offices (prophet, priest, and king), and His first and second advents are all part of the messianic theology of the Psalms. The Israelites knew what it meant to sing of their Redeemer.

Space does not permit me to expound every messianic text, but here are some samples. Psalm 2 reveals Christ as the object of saving faith. Psalm 8 reveals Him as the ideal man. Psalm 16 reveals Him as the resolute servant whose view of His God, His people, and His mission fueled His determination to endure the suffering for the glory that was certain to follow. Psalm 22, one of the places in Scripture that demands the removal of our shoes because we are on holy ground, reveals Christ as the suffering and successful Savior. Psalm 110, revealing Christ as the King and Priest, is a compendium of theological truths concerning the person and mediatorial operation of Christ from His place in the Trinity, to His royal priesthood, to His final triumph over every enemy.

A whole set of psalms designated as royal psalms spotlights the person of the king and always points in some way to Jesus Christ, the ideal King (for example, Psalm 45). Many more psalms either in part or in whole, in fact or in type, direct attention to Christ. When you find Christ in the Psalms, remember that you have found Him in the book of worship and song. That is essential. Any biblical paradigm for worship will have Christ as a principal part. The Psalms make it unmistakably clear that kissing the Son—that is, paying homage to Him—is foundational to true religion and to true worship (2:12). Acceptance before God is always in reference to Christ. That was true then; it is true now.

16

The Formula for Worship

THE PSALMS

Not all psalms are the same. Some are communal; others are individual. Some are joyful; others are doleful. Some confess sin; others claim righteousness. Some exude confidence; others express doubt and even despondency. Some make petitions; others render praise. Some are logically reasoned; others are emotionally random. Any regular reading of the Psalms draws attention to this diversity; it can't be missed. It is not supposed to be missed since every psalm with its own particulars is the product of divine inspiration and therefore the testimony of divine intent. In one way or another, each psalm is a part of the divinely defined paradigm to instruct and to guide to proper worship.

The Psalms constitute a formula for worship that details the kind of things that God expects and desires from a worshiping people.

Praise and Thanksgiving

Since true worship is all about God, praise and thanksgiving for His person and for His works are always integral elements in biblical worship. Although expressions of praise and thanksgiving magnifying God's name and celebrating the manifold evidences of His greatness occur in most psalms, some psalms exclusively eulogize the Lord. They usually include imperatives to praise, reasons for praise (focusing on the Lord Himself or on His creative and redemptive works), and resolutions to praise again. These psalms wholly given to praise and thanksgiving are often designated as hymns. Hymns are sometimes but not always marked by a literary device called *inclusio*, which simply means that the beginning and the end are the same or very similar. Here are some hymn examples. Psalm 8 begins and ends with a pronouncement of God's greatness: "O LORD, our Lord, how excellent is thy name in all the earth!" (vv. 1, 9). In between the two declarations, the psalmist gives evidences of God's glory, grace, and greatness that prove His excellence. Psalm 103 begins and ends with a call to personal worship—"Bless the LORD, O my soul" (vv. 1, 22). Between the imperatives to bless the Lord are reflections on the multiple and varied manifestations of God's mercy and might that motivate the ascription of blessing. Psalm 135 (like Psalms 146–150) starts and finishes with "hallelujah"—"Praise ye the LORD" (vv. 1, 21). The first hallelujah leads to a delineation of God's goodness and greatness with specific descriptions of His grace, uniqueness, sovereignty, eternal immutability, and compassionate care, all of which give justification for praise. The only fitting conclusion is another hallelujah. Psalm 136 begins and ends, "O give thanks unto the LORD (or "the God of heaven" as in v. 26)…for his mercy endureth for ever" (vv. 1, 26). This psalm also repeats the closing refrain in every verse "for his mercy endureth for ever." The statement occurs twenty-six times but not once too often considering the multiple reasons for giving thanks in celebration of who the Lord is, of what He can do, and of what He has done in terms of creation, redemption, providential care, and timely grace.

Confession of Sin

Drawing near to God in worship has restrictions. Psalm 24 poses a question, the answer to which would seem to disqualify most of us from worshiping God at all: "Who shall ascend into the hill of the LORD? or who shall stand in his holy place? He that hath clean hands, and a pure heart" (vv. 3–4). Without those clean hands and pure hearts, worship is impossible. Sin defiles and hinders fellowship with God—something we know both theologically and experientially. But God in His grace and mercy has provided the means for cleansing from sin, thus fitting His worshipers for His presence; He has marked the path leading to forgiveness. David testified that confessing sin really works: "I acknowledge my sin unto thee, and mine iniquity have I not hid. I said, I will confess my transgressions unto the LORD; and thou forgavest the iniquity of my sin" (Ps. 32:5). The Psalms illustrate what God expects in the kind of confession that not only leads to restoration for fellowship but also constitutes a necessary component in worship.

Expressions of confession and pleas for divine mercy occur throughout the Psalter, but seven psalms are traditionally classified as penitential (6, 32, 38, 51, 102, 130, 143). Psalm 51 is perhaps the best known of the penitential psalms, occasioned by David's sin with Bathsheba. The logic and progression of his confession provide a good example to follow in both individual and corporate settings. David begins with a plea for forgiveness, making no excuses for his sins and acknowledging that if forgiveness comes, it comes from God's grace, mercy, and compassion (vv. 1–9). He then pleads for a spiritual renewal and restoration to joy and fellowship in God's presence (vv. 10–13). Finally, he argues the link between his being forgiven and the worship experience (vv. 14–16). All of the outward exercises of worship are pleasing to the Lord when accompanied with the sacrifices of a broken spirit and contrite heart (v. 17). Confession of sin is part of the necessary humility and submission required of all worshipers in God's presence.

Lamentation

Being in God's presence in spiritual worship is a happy relief from the responsibilities and anxieties of life, but it is not a narcotic that dulls the senses to the stuff of life. A great many things in the world seem to threaten God's people and to even contradict what is true about God. The Psalms teach that worship includes expressing those concerns and petitioning God for defense and deliverance. These psalms, whether dealing with individual matters or community concerns, usually include a cry for the Lord to hear the complaint, a summary of the distressing or dangerous circumstance, a confession of trust in the Lord, a petition for divine intervention to reverse the circumstance, and a resolution to praise the Lord. Psalm 13 illustrates the pattern. David begins by directing a transparent question to the Lord that shows his despair: "How long wilt thou forget me, O LORD?…How long shall mine enemy be exalted over me?" (vv. 1–2). He then makes his petition for the Lord to do something before the enemy prevails: "Consider and hear me, O LORD my God" (v. 3). Finally, he confesses his trust and breaks out in song, praising the Lord for His intervention: "But I have trusted in thy mercy; my heart shall rejoice in thy salvation. I will sing unto the LORD, because he hath dealt bountifully with me" (vv. 5–6).

A legitimate ingredient of worship is bringing God to bear on issues that without divine attendance would seem to jeopardize His glory or at least to obscure our vision of His glory. The circumstances of life—those in our private little worlds or in the larger world around us—have the potential to create a tension in our hearts between experience and creed—that is, what we believe about God. When experience assumes precedence over creed, we don't feel much like worshiping. Walking by sight is always deleterious to walking by faith. The Psalms direct us to factor God into current situations; true religion is always relevant to life. It is good in worship to dwell on God's faithfulness and the sensibility of trusting Him regardless of our circumstances. Praising God tends to put everything else in proper perspective, even life.

Imprecation

Biblical worship includes praying for the vindication of God's glory, His cause, and His people. This vindication often involves His judgment on those who oppose His glory, His cause, and His people. These imprecatory prayers for divine judgment to fall on the wicked reflect a righteous sense of God's justice, a righteous hatred of sin, and a righteous jealousy for God's glory and kingdom (see Psalms 35, 69, 109, and 137). Imperative to our understanding of the imprecatory psalms is the realization that they never involve personal issues or vindictiveness. Both the Old and New Testaments demand love for personal enemies (see Ex. 23:4–5; Lev. 19:17–18; Matt. 5:38–45). Hence, imprecatory prayers are not a biblically sanctioned means of sticking it to personal enemies. That God's people find relief and deliverance when God judges His enemies is a felicitous corollary but never the motive behind a prayer. True prayer always has God's glory as its principal end and driving cause. The imprecatory psalms always reflect the highest motive and are just as much a part of the divinely inspired paradigm for worship as the hallelujah psalms or any other. Christians have every right and warrant both to declare God's word in announcing judgment on the unrighteous and to pray for God's will to be done. Love for God demands both the declaration and the prayer. Consider how the psalmist identified himself with God and follow his example: "Do not I hate them, O LORD, that hate thee? and am not I grieved with those that rise up against thee? I hate them with perfect hatred: I count them mine enemies" (Ps. 139:21–22). To pray for God to execute His righteous judgment on the wicked is equivalent to praying for the advancement and extension of His kingdom. Following this paradigm is part of what Christ Himself instructed about prayer when He taught us to pray, "Thy kingdom come, Thy will be done in earth, as it is in heaven" (Matt. 6:10). An imprecatory prayer that follows the principles of God's paradigm specifies that general petition. To pray for God's kingdom to come is a most Christian thing to do in worship.

Ethical Instruction

True and biblical religion pervades life. In contrast to the postmodern propensity for separating different spheres of life into unrelated compartments, biblical religion demands that a saving relationship with God defines and directs every experience and relationship in life. There can be no disconnect between worship and life. Remember the requirement of Psalm 24 that restricts worship to those who are ethically and morally pure (clean hands and pure hearts). Not surprisingly, in the God-given handbook on worship, ethical demands are placed on would-be worshipers. Psalm 15, for instance, demands honesty and prohibits slander. Psalm 82 demands justice and humanitarian and equitable treatment of the defense-less. Psalm 131 requires humility. Some of the psalms that seem to deal predominantly with issues of piety and ethics are referred to as wisdom psalms (for instance, Psalms 37, 49, 73, 112, 127, 128). Sig-nificantly, standing over the entire Psalter is the contrast between the two ways—the way of the righteous and the way of the ungodly. The godly man must be separate from sinners and must find his delight in God's word (Psalm 1). Before issuing the first imperative to praise the Lord, the Psalms identify the kind of life expected of those who would worship God. The Psalms consistently link life and worship. Worship does not leave religion or God in the realm of theory.

17

A Handbook and Hymnbook for Worship

THE PSALMS

There is no question that the Psalms teach us how to worship; the question is how we are to use the Psalms in worship. What should be their function? David's introduction of a psalm to thank the Lord and celebrate the ark's return in 1 Chronicles 16 illustrates the function of psalms in public worship. Interestingly, the psalm sung first on that day became in the Psalter, either in part or in whole, what we know as Psalms 96, 105, and 106. Similarly, some of the superscriptions identify the liturgical use of particular psalms. Psalm 30, for instance, was for the dedication of David's house. Psalms 120–135 were designated as the songs of ascent, traditionally understood to have been part of the celebration of the pilgrimage feasts. Psalm 92 is marked as a song for the Sabbath. Additional instructions recorded in the Septuagint designate other psalms for specific days of the week (first day—Psalm 24; second day—Psalm 48; fourth day—Psalm 94; sixth day—Psalm 93). First Corinthians 14:26; Ephesians 5:19; Colossians 3:16; and James 5:13 confirm the place of the Psalms in New Testament worship as well.

Evidence is that the early church followed the biblical pattern and incorporated the Psalms into the services of public worship. Certainly, the Reformation with its revival of congregational singing relied heavily on the Psalms, even relying on the Psalms—some would argue—exclusively. The point to be taken is that there is both biblical and traditional precedent for using the Psalms in worship.

It is not my concern to enter into any of the debates or controversies that have arisen regarding exclusive psalmody or inclusive hymnody. I want simply to recommend four functions that the Psalms ought to have in worship.

First, *read the Psalms*. Every worship service must include the public reading of Scripture. Although this public reading should not be restricted to the Psalms, the Psalms by their very nature accomplish much of what is desired in the public reading. With their commands to praise and give thanks, many of the psalms lend themselves to use at the beginning of the service to call the people to worship. In addition, the Psalms exhibit a theological completeness that will keep the whole course of God's redemptive operation in view if they are read systematically.

In *Give Praise to God: A Vision for Reforming Worship*, pastor and author Terry Johnson offers an interesting array of quotations from Martin Luther and the church fathers demonstrating that this was their understanding of the Psalms. In his 1528 preface to the Psalter, Luther refers to the Psalms as a "little Bible." He says, "In it is comprehended most beautifully and briefly everything that is in the entire Bible." He calls it a "short Bible," in which is provided an "entire summary" of the whole "comprised in one little book." Before him, Athanasius (ca. 293–373) referred to the Psalter as an "epitome of the whole Scriptures." And Basil (ca. 330–379) called it a "compend of all divinity." All that the Bible teaches is found in summary form in the book of Psalms.

Second, *pray the Psalms*. Since so many of the psalms are themselves prayers addressed directly to the Lord, following the paradigm requires praying—the specifics as well as the patterns. Although not a paragon of ministerial compassion or concern, Jonah teaches us something about the Psalms and praying in Jonah 2. His prayer from the belly of the great fish is a casebook example of what it is to saturate prayer with scriptural language. Almost every line of his prayer is either a direct quotation from or very close allusion to some

line from the Psalter (just look at the cross references in your Bible).
Though he repeated the words of Scripture, he adapted and applied
the truths to his unique need and circumstance. Think what we will
of Jonah, his knowledge of Scripture that surfaced in his most distressing and disgusting environment depicts a man who knew how
to pray. His prayer was in a very private setting, but its pattern and
example are appropriate for public praying as well. A key point to
remember is that Jonah did not simply recite scriptural language;
he really prayed using scriptural terms. There is hardly a better way
to learn to pray than to pray through the Psalms, personalizing the
inspired words. There is hardly a better way to insure that public
praying is scripturally sound than to utilize the words of Scripture.
Spontaneous praying does not preclude using the Psalms.

Third, *preach the Psalms*. It is significant to me that the first sermon preached on the day of Pentecost was based on a text from
the Psalms. After Peter appealed to Joel's prophecy to explain what
was happening on the eventful day, he began to preach Christ, taking Psalm 16 as his text, and he didn't finish before commenting
on Psalm 110 as well (Acts 2:25–36). Acts refers to more than one
apostolic sermon that used the Psalms (see, for instance, Acts 4:25
referring to Psalm 2). In light of the full compendium of theological
truths and life issues addressed in the Psalms, any preacher ought
to find abundant sermon material. Once he learns something about
the structure and style of the poetry, he sees that the Psalms almost
outline themselves. They are eminently "preachable."

Fourth, *sing the Psalms*. Among other purposes, the Psalms were
made for singing. That they were sung in their original settings and
continued to be sung in both Jewish and Christian worship is indisputable. Psalm singing has a rich history, especially in Reformed
worship traditions but particularly among the Scottish Covenanters.
Singing the Psalms will help dispel what has become a common
notion even among the most conservative that singing is preparatory for worship. Proper singing is not preparatory for worship; it

is worship. Singing the Psalms, the divinely inspired hymnbook, is singing what God wants sung.

In his preface to the Psalter, Calvin comments on both the words and the tunes to be sung in worship:

> Moreover, that which St. Augustine has said is true, that no one is able to sing things worthy of God except that which he has received from him. Therefore, when we have looked thoroughly, and searched here and there, we shall not find better songs nor more fitting for the purpose, than the Psalms of David, which the Holy Spirit spoke and made through him. And moreover, when we sing them, we are certain that God puts in our mouths these, as if he himself were singing in us to exalt his glory.

And then with reference to tunes, he says, "Care must always be taken that the song be neither light nor frivolous; but that it have weight and majesty (as St. Augustine says), and also, there is a great difference between music which one makes to entertain men at table and their houses, and the Psalms which are sung in the Church in the presence of God and his angels."

Even human-composed hymns ought to follow the patterns and themes suggested in the Psalms; that's what paradigms are for. I would suggest that singing the Psalms is a safeguard against singing inappropriate hymns and spiritual songs. Singing the Psalms and using them as a pattern for singing other things will insure the proper kind of words. Since the tunes have not been preserved and thus were not inspired, common and sanctified sense must operate. This is the notion expressed by the Westminster Confession of Faith when it says, "There are some circumstances concerning the worship of God…which are to be ordered by the light of nature, and Christian prudence, according to the general rules of the Word, which are always to be observed" (1.6). I will not venture commentary beyond my competence about music style, but I will make a statement reflecting common and sanctified sense. The tunes ought to fit the words and be fit for the One to whom the songs are directed. Remembering that worship singing is not for personal entertainment but for service to God will automatically exclude tunes and music styles that are associated with secular or worldly contexts. I'm not saying that contemporary tunes are inherently bad; the date of composition is not the issue. Something written yesterday might well be appropriate and honoring to God; something written centuries ago might well be spiritually disgusting. The melodies ought to match the words. Joyous psalms ought to have joyous tunes. Praise psalms ought to have majestic tunes. Penitential psalms ought to have doleful tunes. Some things just make sense. Sing the Psalms.

The Psalms teach us that we are to meditate on God, His person, His works, and His Christ. The Psalms teach us to declare, to describe, to praise, to give thanks, to pray, to vow, and to sing. The Psalms not only teach us the patterns for worship; they teach us to worship. God has given us a handbook and hymnbook all in one place. Let's use it to His glory.

18

Christ of Saving Faith

PSALM 2

Psalm 2 is the first explicitly and uniquely messianic psalm. It is a royal psalm that shows the ideal and inviolable fulfillment of the Davidic covenant. The psalm progresses in four distinct stanzas marked by four different speakers: rebels, the Lord, the Messiah, and the narrator (ultimately, the Holy Spirit). Each stanza expresses a particular attitude about the Messiah with a climactic warning that our attitude toward the Messiah determines our eternal destiny.

Stanza 1: Rebels

In the first three verses, the rebels speak and *oppose Christ's authority*. Although the rebels include every race and every class from every age who are naturally alienated from God, the raging, plotting, and general hostility against Christ found its most grievous demonstration in the strange alliances between Jews and Gentiles and between Pilate and Herod in the trial and execution of Christ. The object of all the scheming hatred was the Lord and His Messiah. Desiring freedom from divine restraint, the rebels combined their hatred in a futile attempt to sever the "bands" and "cords" of Christ's authority by putting Him to death (see Acts 4:27–28). We know that God used their plot as the means of effecting His eternal plan for our redemption in Christ. "Him, being delivered by the determinate counsel and foreknowledge of God, ye have taken, and by wicked hands have crucified and slain" (2:23). That's what Peter said right to the face of some of the conspirators.

Stanza 2: God

In verses 4–6, God speaks and *confirms Christ's authority*, thus highlighting the futility of any attempt to thwart God's purpose in Christ. The contrast between the scheming agitation of world leaders and the serene, supreme sovereignty of the Lord (Adonai, the real King), who sits laughing at their efforts, would be comical if it were not so tragic. His sitting in heaven testifies to His absolute authority to actually accomplish whatever He pleases (Ps. 115:3). God is not just a passive witness to what takes place in the world. He sits on a throne to rule, not "in the stands" to watch. His laughing at those who conspire against His purpose is a bold statement emphasizing the absurdity of their futile efforts. His holding them in derision is literally "to stammer disrespectfully in their face." What a vivid image of God's "getting in sinners' faces" to ridicule them and establish His infinite superiority and power to consume the rebel in a moment were it not for His longsuffering. After He mocks, He speaks. Notwithstanding the rejection of Christ's authority by sinners, the Lord declared that He had set His king on the holy hill of Zion (Ps. 2:6). The word "set" literally means "to pour out" and refers to God's consecrating and exalting Christ to the position of authority. That is His resolute purpose, and nothing could or ever can alter it. The kingdom of God and His Christ is not a democracy. Whether people submit or not, Christ is the King.

Stanza 3: Messiah

In verses 7–9, Christ Himself speaks and *affirms His own authority*. This indeed is holy ground as the Messiah reveals what the Father, in the privacy of eternity, had promised Him. Three truths stand out in Christ's speech. First, messiahship is based on God's certain decree ("I will declare the decree," v. 7). The word "declare" includes the idea of detailing, listing, or enumerating. He is going to detail some of the elements of the decree, the obligations and rules that defined the covenant agreement between Himself and the Father concerning the whole mediatorial work of redemption. This is language of certitude, and it should generate confidence and joy that God's decree concerning Christ and, consequently, salvation is irreversible, irrefutable, and unfrustratable.

Second, Christ stood in a unique relationship with God the Father ("Thou art my Son; this day have I begotten thee," v. 7). This was not a prophecy to Christ that He would become the Son at the incarnation; it was the eternal declaration of the existing sonship. Although this statement has direct bearing on "official" messianic sonship, the language demands that this be viewed as a direct statement of the essential Trinitarian sonship of the second person of the Trinity, the eternal Son of God and chosen Mediator. The statement "this day have I begotten thee" has caused some confusion, but it is a key statement for proper understanding of the psalm's intent. The problem is that we tend to think of something begotten as having had a beginning. That Christ is the eternal Son of God and begotten at the same time seem to be mutually exclusive. How can both be true? The problem is more apparent than real. Although the word "begotten" can be used metaphorically, it usually refers to a familial rather than official relationship. This is why I say that the focus here is on the eternal Trinitarian relationship. Again, the word usually—though not consistently—takes a distinct form depending on the subject of the verb (whether the mother, father, or midwife). In this text, the form used usually refers to the mother's giving birth. It would be ludicrous and blasphemous even to hint that God the Father was the mother of Christ. The point is that the word is used not to suggest in any way a beginning of existence but rather to underscore the existence of a Father-Son relationship.

Happily, the New Testament uses this verse in such a way as to confirm this interpretation: the word speaks of the existence and not the inception of a relationship. In his sermon at Antioch in Pisidia, Paul specifically alluded to the second psalm and appealed to the statement "Thou art my Son, this day have I begotten thee" as biblical proof that God had raised up Jesus from the dead (Acts 13:33). That the Father had already spoken from heaven declaring Christ to be His Son at the baptism and transfiguration precludes interpreting the resurrection as the beginning of sonship. Romans 1:4 explains why Paul used Psalm 2 in connection with the Lord's resurrection: by the resurrection God declared in power that Christ was His Son. The resurrection was the conclusive, irrefutable evidence of who Christ was. It vindicated and confirmed His every claim, not the least of which was that God was His Father (see, for instance, John 8:16–29).

The third truth in Christ's speech concerns His universal inheritance and unwavering authority. One of the details of that eternal agreement was that the Father would give a people to His Son. This same promise is in Isaiah 53:10. If the Servant would offer Himself for sin, He would see His seed. So according to the passage in Psalm 2, the heathen throughout the world would be Christ's for the asking. This divine offer of a people throughout the world evoked David's acknowledgment that the Seed promised through his family line was a revelation of truth for all humankind (2 Sam. 7:19). The promise of Messiah in the Old Testament was never a uniquely Jewish promise. Knowing what the Father promised the Son heightens the significance of the Great Commission that Christ gave His church to evangelize the world. Evangelism is the divinely intended means of claiming all that belongs to Christ. That ought to increase zeal and boldness in every evangelistic effort. All people will in one way or another submit to Christ's authority. He conquers either by grace or by the rod of iron. Sooner or later, every knee will bow and every tongue will confess that Jesus is the Lord, the only Christ of God.

Stanza 4: The Holy Spirit

That threat is a fitting transition to the climactic final stanza in which the narrator *recommends submission to Christ's authority* (vv. 10–12). If anything is clear from the last stanza of this song, it is that eternal destiny is linked to relationship with the Son. Since it is impossible to frustrate God's eternal purpose in Christ, the best thing to do is to submit to it. With a series of five imperatives, the narrator appeals to people to submit to Christ. Being wise means to act wisely, setting aside the foolishness of rejecting Christ. Being instructed means to become teachable, setting aside the arrogance and obstinacy of self-will. Serving the Lord with fear means to surrender humbly to His authority, recognizing that He is the Lord, the Sovereign. Rejoicing with trembling means to find contentment and true happiness in the awareness and fear of the Lord. Kissing the Son means to embrace Him in homage and worship. The consequences of obeying or disobeying this gracious invitation were and are fixed. Irresistible wrath is on those who do not submit, and indescribable blessing is on those who do. Those who refuse Christ will perish. Those who seek refuge in Christ as the only place of safety are saved. In the truest sense, it is Christ who rescues the perishing. Note that these commands to trust Christ or suffer the consequences are not prophecies of how people would be saved after the incarnation. Christ was the only object of saving faith in the Old Testament dispensation just as He is the only object of saving faith now.

19

A Psalm for Christmas

PSALM 8

The messianic content and intent of Psalm 8 are confirmed four times in the New Testament. In answer to His enemies and would-be conspirators who protested the children's praise of Him on Palm Sunday, Jesus asked them if they had never read, "Out of the mouth of babes and sucklings thou hast perfected praise" (Matt. 21:16, quoting Ps. 8:2 and reflecting the interpretation of the Septuagint). Twice Paul explains Christ's resurrection, exaltation, and dominion in terms of Psalm 8 (1 Corinthians 15; Ephesians 1). Most significantly, Hebrews 2 interprets Psalm 8 as a description of the incarnation and earned exaltation of Christ. The whole psalm is a song highlighting the greatness and grace of God that points to the Lord Jesus as the only means by which fallen man can come to the enjoyment and experience of the privileged rank God assigned to human beings in creation.

Although verses 5 and 6 are the principal messianic statements, thus having independent significance, they are an integral part of the argument of the whole psalm. I want to focus my comments on these two verses, but I must first set them in the overall context. That the psalm begins and ends with the same statement marks this as a hymn of praise: "O LORD, our Lord, how excellent is thy name in all the earth!" This refrain says three things about God that reveal His glory and establish the topic for thanksgiving.

First, the names the psalmist uses reveal God's glory. "LORD" is Jehovah and identifies God as the covenant Savior of His people. Although this name reveals much about God's eternal self-sufficiency and absolute independence (I Am That I Am), it is uniquely the salvation name that He revealed in covenant promise. The title "Lord" is Adonai: it identifies God as the absolute Sovereign over everything. He is the owner, the master, the King of kings and Lord of lords. That His name is excellent declares that His entire being, with every infinite, eternal, and unchangeable perfection, is majestically glorious throughout the earth. The Lord our Savior has fixed His glory indelibly over all creation.

Having established the fact of God's glory, second, the psalmist David testifies to God's greatness and expresses his amazement that such greatness could be so gracious and condescending (vv. 2–4). The praising babes and sucklings testify to God's ironic use of weak things to confound the mighty. His using frail and defenseless beings to silence His enemies demonstrates His great power. This is a particular group of children who evidence far greater spiritual perception than religious leaders and professionals when they sing their hosannas to the Lord Jesus. Along with the infant chorus, the immense creation of the universe declares the same great glory. Notwithstanding the incomprehensible vastness of the universe, its existence is but the intricate finger work of God. If such an immense universe with all its complexities is but finger work, how infinitely great must be the "fingers" that created! From the beginning of creation until the end of time, the heavens have constantly declared and will unceasingly declare the glory of God (see Ps. 19:1). If the heavens are preaching and singing anything, it is "My God, how great Thou art."

Finally, considering the vastness of creation with its unfailing testimony to God's greatness raised the question in David's mind as to why God would give such special attention to man. He used two designations that contrasted man's puniness with creation's vastness: "What is man, that thou art mindful of him? and the son of man, that thou visitest him?" (Ps. 8:4). The first word, "man," underscores man's frailty, mortality, and impotence. The second expression, "the son of man [*adam*]," also represents man's inherent weakness and insignificance as earthy. Could this part of the psalm have been in Paul's mind when he said of Adam, "The first man is of the earth, earthy" (1 Cor. 15:47)? I think so. Sadly, man did not live up to what God made him to be. Made upright, he fell into sin (Eccl. 7:29). Yet notwithstanding the failure and frailty, God, with divine purpose, set His mind and special attention on man (the meaning of "visit"). The Lord intervened in the affairs of man. The thought of that condescending grace amazed David. This statement of the grace God deigned to bestow is the transition to the messianic text.

Verses 5 and 6 attest to man's creation in the image of God and his subsequent dominion over everything else created. The Genesis account clearly sets Adam apart from the rest of creation as the only being created in God's image and the only created being requiring the breath of God to live. Although there are several significant implications of man's having been created in God's image, the main reflection of it in Genesis was Adam's being commissioned with dominion over the rest of creation. It was not long before Adam fell, plunging his entire race into sin, making dominion a struggle, and severely marring, though not losing, the image of God. Psalm 8:5–6, however, speaks of a man who honorably and unfailingly fulfilled the high station God intended for man. It points to the "last Adam," "the second man." Whereas the first man was of the earth, "the second man is the Lord from heaven" (1 Cor. 15:45–47). Everything the first Adam lost, the second Adam regained. This points to Christ, who, being the eternal Son of God, became the ideal Man. In absolute perfection Jesus Christ was the "image of the invisible God" and the "brightness of his glory, and the express image of his person" (Col. 1:15; Heb. 1:3). I would suggest that Psalm 8 provided the foundation theology for Paul's analogy between Adam and Christ.

The New Testament helpfully confirms the messianic intent of this text, but it does not create it. Messianic clues and the ideality/uniqueness principle contextually point to Christ. The first clue comes from the opening statement, "Thou hast made him a little lower than the angels" (Ps. 8:5). The word "made" is not a word of creation that we would expect if the reference were to the first Adam. Rather, it literally means "to diminish," "to take away from," or "to deprive." The very meaning of the word requires the existence of the object or person being diminished. Adam, obviously, had no existence prior to his creation, but Christ eternally existed prior to His birth. It is a most vivid term to describe the humiliation of the incarnation. It parallels closely Paul's great incarnation passage declaring that Christ, being in the form of God, "made himself of no reputation" (Phil. 2:6–7). The word translated "a little lower" can be a temporal as well as a spatial word. The idea is that for a little while, God positioned His Son beneath the status of angels. The humiliation element of the incarnation was not forever; it lasted only long enough for Christ to perform the necessary obedience to merit and restore life to the race of which He was the head, the second Adam. In this temporary humiliation He, "by the grace of God," tasted "death for every man" (Heb. 2:9).

Unlike the first Adam, who had the glory and lost it, the second Adam started in humiliation and regained the honor and glory. The logic and order of verse 5 parallel Paul's in Philippians 2. After Christ humbled Himself, becoming obedient unto death, God highly exalted Him. Similarly, Peter saw in the resurrection, ascension, and session of Christ at God's right hand that Christ and the angels were again both in their right place (1 Peter 3:21–22). "All things" put "under His feet" (Ps. 8:6) pictures triumphant victory; all power and authority belong to Christ. He earned it, and He deserves it. Paul applied this merited exaltation both to Christ's mediatorial kingship over His church (Ephesians 1) and to the end of time when the last enemy, death itself, is destroyed (1 Corinthians 15). While the specific details may not be as obvious in Psalm 8 as in the New Testament, the essential theology is the same. Psalm 8 is indeed a Christmas song. The Messiah as the ideal Man was and is something to sing about: "Joy to the world! The Lord is come."

20

Christ, the Resolute Servant

PSALM 16

The New Testament confirms the messianic significance of Psalm 16. On the day of Pentecost, Peter appealed to Psalm 16:8–11 as his proof text for the resurrection of Jesus Christ. In so doing, he made it clear that David was a prophet who knew full well that he was writing about Christ (Acts 2:25–31). Similarly, Paul appealed to Psalm 16:10 as proof of Christ's resurrection, making it clear that the statement had no reference at all to David, whose dead body stayed buried and saw corruption (Acts 13:35–36). In the light of that inspired authority and confirmation, there can be no doubt that at least verses 8–11 of Psalm 16 have direct and unique reference to Jesus Christ. The question is whether the first seven verses are also messianic or there is a jump from David to his greater Son between verse 7 and 8.

I would suggest that the entirety of Psalm 16 refers to Christ. I do not see anything in the psalm that requires a transition from David to Christ or that does not have legitimate messianic relevance. I am happy to admit that there are statements in the psalm that can in some circumstances apply to all believers; that should not surprise us in view of the fact that Christ's humanity was a real humanity and that He endured and experienced the stuff of life. It is always good for us to see our union with Christ and His identification with us.

Although the term *servant* does not occur in the song, the thing that seems most impressive about the song as a whole is the absolute resolve and determination of Christ to fulfill His mission in submission to the Lord. Although it was the prophet David who wrote down the words, this psalm records for us the mind of Christ Himself: how He viewed His God, His people, and His mission.

Christ and His God

The first lesson concerns Christ's view of God. As the Messiah, He trusted the Lord, depending on Him and delighting in His will. The opening petition for preservation was a prayer that God might watch over Him, guarding and keeping Him as a shepherd would his sheep (v. 1). How often from the manger to Gethsemane did the Father answer that prayer as the Lord Jesus was delivered over and over again from the plots of rulers, anger of crowds, and onslaughts from the devil himself? The analogy of Scripture not only parallels this theme of divine preservation of the Messiah but also warrants our seeing Christ in this psalm as God's Servant. According to Isaiah, the Lord said to the Servant, "In an acceptable time have I heard thee, and in a day of salvation have I helped thee: and I will preserve thee, and give thee for a covenant of the people, to establish the earth, to cause to inherit the desolate heritages" (Isa. 49:8; see also 42:6). That Christ regarded the Lord as His portion and the one who maintained His lot in life is also expressed in His conscious sense of dependence on God (Ps. 16:5). This language links Christ with the priesthood, whose only inheritance was the Lord (Deut. 18:2). What the Levites imperfectly typified, Christ fulfilled perfectly. Ironically, He who created the world had no place even to lay His head while in the world, but daily He knew the fellowship and communion of His Father.

Most outstanding is Christ's determination to do the will of God. Although somewhat difficult to translate, the closing line of Psalm 16:2 is a synopsis testimony of Christ's total commitment to God. Let me offer this translation: "Thou art the Lord; My happiness is not in addition to Thee." The sense is simply that Christ found His contentment in and directed His goodness to the Lord only. With unrelenting resolve, Christ set Himself to accomplish the purpose for which He came into the world. As the ideal Prophet,

daily He received His instructions from the Lord: "I will bless the
LORD, who hath given me counsel: my reins also instruct me in the
night seasons" (v. 7). Compare this verse with another of Isaiah's
Servant Songs (Isa. 50:4–5) for this same focus. In both texts, God's
instruction to the Servant was followed with perfect and resolute
obedience and with the inflexible determination to keep the Lord's
presence and purpose foremost in His thoughts and life (Ps. 16:8).

Christ and His People

The second lesson concerns Christ's view of His people. Two statements in particular stand out in verse 3 and verse 6. From verse 3
we learn that what Christ did in fulfilling the will of God (v. 2), He
did with respect to or in reference to His people: "To the saints that
are in the earth, and to the excellent, in whom is all my delight." The
saints are the holy ones, those who are set apart as the beneficiaries
of the mediatorial work of Christ—those who are saved. The term
"excellent" further defines the saints as those who enjoy special rank
and privilege of position. The point is very simply that Christ's people
are special to Him.

From verse 6 we learn that Christ was confident that a people
had been given to Him and that therefore His mission would not be
in vain: "The lines are fallen unto me in pleasant places; yea, I have
a goodly heritage." Notwithstanding the frequent use of this verse
in testimony meetings, expressing thanks to God for station in life,
the messianic significance of this verse takes us right back to the
eternal promise to Christ that He would see His seed (Isa. 53:10)
and have His own house, "whose house are we" (Heb. 3:6). The word
"line" designates a rope or a cord and refers to an allotment that
would be marked off by the measuring cord. According to Deuteronomy 32:9, "The LORD's portion is his people; Jacob is the
lot of his inheritance." Similarly, in Psalm 2 the Lord offered the
heathen and the uttermost part of the earth to Messiah as His
inheritance and possession. That is precisely the idea in this context.
His saints and excellent ones are His inheritance who will populate
His glorious kingdom. Believers have a part in verse 6 after all; they

are the goodly heritage. That is a blessing that far exceeds any temporal placement in this life.

Christ and His Mission

The third lesson concerns Christ's view of His mission. This brings us specifically to the portions of Psalm 16 used in the New Testament. Christ knew from before His incarnation the direction and the end of His mission. He knew that glory would certainly follow His obedient humiliation and atoning death. According to verse 9, He rejoiced and confidently rested in that certain hope. Verses 10 and 11 fix on two essential elements in Christ's exaltation: the resurrection and the session at God's right hand. Although this psalm does not explicitly refer to Messiah's death, the simple fact that Christ expresses His confidence in a sure resurrection presupposes His knowledge of an antecedent death. The New Testament's interpretation and use of this verse require it to be an explicit declaration of the bodily resurrection of the Messiah from the grave. It has unique reference to Jesus. The Hebrew says the same thing, and this is clear when we remember that the word "soul" designates the person, not just the immaterial spirit, and that the word "hell" can refer to the grave (as it is so translated by the King James Version in about half of its occurrences; v. 10). Christ knew that the Lord would not abandon Him in the grave or allow Him to experience any corruption as dead bodies typically do. The Hebrew terms and parallel structure of the lines (the lines saying the same thing in a different way) make a clear, direct declaration of the real, bodily resurrection of Christ.

Verse 11 ends this prophetic prayer of Christ with His glorious presence at the right hand of God. We refer to this as the session of Christ. This is the place of the present mediatorial work of Christ as He represents His people, having guaranteed for them entrance to where He is. The reference to the path of life that the Lord showed Him from death to glory is the way that will be followed by all His believing people. As the firstfruit of the resurrection, He is the surety of our resurrection. He is the way, the truth, and the life.

Every believer will share in the earned pleasures and glory of Christ, the Savior. But sorrow awaits those who reject Christ for some other god. With sobering words, Christ declares that He will provide neither a sacrifice nor a prayer for those who reject Him (v. 4). This is not a happy note in this song, but it is one that must be sounded loudly.

21

The Wonder of God's Word

PSALM 19:7–14

Psalm 19 is one of the classic texts dealing with the word of God. Its theme is communication: God communicating to us, and we to Him. Structurally, the psalm develops in three sections. In verses 1–6, God communicates through nature. This general revelation is unceasing, understandable, and universal but unable to save since faith comes by hearing the word of God. In verses 7–10, He communicates through His word (special revelation), to which we respond by communicating through prayer (vv. 11–14). There is always a link between God's speaking and our praying: that is communication. The psalm addresses God's revelation through His works and word, but I want to focus our attention on the word. From Psalm 19, I want to think about what the Bible says about itself and how we ought to regard it as our prized possession.

Before we survey the section, pay attention to the parallel structure David uses in describing God's wonderful word. He gives a title, a characteristic, and an effect of the word (vv. 7–8); and then a title and an expanded characteristic of the word without specifying its effect (v. 9). Three broad statements sum up the wonder of Scripture: first, the attributes of the word declare its authority; second, the ability inherent in the word reveals its power; and third, the application demanded by the word is personal. A brief analysis of the six titles for God's word supports this synopsis.

The Law

First, the instruction of the Lord is complete (v. 7). The word "law" is *torah*, the body of instruction. It is the most general word in the Old Testament to designate all of special revelation. Whether in legislation, narrative, prophecy, or poetry, God's word is designed to teach—to reveal what could not be otherwise known. Its characteristic is that it is perfect. It is complete, lacking nothing. This obviously does not refer to the canon since much of the canon was yet to come from David's perspective. But it does mean that all the issues of necessary truth had been revealed at least in seed form. But certainly for us, God's word is complete in every way. The canon is complete, and God has spoken to us directly in His Son, His final Word (see Hebrews 1). That Jehovah is the source of this instruction elevates its importance even more. The covenant God of salvation has insured that we have what we need. His word shows the way to eternal life as well as maps the course for daily life. Its effect is the conversion of the soul. This means that it touches every part of life. The word "convert" has the idea of restoring, revitalizing, or energizing, and the word "soul" refers to the person, the whole man. The all-comprehensive message of God's revelation addresses the needs of the entire man. In Scripture, we have instructions for what we need to know for life and for death.

The Testimony

Second, the testimony of the Lord is trustworthy (v. 7). The word "testimony" refers to self-attestations. What we know of God is not relative theory or make-believe; God is not a figment of imagination. We know of Him what He has chosen to reveal about Himself. We must stand in wonder when we consider what God has chosen to reveal: a personal God who is the Creator and Sustainer of all, the Redeemer of His elect, the Judge of unrepentant sinners—and so much more!

His self-attestation is "sure." This word means "reliable" or "dependable." Whatever God says is true; it is a word that cannot be destroyed or proven wrong. It is worthy of belief. The effect of this reliable word is that it supplies our basic needs. The text specifically says that it makes "wise the simple." The point is that God addresses us where we are to minister to our needs. Those who are simpletons need wisdom, so God's word gives them wisdom. By extension, the implications are far-reaching. For those who sorrow, there is comfort; for those who sin, there is rebuke and warning; for the wayward, there is direction. The point is that whatever we need, we can find answers in the word of God.

The Statutes
Third, the precepts of the Lord are right (v. 8). The word "statutes" refers to what God has revealed from the vantage point of omniscience. He knows all that is knowable, things both actual and possible. He knows all simultaneously—both macroscopically as a whole and microscopically of all the parts. So what He has spoken from His divine oversight He has spoken on purpose with full knowledge of all our needs. There is not one wasted word in Scripture.

The word "right" (v. 8) means straight, referring to the right path to take. Without God's word, we would remain irretrievably lost. The waypoints to life and safety are clearly marked. As a consequence, God's word rejoices the heart. "Rejoicing" has the idea of being content or satisfied. Scripture has the power to bring satisfaction to our innermost being regardless of external circumstances. So many people never find contentment in life because they are trying to find it in all the wrong places. But because God knows exactly what we need, He has recorded in His word what we need. God will not disappoint His people when they seek their joy and contentment in Him.

The Commandment
Fourth, the commandment is clear (v. 8). This means that God's word consists of authoritative declarations, not suggestions or options. God means what He says, and it is imperative to get His point. Too often we hear what we want to hear, but discerning what He means is crucial. His is a living word, but it is not a floating message that

changes with time or circumstance. His intention must determine our response. The word "pure" means clear, bright, and radiant. It shines light on the path, giving clear directions to follow. The Bible is not filled with hidden codes designed to conceal the divine will, but rather with revelation to communicate that will to us. Granted, some things are easier to understand than others, but there is a message for all to comprehend, whether the layperson or the scholar. Significantly, this bright and shining word enlightens the eyes (the symbol of understanding) by giving discernment and putting everything in life in its proper perspective.

The Fear

Fifth, the fear of the Lord is pure (v. 9). What a title for the Bible this is! The word "fear" is a figure of speech (metonymy) designating the effect for the cause. God's word (the cause) produces fear (the effect). In Scripture, God allows Himself to be known, and to know God as He reveals Himself to be produces fear. The fear of God is that awareness of God that generates awe in the heart and obedience in the walk. The format of the psalm shifts at this point. Rather than stating characteristic and effect, it expands the characteristic. The first thought is it is "clean," meaning "refined or free from any defilement, impurity, or defect." Second, the word endures forever; it is eternally settled in heaven and thus imperishable. This implies as well that the relevance of the word is timeless and universal.

The Judgments

Sixth, the judgments of the Lord are perfect (v. 9). The word "judgments" refers to the record of God's decisions. The Bible is a casebook of the divine will. A casebook sets the precedence for determining proper actions in various situations. The Bible, therefore, is to be consulted in making the decisions of life. That they are true and completely righteous describes these decisions as perfect. They conform to and declare the Lord's absolute standards of what is right in terms of both doctrine and duty. It is imperative, then, to take heed to what He says.

The closing verses (vv. 10–14) reveal something of David's wonder over what he possessed in the revelation he had. The conclusion that God's word is more desirable than gold (the symbol of wealth) or honey (the symbol of pleasure) is logically appropriate (v. 10). For us, the Bible is a common possession. Many of us possess multiple copies—even in different languages. Although it is a common possession, nothing we possess is of any greater value; it has uncommon worth.

Finally, verses 11–14 demonstrate the link between God's word and prayer. Prayer should always flow from the word. In the light of God's word, David prayed for personal purity and pleasing behavior before the Lord. That is the pattern for us to follow. Let us stand in constant wonder that God has spoken to us and resolve to live in the light of that amazing word. It is so easy to get used to the most wonderful things and take them for granted. May that never be our attitude about this book. We confess that Scripture is our only rule for faith and practice. Let's live like we really believe it.

22

Christ, the Suffering and Successful Savior

PSALM 22

Psalm 22 is one of the places in Scripture that demand the removal of shoes because it is holy ground. It has been appropriately labeled the Crucifixion Psalm. It is hard to imagine that any Christian could come to this song without being confronted with thoughts of the suffering Savior. As a preacher and teacher, I confess this is one of those places that on the surface seems so easy to preach or teach and yet defies every effort to scale its height or plumb its depth. In this venue, I cannot begin to give a full exposition of the psalm, but I can suggest some things to consider and meditate on as you read it.

This psalm is messianic from beginning to end. It divides into two main parts marked by a significant transition statement in verse 21. The first division concerns the suffering Savior (vv. 1–21); the second division concerns the successful Savior (vv. 22–31). Perhaps because the details of the suffering are so explicit and because they parallel so closely the gospel narratives of the crucifixion, the first division is better known. But the second division finishes the gospel theology by moving to the resurrection and beyond.

Between the suffering and the success is a one-word transition: "Thou hast heard me." It's one word in Hebrew, anyway. I would translate verse 21 like this: "Deliver Me from the mouth of the lion and from the horns of the wild oxen. Thou hast answered Me." This translation highlights the shift from the series of requests to a fact. A contrast occurs. Logically as well as grammatically, the last word is set off from the preceding petitions that begin in verse 19. The Lord expresses His confidence that His prayers have been heard and then in the next section begins to detail the answer to those prayers. The second division makes it clear that all the suffering of the first division was not in vain.

As you meditate your way through this psalm, do so with what should become an overwhelming impression that you are reading what the blessed Savior said, thought, and prayed while He was suffering vicariously for His people on the cross. The New Testament reveals that the initial lament was audible: "My God, my God, why hast thou forsaken me?" (Matt. 27:46; Mark 15:34). There is no indication that the crowd could hear the rest of the prayer, but God heard. In this psalm, we are allowed into the mind and soul of the Savior. This is holy ground.

The Suffering Savior

The first division highlights three spheres of suffering endured by the Savior. He suffered before the holy God (vv. 1–5), by cruel men (vv. 6–11), and in His whole person, body and soul (vv. 12–18). The opening stanza (vv. 1–5) brings us to the heart of the atonement. The simple answer to Christ's agonizing "Why hast thou forsaken me?" is that God forsook His Son so that He could forgive us. With our sin and guilt imputed to Christ, He who knew no sin, having become sin for us, took the full force of God's just and necessary wrath against our sin. While Christ was suffering on the cross, God dealt with Him in terms of us. I confess a total inability to explain the utter dereliction of Christ that is expressed by this statement; it boggles the mind. It declares how absolutely offensive sin is to the holiness of God and how absolutely gracious God is in giving His dear Son to be the only Savior.

The second stanza (vv. 6–11) testifies to the cruelty of spiritually blind men who can look directly at the cross and reject the Savior. Note how closely Isaiah 53 echoes the language of verse 6 that describes the natural perception of Christ by unbelievers. He was despised and rejected, a Man of Sorrows indeed. Note how

closely Matthew 27:39–44 and Luke 23:35–39 reflect the actual
taunts of verses 7 and 8 made by the spectators, religious leaders, and
soldiers surrounding the cross. The One who in heaven had heard
the praise of pure angels, on the cross endured the mockery of puny
men. Whether then or now, it is impossible to look at the cross of
Christ without some reaction. Better to kiss the Son, as Psalm 2
recommended, than to join the mockery and unbelief that doom the
soul to destruction.

The final stanza (vv. 12–18) vividly describes the immense agony
Christ experienced on the cross. Part of the agony was in His innermost being as the bestial crowd hurled their hatred toward Him.
Described as "strong bulls" (v. 12); "a roaring lion" (v. 13); starving,
mangy, wild dogs (v. 16); and wild oxen (v. 21), the crowd inflicted
pain that whips and nails could not. Part of the agony was physical
torture that defies comprehension. Christ was exhausted with burning anguish (v. 14); His bones were disjointed (v. 14) and His body
stretched (v. 17); He endured intolerable thirst (v. 15); His hands
and feet were pierced (v. 16). Adding insult to all the immense injury
was that He was totally naked in public shame. The soldiers took His
garments and cast lots for the meager robe, His last material possession (v. 18). When Adam and Eve brought the curse on humankind,
plunging the race into sin, God in His grace provided garments to
cover the shame of their nakedness. On the cross, the Lord Jesus,
reversing the curse, was void of even that token of God's grace. He
paid the price of sin in complete shame.

Yet I see a twofold irony in His nakedness. On the one hand,
while He was naked He wove for us a garment of salvation, clothing us with a robe of righteousness (Isa. 61:10). On the other hand,
what appeared to be an evidence of defeat was in reality the ultimate
victory. It was normal procedure for soldiers to cast lots to divide the
spoils of those they had conquered. But this booty was so paltry that
sharing it would give them nothing; they cast lots to see who would
take the whole prize. It seemed as though wicked men had won the
day against Christ. The irony is that in His death, Christ won the
day. The cross crushed the serpent's head, and in just three days the

victory over death and Satan would be declared by the resurrection of Christ from the grave.

The Successful Savior

The second division reveals a most obvious shift from suffering agony to joyous celebration. Even as He suffered and died, the Savior was confident of the success of His mission; the joy was always before Him. His success is the subject of praise (vv. 22–24). It is significant that the first statement of the Savior's activity is that He declared God's name. Declaring God's name is prophet work. The Lord Jesus had staked His entire reputation and messiahship on His prophecy that God would raise Him from the dead. The resurrection sealed and confirmed Jesus Christ as the ideal Prophet. His life after death was the ultimate answer to all His prayers and petitions for deliverance (Heb. 5:7). What a message this was to proclaim to His brethren (see Heb. 2:12 for the unmistakable reference to Christ). The entire congregation of those who feared the Lord joined in praising God for the answered prayer in delivering the suffering Savior from His affliction, from death to life.

His success is also the surety of life for His people (vv. 25–29). In a most remarkable statement, the Savior pledges to fulfill His vows to those who fear the Lord. Verses 26 and 27 define the vow: He promises life and satisfaction to all throughout the world who will seek and turn to the Lord. Eating is a common image in both Testaments to picture the personal appropriation of faith. Just as eating sustains life and brings physical satisfaction, so faith in Christ brings life and spiritual satisfaction. Christ said that those who eat and drink of Him will never hunger or thirst again. Finding satisfaction and life in Christ is vital because "none can keep alive his own soul" (v. 29).

The climactic statement of His success is that there is a guaranteed seed (vv. 30–31). The seed that the Father had promised Him (Isa. 53:10) will in fact serve Him. Although the seed is fixed by promise, the means of claiming that seed for Christ is equally fixed. Faith comes by hearing the word of God. So according to this passage, the message concerning the Lord will be recounted (repeatedly told) to a generation. The word "generation" designates contemporaries of any particular span of life. The declaration of His righteousness to a people not yet born (this refers to us, you know) suggests that every generation has the duty and privilege to pass on the gospel truth to the next. The message for the future people was simply "he hath done." That says it all. Whatever had to be done for the salvation of guilty sinners, the suffering and successful Savior did. On the cross He declared, "It is finished," and it was. Nothing else need be or can be done to add to the work of Christ. To realize that we are part of that unborn people in the mind and heart of Christ on the cross and destined to hear the message of Christ is an overwhelmingly thrilling thought. Ought it not compel us to tell our generation the good news that Jesus saves?

23

A Theology of Trouble

PSALM 30

"Man that is born of a woman is of few days and full of trouble" (Job 14:1). This is one of those texts of Scripture that needs no explanation or exposition. Virtually every day of life confirms the truth; virtually every day we experience the tension between what we know to be true by faith and what we feel to be true by sight. We affirm by faith with Paul that if God is for us, none can be against us (Rom. 8:31), but the fact remains that so many things in life seem to be against us.

Significantly, the same apostle wrote to the Thessalonians about the afflictions to which the church was appointed (1 Thess. 3:3). The apostle himself experienced trouble on every side (2 Cor. 11:23–27), but through it all he testified of the sufficiency of God's grace (12:9). Paul knew that God's faithfulness was great and that His mercies were fresh every day to meet whatever the challenges of trouble.

Christianity is a life of self-insufficiency during which we must depend on God. Experiencing trouble is a key means of generating a renewed sense of dependence on God. In many ways, Psalm 30 is an exposition of that truth; it illustrates a theology of trouble designed to teach us to depend on God regardless of circumstances. David wrote this psalm after he had experienced some wave of trouble and records three key lessons he learned that would be good for us to learn as well. The historical context, suggested by the superscription, was most likely at the dedication of the altar on the threshing floor of

Araunah after the divinely sent plague in punishment of his numbering the people (2 Samuel 24).

Lesson 1: Without Trouble, We Often Miscalculate Reality

Lack of trouble can generate a false sense of security: "And in my
prosperity I said…" (v. 6). The word "prosperity" does not refer
to wealth but rather to undisturbed and careless ease, a quiet and
relaxed complacency. This was a strange place to be for David, whose
career was marked more by battles, betrayals, and opposition. David's
numbering the people was a reflection of his self-sufficiency as he
rested in the security of the magnitude of his might and the greatness of his mighty men. In the time of prosperity, he looked more on
his resources than on the Lord.

Tragically, there is something about prosperity that makes God's
people forget Him (see Deut. 8:7–20). Lack of trouble can also lead
to foolish boasting. David made two statements in his ease that
revealed unfounded pride: "I shall never be moved," and "LORD, by
thy favour thou hast made my mountain to stand strong" (vv. 6,
7). He regarded himself as invincible with a Peter-like arrogance
that boasted against ever denying the Lord, only to succumb to the
first temptation. Granted, he piously credited God with making his
mountain strong, but the statement "my mountain" says volumes
regarding David's perspective. All too easily we can fall into the
same frame of mind and expression. We all too easily, even when
giving recognition to the Lord for His work, refer to "my church,
my service, my [fill in the blank]." When all seems to be going well,
we so easily miscalculate reality. We must learn to depend on God
in the good times as well as in the bad. But there is something about
good times that adversely affects the memory. It has been said that
sunshine is more dangerous than storms. Spiritually speaking, that,
unfortunately, is true. It doesn't have to be, but without trouble we
tend to forget.

Lesson 2: In Trouble We Are Often Confused

The trouble that came to David was contrary to expectation: "Thou didst hide thy face, and I was troubled" (v. 7). God's hiding His face was a symbolic gesture of divine displeasure over David's expression of self-confidence. To say the least, David was shocked that God turned away from him in this manner. The word "troubled" more vividly has the idea of being horrified out of one's senses, of being disturbed out of ease. During a moment of ease, David numbered the people as an expression of his self-dependence. God intervened with the plague to bring David back to reality.

As is frequently the case, the hard providence of the Lord leads to struggles of reason. Often, the more we affirm the sovereignty of God in His work of providence, the more apt we are to be dismayed when trouble comes. Since God is in control of all things, why do bad things happen? This was David's question as he at first misunderstood what God was doing. His initial action was to cry to God and make supplication (v. 8). That was the right thing to do, but what he prayed betrayed his self-pity and his confusion about what God was doing. Things did not make sense, and he reasoned that God had erred, seemingly not thinking through the consequences of His chastening work: "What profit is there in my blood, when I go down to the pit? Shall the dust praise thee? shall it declare thy truth?" (v. 9). Even in his reasoned struggles, his focus was still on self. God was using the trouble to teach David again how much he needed the Lord, but in his foolishness, David thought that God needed him. He reasoned that God was going to lose a worshiper and a servant because of the trouble. How could God's glory be served without him? It didn't make any sense.

There is a natural tendency to misinterpret what God does when we don't understand it. This is demonstrated in the scene in Egypt between Joseph and his brothers before Joseph disclosed his identity. His brothers interpreted Joseph's behavior toward them to be harsh and unfair, but behind the scene Joseph wept in evidence of his compassionate heart for them. We sometimes respond to God the same way. We interpret what we see or experience as being harsh or unfair.

If we could only see behind the scene, we would see a God who has our best interest at heart and is in reality doing us good.

Lesson 3: Above Trouble, We Are Able to Put Things in Proper Perspective

Trouble should be a sanctifying experience. The psalmist elsewhere said, "Before I was afflicted I went astray: but now have I kept thy word" (119:67); and "It is good for me that I have been afflicted; that I might learn thy statutes" (v. 71). In Psalm 30, David finally gets it. Affliction brought him to the place of recognizing that his help was in the Lord and that he must completely depend on Him. The first thing he does is to pray (v. 10). But unlike the prayer expressed in verses 8 and 9, where he reasoned from what he perceived to be his worth to God, here he pleads for what he does not deserve. "Have mercy upon me" is, more literally, "Be gracious to me." The appeal to grace puts the focus directly on God and away from self, right where it needs to be. This petition is always in proportion to the sense of dependence on God.

His living above the trouble that began with prayer was sustained with joy (vv. 5, 11). Troubles come and go and sometimes stay, but it is possible to experience joy through every circumstance. Weeping in the midst of trouble is only temporary, just an overnight lodger, in view of God's purpose for sending the trouble (v. 5). The weeping transitions to joy because God turns mourning to dancing and exchanges sackcloth, the symbol of sorrow, for a belt of gladness (v. 11). This change of attitude is unrelated to any actual change of circumstance. We can live above trouble even in the middle of it. As the psalmist testified, "Trouble and anguish have taken hold on me: yet thy commandments are my delights" (119:143).

Living above trouble finds expression in praise (vv. 1–4, 12). The beginning of the psalm indicates that David had learned his lesson and had put things in proper perspective. He begins with praise, extolling the Lord by regarding Him as high and exalted (v. 1). His praise is reasoned and extensive. He praises the Lord because his enemies have been silenced (v. 1), because he has been forgiven (the sense of being healed in v. 2), and because he has experienced deliverance from trouble (v. 3). Praise is an effective means of moving attention away from self and thus the source of discontentment at God's providence. Praise highlights God and breeds contentment in all His works. The ending of the psalm underscores the extent of David's praise as he confesses his objective to devote and engage all of his assets (the significance of "glory" in v. 12) to praising the Lord forever. This is the key lesson to learn.

Glorifying God and enjoying Him is our chief end. With that purpose in view, the troubles of life are not hindrances to praise but rather reasons for it. There is hardly a better way to glorify and enjoy God than living in conscious dependence on Him. He aids us to live that way by bringing a bit of trouble from time to time: "In the day of prosperity be joyful, but in the day of adversity consider: God also hath set the one over against the other, to the end that man should find nothing after [H]im" (Eccl. 7:14). Faith sees theology in the time of trouble.

24

How Faith Looks at Life

PSALM 37

Faith is not the stuff of dreams. Faith is practical and realistic because it engages God, the one great and absolute reality. To trust Him is to enter the world of fact, not fiction or make-believe. Naturally, we arrive at knowledge by observation; we tend to believe the report of our senses. After all, seeing is believing. Biblical faith, however, introduces another element: believing is seeing. It is by faith that we know, regardless of what we see. The problem of living by faith is very simply that it is all too easy to walk by sight. The tension between what we believe and what we see is sometimes overwhelming. It seems that this tension that is all too frequent in our hearts bothered the inspired psalmists as well. How many times in the Psalms do we find discouragement over this or that, and how many times do we see the inspired psalmist praying and praising his way out of that despair? The Psalms constantly remind us that unless there is the constant use of the means of grace we will revert to the same problems over and again.

Psalm 37 is one of a trilogy of psalms (along with 49 and 73) that directly addresses the issue of the apparent inequities of life, particularly the prosperity of the wicked. The psalm is an acrostic (each unit beginning with the sequential letter of the alphabet) in four stanzas: (1) counsel not to fret (vv. 1–11); (2) the temporary prosperity of the wicked (vv. 12–20); (3) the certain reward of the righteous (vv. 21–31); and (4) a final contrast of fates (vv. 32–40).

In this meditation, our attention will be on the first stanza, where three times we are commanded not to fret (vv. 1, 7, 8). The Hebrew word has the idea of getting agitated, heated, or bothered. If we are not to get hot and bothered by the stuff of life, we should follow the counsel as to how faith should look at life.

The Future Look

Psalm 1 contrasts the righteous and the wicked, and clearly it is the righteous who experience and enjoy the blessing. Yet so often the opposite appears to be the case. The prosperity of the wicked is something that can grate on faith. The most spiritual men have been bothered by it, as Jeremiah confessed more than once (Jer. 12:1; 15:17). But appearance and reality do not necessarily equate, and looking to the certain future puts things in the proper perspective. Faith's future look puts two things in focus.

First, the future is bad for the wicked (Ps. 37:2, 9, 10). It is a sobering truth that this life is the best it will ever be for the wicked, and this life is so brief. The text makes this point both figuratively and literally. The wicked are like grass, a common image for that which is weak, transient, and perishable (see Pss. 90:5–6; 103:15–16). It doesn't take long for grass, which for a while appears lush, to wither and lose its beauty as the seasons change. So it is with the wicked. Verses 9 and 10 make the point directly: they will be cut off in a little while and be no more. Divine justice prevails; the triumph is short, and the weeping is everlasting. Here, then, is the folly of fretting over something that is so temporary. Not fretting does not mean that we are to rejoice in their coming calamity. On the contrary, if temporal tragedy generates efforts to alleviate suffering, how much more should the prospect of eternal tragedy move believers to warn the wicked of impending judgment lest they repent?

Second, the future is good for the righteous (vv. 9, 11). There is a promise to the meek (those who are afflicted and oppressed) that they will inherit the land (see Matt. 5:5), implying rest and enjoyment of God's presence, and that they will take delight, or literally "pamper themselves," in the enjoyment of peace. This

prospect belongs to those who wait on the Lord. To wait is to hope
with confident expectation and anticipation in what God will do.
Waiting actively with importunity is the future focus of faith. It is
not wishful thinking; it is confidence in God's unfailing word.

This is the bottom line: the sight of eternity puts the experi-
ences of time in the right perspective. Paul learned the secret of this
(2 Cor. 4:17–18), and so should we.

The Godward Look

Biblical faith is always objective; the object of faith determines its
value. The focus of faith is God; this is why it is not a vain or useless thing to wait on the Lord. It is looking to God that provides
contentment in life regardless of circumstance. Although eternity
puts things in perspective, our religion is not just a narcotic to tide
us over to eternity. There is a way to be content, to be satisfied—dare
I say, to be happy in this life. It is a preoccupation with the Lord that
achieves perfect peace (see Isa. 26:3–4). The text suggests five steps
to finding contentment.

First, *trust in the Lord* (vv. 3, 5). To trust is to find safety, refuge, and
security. Finding in the Lord our refuge generates the confidence
that in Him all must be well and thus enables us to submit to His
will, whatever it may be.

Second, *dwell in the land and graze on faithfulness* (v. 3). This is the
literal translation reflecting the imperatives in the Hebrew that
together form a unit of thought. In the Old Testament, the land
concept was symbolic of God's presence; thus, dwelling in the land
was always conditioned by faith and obedience (see the warnings of
Moses in Deuteronomy 27–28). So the first imperative is a call to
faith to take up residence where God is. In residence with the Lord,
we are to nourish ourselves consistently in God's steadfastness. The
word "faithfulness" (translated "verily" in the King James Version) is
the same word Habakkuk uses to describe how the just are to live
(Hab. 2:4). Living by faith is feeding on the Lord.

Third, *delight in the Lord* (v. 4). To "delight" is to make merry over, even to pamper oneself—perhaps an odd expression, but it vividly pictures how we should be overwhelmed with the God of covenant grace and find in Him what really makes us happy. If it is in the Lord that we seek contentment, then we will not be disappointed because God's desire is to draw near to us as we draw near to Him (James 4:8). The Hebrew reads, "Take delight in the Lord so that He can give you the desires of thine heart." It is as though the Lord is "waiting" for us to delight in Him so He can grant us what we desire (what we delight in), which is the rich experience of Himself.

Fourth, "*commit thy way unto the LORD*" (v. 5)—literally, "roll upon the Lord your way." We are to cast all our cares, anxieties, and nagging concerns to Him with the confidence that He will take care of them. Implied in the rolling over to Him is the leaving of what we roll. Too often in prayer we cast our cares on Him and take them back when we say amen.

Fifth, "*rest in the LORD, and wait*" (v. 7). The Hebrew word translated "rest" means "to be quiet" or "keep still"; in other words, just calm down. It is the opposite of the fretting and agitation that occurs so naturally. We can know contentment as we look to God with that patient expectation that all will be well. Evaluating our life by comparing it with another's life will never bring contentment. Looking to God and enjoying Him is how faith ought to look at life.

Thus, looking to the future and looking to God are the right ways for faith to look at life. It follows that if we look at life rightly, we will live rightly as well, since thinking always determines behavior. The psalmist sums up the proper lifestyle for God's people in simple terms: "do good" (v. 3), and don't do bad (v. 8). That is the essence of sanctification's mandate, to die to sin and to live to righteousness. That is a good way to live and is possible only through faith. What we see can so easily bother us, but we must not be blind to what is more real than sight. Only those realities can keep us calm and content. Faith enables us to live in reality.

25

Formula for Security

PSALM 91

These are scary times. Danger seems to lurk everywhere; there seems to be no safe place on earth. Fear and paranoia reign in most of society. It would be foolish to deny that the dangers and threats are real, and we must not—even in the exercise of our faith—presume that we are immune. Yet even in the places of danger through which we must walk with our eyes open to reality, we can and should enjoy peace and confidence. The God who will keep us forever keeps us now. He neither slumbers nor sleeps, and He is our refuge and strength, a very present help in trouble. Therefore, we should not fear even if the earth should change (see Psalm 46).

Psalm 91 develops this theme of the present security believers have in the Lord. It reminds us that the saving, protecting, strengthening power of God is the personal experience of believers through all the trials, terrors, and temptations of life. Although anonymous, there is a good tradition that attributes the psalm to Moses, who in Deuteronomy 33:27 testified that the eternal God is our refuge and underneath are His everlasting arms. Throughout his career, Moses was in constant danger and distress, but God never left him without His presence, provision, and protection. This psalm is an expression of faith at its best. It is the poetic version of Paul's bold statement, "If God be for us, who can be against us?" (Rom. 8:31). To live in the spirit of this psalm is to be fearless in all the circumstances of life. This hope and confidence is not just a whistling in the dark; it is a real possibility as we focus on the Lord and not the surroundings. The psalmist sets before us three ways to experience and enjoy the security that is founded in the Lord.

How to Stay Sane in a Crazy World

The person of the Lord is the basis for our sanity in a world that in many ways makes no sense. The more of our attention that we focus on the Lord, the greater will be our confidence that He is in control and is trustworthy as our faithful God. In the first two verses of Psalm 91, the psalmist directs attention to the Lord with four titles that declare significant propositional truths about who God is and what He is to us.

First, *He is the Most High; therefore, He owns us.* The first occurrence of this title links the statement of God's exalted status over all creation with the fact that He is the "possessor of heaven and earth" (Gen. 14:19). The Lord's ownership of the world is the corollary to His creating the world. He owns what He has created, and He has the right to rule what He owns. Indeed, He owns the cattle on a thousand hills, the wealth in every mine; the fullness of all the earth is His. There is nothing that is outside the realm of His rule. God's people happily confess that the Lord has made them, and therefore by virtue of that creation they belong to Him (Ps. 100:3). But believers can also confess that God doubly owns them, both by creation and by redemption. Consequently, they are His prized possession and the objects of His special care.

By faith, believers should take up their residence in the secret place of the Most High. The secret place refers to a hiding place, an asylum. What a place of safety that is! To dwell with the Most High God is to be out of the reach of those who would harm. Certainly, to be "in heavenly places in Christ" spiritually (Eph. 1:3) should translate into temporal confidence regardless of circumstances.

Second, *He is the Almighty; therefore, He sustains us.* The title Almighty is *Shaddai*, which reveals the Lord as the one who provides for and

nourishes His people. He is the keeper of every promise. He is sufficient to meet every need because He has the will, heart, and power to
do so. By faith, believers should abide under His shadow. To "abide"
literally means to keep on spending the night. In the Old Testament,
the shadow was a common image of a host/guest relationship. The
host assumed the responsibility for the complete welfare of his guest,
including protection and provision. To "spend the night" with the
Lord is to be not only secluded from danger but at rest knowing that
God has assumed the responsibility for our care. *Shaddai* keeps His
word and fulfills His obligations.

Third, *He is the "LORD"; therefore He saves us.* This title is Jehovah, the
very name of the covenant-keeping God. Because He is the covenant
God, believers should have confidence in His saving faithfulness.
Significantly, the psalmist expresses his personal faith: "I will say of
the LORD, He is my refuge and my fortress." The "refuge" refers to
a shelter, and the "fortress" refers to a mountain stronghold—places
of safety and deliverance. This is a truth about God to live by; it is
not abstract theology. That God is safety and deliverance means little
if it is not true experientially. We must prove what we profess to
believe by our actions. When in danger, flee to Him.

Fourth, *He is "my God"; therefore He is able.* God is the general term
for deity and declares Him to be the transcendent Creator who is
infinitely powerful. By faith the psalmist claims a personal relationship with this transcendent God and confesses his trust. To trust
is to find safety in the object of trust, and the psalmist knows that
his God is reliable and trustworthy. God would not let him down
because under him were the everlasting arms of the omnipotent and
eternal God.

How to Be Safe in a Dangerous World

Verses 3–13 detail God's providence to accomplish the desired end
of His glory and His people's good. The psalmist highlights three
thoughts about God's protection.

First, *His protection is all encompassing* (vv. 3–4, 10–12). Verse 10 is the summary, all-inclusive statement: "There shall no evil befall thee." "Evil" refers to danger, trouble, or calamity; nothing is exposed to the onslaughts against us (see the complete armor of Ephesians 6). Specifically, God provides safety against external threats (v. 3). The bird snare (a net to entangle and filled with bait to allure) and the noisome pestilence (literally, pit of destruction) refer to all the man-made or spiritual perils that can bombard the soul. For this reason, we should pray as Christ instructed: Deliver us from evil, and lead us not into temptation. Also, God provides safety in His loving care (v. 4). With a beautiful image, the psalmist compares God's protection of His people to feeble little chicks who are subject to the snare but who find safety under the wings of the mother hen, exposing herself to danger while sheltering her chicks. Isaiah explained this when he said of the Lord's presence with the wilderness generation: "In all their affliction he was afflicted, and the angel of his presence saved them: in his love and in his pity he redeemed them; and he bare them, and carried them all the days of old" (Isa. 63:9). The image shifts in the second part of verse 4, but the truth is the same. The Lord's unfailing word is a shield (that which covers the body) and buckler (the round movable shield to ward off well-aimed assaults). Finally, the psalmist instructs that God provides safety through the operation of angels, those ministering spirits who are the agents of His providence (vv. 11–12). They guard like a shepherd watching over a flock and like a nurse who lifts up a child into her arms. Angels are spiritual beings operating beyond sight, but operating nonetheless.

Second, *His protection is personal* (vv. 7–9). Believers are special to God, and His care for them is discriminating. His people are restricted to the sidelines as spectators of the calamity that will befall the wicked. Trouble may be all around that threatens faith in the good providence of God, but the wonderful fact is that no one who trusts God will ultimately fall. His purpose stands, and no believer will ever be subject to the judgment of the wicked.

Third, *His protection demands a response* (vv. 5–6, 13). The demanded response is fearless boldness. With forceful language the psalmist commands, "Thou shalt not be afraid" (v. 5). Not fearing in scary situations (terrors, arrows, pestilence, and destruction) is walking by faith and not by sight. Not to be afraid of the fearful things that can be seen requires consciousness of a greater power that is unseen but infinitely more real. The fear of God dispels fear of everything else. Why should we fear the stuff of this crazy world if we believe that He owns and rules all that is? This kind of faith generates action and confidence to conquer the things that otherwise would cause the fear (lions, adders, and dragons). Resting in providence is active, not passive.

How to Be Satisfied in an Uncertain World

In verses 14–16, the Lord interrupts the inspired poet and speaks for Himself concerning His own, thus reinforcing the guarantee of salvation both in time and for eternity. Knowing that nothing can separate the believer from God's love is grounds for satisfaction.

First, *God promises mutual love* (v. 14). Love reciprocates. We love God because God first loved us, and as we love, He keeps evidencing His love for us. To "set his love" literally has the idea of being attached to, referring to an intimate clinging or cleaving to the object of the love. Knowing God's name refers to an intimate relationship to His person. God's promise is to deliver and exalt those who love and know Him by bringing them near to Him. As James said, "Draw nigh to God, and he will draw nigh to you" (James 4:8). As we are brought near to Him, we can live in confident satisfaction even in the midst of turmoil.

Second, *God promises His presence* (v. 15). This is the key thought and foundational to contentment. God does not promise that there will not be trouble, but He does promise that He will be with His people in the midst of trouble. This is the Immanuel concept that is so precious to believers. Regardless of circumstances, God is with His people, and He answers them in their distress (see Ps. 34:6).

Third, *God promises satisfaction* (v. 16). When God's people rest in His love and presence, they will be content in whatever state they are in. God is never a disappointment, and He promises to satisfy with long life and salvation. Dying old or young is not the issue but rather living out the measure of one's allotted days with satisfaction and readiness to leave this life for the next. Satisfaction and security come when we realize that our times are in His hands, and there is no better place to be.

26

Christ, the King and Priest

PSALM 110

The New Testament quotes Psalm 110 fourteen times—more than any other text in the Old Testament. In each instance, it applies the psalm to Christ. This psalm is a compendium of theological truths concerning the person and mediatorial operation of Christ, from His place in the Trinity to His royal priesthood to His final triumph over every enemy. The argument of this psalm flows from the two propositions in verses 1 and 4, which are most frequently quoted in the New Testament.

Kingship

The first proposition is that *Christ is king.* Three issues about Christ's kingship stand out in this section: who He is, where He is, and what He does. The opening words identify Christ: "The oracle of Jehovah to my Sovereign" (my translation). The word "oracle" is more common to the prophets than to the poets, but here David speaks with prophetic authority as he records the communication between Jehovah and His Son, David's superior Seed. The particular form "my Lord," which I translated "my Sovereign," is key to the argument and an essential point in some of the New Testament quotations. There is a subtle yet significant difference between this form and the form that invariably refers to deity. The word *Adonai* always refers to God, including Christ specifically. The word here is *Adoni*—not a big difference. Even though this form does not necessarily designate deity, it does designate one who is the superior owner and master. For David, the king and highest superior on earth, to acknowledge One to be his superior and master and sovereign was an expression of his faith in the covenant promise that the ideal King coming through his family line was indeed the Messiah. This form (*Adoni*) does not preclude the deity of David's confessed Sovereign; that is just not the point he is making here. Instead, here is the point that Christ focused on in one of His contests with the Jewish religious leaders to prove His messiahship and to prove that David knew it. His logic was irrefutable (Matt. 22:41–46). Who is Christ? He is David's King, the one, true mediatorial King.

Jehovah's word to Christ answers the question of where He is: He is sitting at the right hand of God. God's right hand is a unique position of honor, exaltation, and majesty. Theologically, this refers to Christ's session. It is a position that He earned by His mediatorial obedience. That He sat down suggests that the work of redemption was done, and that He sat down at the right hand suggests that the work was well done.

What Christ does is rule. This is what kings do. His session is not passive; He will continue to rule from His place of honor until every enemy becomes His footstool. The psalmist is presenting the relatively common contemporary image of a conqueror with his foot resting on the neck of a defeated enemy as a gesture of victory. That He is ruling with His royal scepter ("the rod of thy strength," v. 2) in the midst of His enemies indicates that all the enemies are not yet subdued but that they most certainly will be (see 1 Cor. 15:24).

Proverbs 14:28 says that "in the multitude of people is the king's honour." The psalmist, therefore, fittingly draws special attention to those who are ruled by the messianic King. The contrast between His subjects is significant: they are either enemies or a willing people. He rules and conquers either by grace or in wrath, but either way, He certainly rules and conquers. Grace transforms enemies of Christ into soldiers of Christ. Having Christ ruling from the heart is eternally better than having His foot on the neck.

Priesthood

The second proposition is that *Christ is priest*. The uniting of the kingly and priestly offices invariably points to Christ. After the establishment of the official Aaronic priesthood and official Davidic kingship, the offices of king and priest were distinct. Only in the ideal King and ideal Priest would these two mediatorial operations be united in a single person.

Psalm 110:4 is a theological benchmark in Old Testament revelation. It resolves the paradox of how one person could fulfill these two offices that formerly were represented by two distinct tribes and families. How could Messiah be from the tribes of Levi and Judah at the same time? Obviously, He could not. From the beginning of Aaron's priesthood, the Lord had built in some factors that pointed to the obsolescence of Aaron's temporary priesthood. Remember that Genesis, with its record of Abraham's encounter with Melchizedek, was written to the same people at about the same time as the details establishing and explaining the Levitical priesthood. From the beginning, God made it clear that there was a priesthood superior to Aaron's. David understood and declared that the Messiah's priesthood was not after Aaron's order but after Melchizedek's. All you have to do to see the importance of this benchmark declaration is to read the book of Hebrews.

Three important elements of Christ's priesthood are presented in verse 4. First, Christ is a priest on the authority of God's irrevocable decree. What God says without oath is both sure and steadfast. For God to swear is to heighten and intensify the certainty of what He says. The certainty of the decree is strengthened even more by the promise that He will not repent, which simply means that He will never regret His decision or change His immutable mind. This stands as a stern warning against attempts to approach God apart from this one and only Priest whom He has chosen and ordained.

Second, Christ is a priest forever. Unlike Aaron, Christ would not be the head of a dynasty of priests; none would follow Him because His priesthood was perfect and effective. Hebrews explains the significance of this far better than I can: "But this man, because he continueth ever, hath an unchangeable priesthood [i.e., not transferable, not to be passed to another]. Wherefore he is able also to save them to the uttermost [i.e., completely and finally] that come unto God by him, seeing he ever liveth to make intercession for them" (7:24–25).

Third, Christ is a priest after a special order. He is like Melchizedek. Apart from the historical introduction of Melchizedek in Genesis 14, Psalm 110 is the only other Old Testament reference to him. The book of Hebrews, however, expands and explains why and how Melchizedek's priesthood was so superior to Aaron's and why it prefigured so well the priesthood of Christ. The ideal Priest would also be the ideal King, the King of righteousness and of peace. The order of Melchizedek resolves the tension between kingly and priestly functions that could not be resolved outside of Jesus Christ. Not only is the union of the two offices in a single person unique to Christ, but so is the union of the two virtues. The name Melchizedek literally means "king of righteousness," and according to the Genesis record, he was the king of Salem, which means "peace."

That is a most amazing combination of virtues when we realize that righteousness and peace have not coexisted in any created person since the fall. Man's unrighteousness renders peace with God impossible. But in the perfect Man, the perfect Priest who represents His people, "mercy and truth are met together; righteousness and peace have kissed each other" (Ps. 85:10).

Perhaps to emphasize that this decreed Priest of verse 4 is the same exalted King of verse 1, the activity of the Priest in the closing verses relates more to kingly operations than to priestly functions. Whereas verses 2 and 3 seem to describe aspects of Christ's present rule, verses 5–7 jump ahead to the final contests in which every last one of His enemies becomes His footstool. These verses emphasize His just wrath against His enemies. The language is graphic and fearfully wonderful. According to verse 5, in the day of His wrath, He with the Lord at His right hand will irreversibly beat into pieces opposing kings. According to verse 6, He will execute justice on sinners, heaping up their dead bodies in rotting piles—not a pretty picture.

But most significantly, He will "wound the heads over many countries." Interestingly, the word "wound" is the same word translated "strike through" in verse 5. Since the word literally means to beat into pieces, this would be a fatal blow. Also noteworthy is that the word "heads" is actually the singular form "head." I don't think I am going too far in identifying this head as Satan himself, who in that last day gathers the nations in his last-ditch effort against Christ (see Rev. 20:7–10). Not only does this point ahead to that future and final victory over Satan but it also points back to that first gospel promise that the Seed of the woman would crush the head of the serpent (Gen. 3:15). Isn't it thrilling how everything ties together in God's Word?

Finally, verse 7 describes Christ's ultimate victory. Having crushed Satan's head, He lifts up His own head in triumph and glory. With His head held high, He rests His feet. Certainly those who have in grace already submitted to this King-Priest can rejoice and lift up their heads with Him, knowing that their redemption draws nigh (Luke 21:28). This psalm stands as testimony that Christ will fulfill every mediatorial duty necessary for our salvation. It also stands as a warning to sinners who have not submitted to Him to submit before His mercy gives way to wrath.

27

The Birth of Immanuel

ISAIAH 7

The coming of the Son of God in human flesh is the best news that helpless and doomed humanity has ever heard. In the fullness of time—at the appropriate and eternally determined moment—the virgin conceived and bore a son. And what a Son He was: Son of God and Son of Man! The Seed of the woman through the seed of Abraham and then of David would be the source of blessing for the whole world.

Christ's birth started something; it inaugurated a new day. The incarnation made the difference between light and darkness, life and death. The message of Christ, particularly the Old Testament revelation of the messianic hope, is often set in contexts of darkness, gloom, and despair. Christ is always God's answer to man's problem. Prophesying about Christ as God's answer to man's need was part of the genius of Isaiah as a preacher of the gospel. Isaiah 7–12 is the Book of Immanuel and contains three great "Christmas texts" that declare the gospel—the good news that shines the light of hope into a world that otherwise would remain in total darkness.

The trilogy is set in the context of Assyrian domination. Assyria was a ruthless and pagan power that threatened the existence of the covenant nation and consequently seemed to jeopardize the progression of God's redemptive purpose. Assyria was a key contributor to that ongoing hostility between the Seed of the woman and the seed of the serpent that was all part of God's redemptive plan (Gen. 3:15).

Although the days were dark, Isaiah's prophecy of the certain coming Christ was God's "not-to-worry" message to His anxious people
that everything was on track to the fullness of time. Isaiah sees the
darkness dispelled by the dawn of the messianic day of salvation. His
Immanuel Trilogy declares truths about both the person and work
of the Messiah and wonderfully declares the gospel. The first in the
series declares the birth of Christ and thus introduces the great mystery: God was manifest in the flesh.

Matthew 1:23 removes any doubt that Isaiah's prophecy of the
virgin birth refers directly and uniquely to Jesus, the son of the virgin
Mary. To Isaiah's generation the virgin birth was to be confirmation
of divine deliverance from the hostile forces (Assyria and Syria) that
threatened national freedom. To every generation, the virgin-born
Immanuel is confirmation of God's gracious purpose of deliverance
from hostile powers far greater than any national enemy—indeed,
deliverance from the enemies of the soul. The prophecy highlights
two important truths about the incarnation of the Son of God.

The Supernatural Birth

Isaiah 7 begins with Isaiah's admonition to Ahaz to trust the Lord
for deliverance from the impending threat of an Israeli-Syrian
coalition. If he would only believe, he would be established (v. 9).
Isaiah offered him any extraordinary sign of his own choosing to
confirm the certainty of God's word. In his unbelief, Ahaz rejected
the offer (vv. 11–12), but God gave a sign anyway—just not to him.
His rejection of the personal sign (note the singular "thee" of v. 11)
led to God's giving to the nation (note the plural "you" in v. 14) what
would be the most extraordinary confirmation in the history of the
world that the Israeli-Syrian threat would come to nothing. Indeed,
when the sign occurred, both kings would be long forsaken (v. 16).
The stupendous sign given to Judah marked the fullness of time and
changed everything for everybody.

The sign was to be an extraordinary birth of an extraordinary
Son. Isaiah announces the incomprehensible birth with the inter-
jection "behold" (v. 14). This is like putting an exclamation point at

the beginning of a sentence to call special attention to something remarkable. What he was about to say defied human experience and understanding: a virgin was about to conceive and bear a son. A supernatural birth was going to happen.

Although some interpret the word "virgin" to refer merely to a young woman of marriageable age, the word that Isaiah uses is the only word in the Old Testament that designates a virgin in the strictest sense of the term without any additional qualification (v. 14). That she was also young and marriageable may be true enough, but that is not the issue. Certainly her giving birth would not be contrary to the norm if age were the only thing designated. Wherever this word occurs in the Old Testament, the purity of the young lady is assumed. There is another word translated as "virgin" in the King James Version, but it can refer to a widow (Joel 1:8), someone who had been married. When it does refer to a sexually pure virgin, it requires the further restriction that no man knew her (e.g., Gen. 24:16). If Isaiah had used that word without further qualification, the nature of this announced birth could be open to interpretation. Instead, guided by the Holy Spirit, he uses a word that clearly refers to a young woman who is a virgin. This restricted understanding of the word is reflected both in the Septuagint and in Matthew's quotation. The meaning of the Greek word is undisputed in its reference to a virgin in the narrowest sense and thus silences any contrary interpretation. This portion of the Old Testament would have been translated at least 150 years before Jesus of Nazareth, so it cannot be charged with choosing a word because of a Jesus bias. The translators used the Greek word for virgin simply because they were translating the Hebrew word for virgin. That the divinely inspired Matthew uses the same word settles the question about the nature of this sign-birth.

How a virgin could conceive and bear a son is beyond human explanation. The virgin birth of Christ, a cardinal truth of Christianity, is a mystery and the most stupendous miracle of all of God's supernatural acts. To explain it is beyond human ability; to deny it is outside the bounds of orthodoxy. The fact of it is gospel.

The Extraordinary Person

A virgin birth alone would be wondrous, but the Son born of the virgin magnifies the wonder beyond wonder. The miraculously born Son is Immanuel, "with us is God."

God's presence with His people is a theme that runs throughout Scripture, and in one manifestation or another was the experience of His people in the old dispensation. In times of crisis, God often assured His people that He would be with them. God was with the patriarchs when they were threatened in their travels (Abraham, Gen. 26:3; Jacob, Gen. 28:15; Joseph, Gen. 39:2). He promised to be with Joshua just as He had been with Moses (Josh. 1:5) as he prepared for the conflicts in Canaan. God's being with David in his walk through the valley of death produced fearlessness and comfort (Ps. 23:4). It was Solomon's prayer that God would continue to be with his generation as He had been in earlier times—indeed, that He would never leave nor forsake them (1 Kings 8:57). With wide-sweeping application, the Lord promised that He would be with all who would call on Him in times of trouble (Ps. 91:15). God's presence was not just for protection or comfort but for fellowship as well. The tabernacle and then the temple, particularly with the ark of the covenant, manifested Immanuel theology, God's being with His people.

The presence that was known only by faith and via symbol was visibly realized with the birth of Jesus Christ, the Son of God. The virgin brought forth the most extraordinary person: the Son of God became the Son of Man. The invisible God became visible in the person of Jesus Christ, the only Redeemer of God's elect, the only Mediator between God and men. The coming of Immanuel into the world in human flesh is the climax of redemptive history. From the first promise of the Curse-Reverser coming into humanity as the Seed of the woman to the promised seed of Abraham and then to the seed of David, all of time was moving steadily, unfailingly, and sometimes mysteriously to this fullness of time when God sent forth His Son made of a woman (Gal. 4:4). Immanuel, the incarnate God, came to redeem His people by destroying the great enemy, the devil

(Gen. 3:15; Heb. 2:14); to deliver them from the bondage of death (vv. 15–16); and to make reconciliation for them (v. 17). That God was with us visibly in Jesus Christ was and remains the only hope for the world.

Although Immanuel physically is no longer in our presence, the truth of His name remains, for "Jesus Christ the same yesterday, and to day, and for ever" (Heb. 13:8). He is in us, "the hope of glory" (Col. 1:27), and our prospect is that we will always be with Him (1 Thess. 4:17). He continues with His church, and His desire is that He will be with us forever (John 17:24). O come, O come, Immanuel.

28

The Kingship of Immanuel

ISAIAH 9

There is little wonder why Isaiah is often called the fifth gospel. Isaiah 9 is in the middle of what is called the Immanuel Trilogy or Book of Immanuel (7–12), which includes three principal texts so appropriately used every Christmas season. Chapter 7 pointed to the virgin birth of Immanuel, God with us. Chapter 11 will describe the ministry and work of David's most royal Seed. At the center of the trilogy, chapter 9, with its most famous verse 6, identifies the character of the Messiah and the difference His presence makes in the world. This text is set in the context of Assyrian domination that would be followed by the darkness of Babylon, Persia, Greece, and Rome. With prophetic insight and foresight, Isaiah sees all that darkness dispelled by the dawn of the messianic day of salvation.

Isaiah 9 begins with a description of the gloom of darkness without Christ. The political and national bondage is but a picture of the darkness of spiritual ignorance and blindness of the estate of sin and misery into which every person is born—bound by a depraved will, captivated and blinded by the god of this world, dead in trespasses and sins, incapable of escaping the darkness of death. But "the people that walked in darkness have seen a great light" (v. 2). When there is light, the darkness disappears.

Matthew 4:12–17 removes any doubt that Isaiah is looking to the light of Christ that dispels the darkness. The territories identified in Isaiah 9:1 are part of the Northern Kingdom, which was the first to be conquered in consequence of their sins against the Lord. Here is the irony and power of grace: the part of the nation that was first to know the judgment of God was the first to see the light of Christ (v. 2). Galilee, a region so despised by many, was so honored by Christ to be the first to see His miracles and hear His message of peace and salvation. Grace is always amazing. The consequence of the light was the increase of the nation, primarily referring to Christ's kingdom, and the increase of joy (v. 3). In Isaiah's day, Israel was carried captive by Gentile nations; in Christ's new day, Gentiles would be incorporated, grafted into the true Israel of God.

Having predicted the dispelling of darkness, Isaiah gives three reasons for the resulting joy, the last of which brings us to the great incarnation text (note the repetition of "for" in vv. 4–6). The first reason is deliverance from oppression (v. 4), the second is peace (v. 5), and the third is the birth of a child (vv. 6–7). I want to focus on the third reason, which highlights five significant truths about Christ. The text speaks specifically of the kingly office of Christ.

His Identity

The birth of a male child underscores the fact of a real birth and real humanity, establishing the contextual link to the virgin-born Immanuel (Isa. 7:14). The virgin-born "God with us" is now identified as a child born "unto us" (9:6) or, more to the point, "for us." Here is the incarnation: God was manifest in the flesh. He is God; He is man. Wesley's great poetic line says it well: "Veiled in flesh the Godhead see; / Hail incarnate deity." This child was born for our benefit—to accomplish for us by His life and His death all that is required for our salvation.

The parallel statement "unto us a son is given" (v. 6) adds to the identification. This could be translated "a son has been appointed" and points to the great mystery of the Father's appointing His Son in eternity to be the only Redeemer of His elect. The birth did not commence this sonship; rather, this sonship was antecedent to the birth. This is a remarkable Trinitarian declaration: the eternal and only Son of God became the Son of Man in the incarnation. In eternity

God appointed His Son to be the Mediator, and in the fullness of time God so loved the world that He gave His Son (John 3:16). Though the word is not used, this Son is Immanuel.

His Authority

That "the government shall be upon his shoulder" (v. 6) refers to the absolute sovereign authority by which He exercises rule and dominion. Although God is ruler of all by virtue of being God, the particular kingship here is the mediatorial kingship that has been given to Christ whereby all things are put under His feet and He is the head over all things, particularly for and to the church, His people (Eph. 1:22). In this special mediatorial kingship, Christ conquers all of His and His people's enemies. He conquers by grace or by the rod of iron, but conquer and rule He will. This is why the psalmist admonished his readers to "kiss the Son, lest he be angry, and ye perish from the way" and then assured that "blessed are all they that put their trust in him" (Ps. 2:12). Eternal destiny is linked to whether or not there is submission to this rightful King.

His Character

Most instructive are the four titles that declare truths about the nature, person, and dignity of this One born the King, with a particular focus on His deity. First, He is the Wonder of a Counselor (Isa. 9:6). Although translated as separate titles, the Hebrew construction links them together as one. The term "wonder" refers to that which is marvelous, extraordinary, and incomprehensible. It typically describes the acts of God. "Counselor" is a term that is associated with wisdom. Significantly, Isaiah elsewhere uses this combination of words to refer to the Lord of hosts (28:29). So this title attests to the Son's deity, identifying Him as the Wisdom of God, itself a significant messianic title (see Prov. 1, 8; 1 Cor. 1:30; Col. 2:3).

Second, He is "the mighty God"—literally, "God, a hero." This particular word for God always designates deity, and the word "mighty" or "hero" refers to His power and His being the champion of His people. His rule is irresistible, and it is for the welfare of those in His kingdom.

Third, He is the "everlasting Father" (v. 6). This is a single word in Hebrew and has caused some confusion. How can the Son be the Father? The word literally says "father of eternity" and should not be taken as a Trinitarian statement since it is vital to maintain the distinction in persons between Father and Son. The term "father" is an honorific title applied to those in various positions of authority. The Hebrew word designates the one in authority over eternity. So rather than confusing the Trinity, the term appropriately applies to the Godhead since eternity is one of the incommunicable perfections of deity. This is another declaration that the birth of Immanuel was not the beginning of the Son's existence. The eternal Son of God became man.

Fourth, He is the "Prince of Peace" (v. 6). The Hebrew term for "prince" does not designate a king in waiting but rather a sovereign administrator. He is the administrator of peace; He has the authority to bring peace. The title unquestionably points to His work of reconciliation whereby He took upon Himself the chastisement that we deserved with a view to achieving our peace (see Isa. 53:5).

His Perpetual Kingdom

The focus in verse 7 moves from the King to the kingdom and highlights four significant traits. The kingdom is *successful*. It will continually increase as His people shall "be willing in the day" of His power (Ps. 110:3). Every conversion marks a new beachhead in the advance of His kingdom. The kingdom is *unending*. There is no end because there are no successors to replace Him or follow Him to the throne. "His name shall endure for ever" (72:17). The kingdom is *legitimate*. That His kingdom operates from the throne of David identifies Him as the legitimate heir, the ultimate fulfillment of the covenant promise (2 Samuel 7). Indeed, He is Shiloh (Gen. 49:10), the one to whom the promised kingship really and truly belongs. This is one reason Matthew and Luke begin their gospels by tracing so carefully the genealogy of Jesus, to verify that He is the promised and long-awaited King, David's greater Son. The kingdom is *just*. Equity of judgment or justice marks the ideal King. Thus, Christ fulfills perfectly that divine mandate: "He that ruleth over men must be just, ruling in the fear of God" (2 Sam. 23:3). Similarly, Zechariah announced to Zion, "Behold, thy King cometh unto thee: he is just" (Zech. 9:9).

His Guaranteed Success

The coming of the ideal King is certain because God's unfrustratable and eternal purpose guarantees it: "The zeal of the LORD of hosts will perform this" (Isa. 9:7). The divine zeal is the divine energy, passion, and fervor that move the divine plan down its certain course. The title Jehovah of armies ("LORD of hosts") designates God as the commander in chief, who has all power at His command and disposal to accomplish His perfect will. How wonderful it is that His perfect will planned to give us His Son, and in the fullness of time He did.

The coming of the Son of God in human flesh to redeem people from sin is the best news that helpless and doomed humanity has ever heard; it is the gospel. In His eternal Son, the holy Father gave His unspeakable gift to the world of lost and undeserving sinners. Were it not for Christ's birth and what it commenced—the road to the cross—there would be no hope for this old world. But there is hope because Messiah came to save His people from their sins.

29

The Work of Immanuel

ISAIAH 11:1–5

The prophecy of Isaiah is thoroughly messianic. He sets down with amazing detail the virgin birth of Immanuel, Messiah's humble ministry, His vicarious death and resurrection, and His return and righteous rule. Particularly in chapters 7–11, the prophet advances the revelation of God's promise of the coming Savior in three remarkable texts—a trilogy of messianic prophecies that highlight the Messiah's miraculous birth, His royal character, and His work. Together they sum up the essence of the gospel, the good news, the great mystery of godliness: God was manifest in the flesh in the person of Immanuel.

Chapter 11 is entirely messianic, beginning with Messiah's appearance (vv. 1–5), continuing with a description of the idyllic peace of the messianic age (vv. 6–9), and ending with a depiction of His saving work in terms of a second exodus (vv. 11–16). In this final study of the trilogy, I want to give attention to the first section that declares the mystery of the incarnation, the endowments of the Messiah, and His engagements.

The Mystery of the Incarnation

The text focuses on the humble origin and life of the Messiah, who appeared in the fullness of time when all seemed hopeless. Verse 1 uses the titles "rod" and "branch" to refer to Immanuel. Both of these words refer to a suckling that springs up in unexpected places rather than to large boughs on strong trees. The suckling is extraneous growth that is usually regarded as worthless, something to be removed and discarded, or something that sprouts up from the stump of a tree that has been cut down. This gives a remarkable image of the Messiah's humiliation and humble origins. That Isaiah associates the rod and branch with Jesse rather than with David heightens the sense of hopelessness since it was with David that the covenant promise was associated. In chapter 7, Isaiah revealed that Immanuel would come to a kingless land. Indeed, when Christ came, it appeared that the house of David had fallen and become defunct. There was no appearance of royal life in David's line and no heir to the throne apparent. But to the stump of David's house a sprout appeared, giving evidence of life and the certainty of God's unfailing promise of David's royal Seed. What an unpretentious and humble beginning for the King of kings!

By giving evidence of latent life, the terms "rod" and "branch" express hope in God's unfailing promise but also the amazing depths of Messiah's humiliation. Interestingly, the term "branch" that Isaiah uses here is not the same word that occurs elsewhere as a messianic title (Isa. 4:2; Jer. 23:5; 33:15; Zech. 3:8; 6:12). The imagery is much the same, but Isaiah 11:1 uses a different word and is most likely the reference to which Matthew refers when he says Christ was called a "Nazarene" because He lived in Nazareth in fulfillment of Old Testament prophecy (Matt. 2:23). Since the city of Nazareth is not mentioned anywhere in the Old Testament, Matthew's statement must be something other than a geographical reference. The Hebrew word is *netser* and is an obvious sound play (or pun) on the Greek word Nazareth. Nazareth was a despised place; even Nathaniel was skeptical that anything good could ever come from there (John 1:46). So Matthew is saying that Christ's living in Nazareth (a despised village) was a manifestation of Messiah's being a "suckling" (a *netser*, that often-unwanted growth). He could have translated the Hebrew word but chose to transliterate it because it sounded similar to Nazareth. The point, however, is clear: from heaven's glory God sent His Son to be born in a barn to a poor family of David's line who lived in a most humble place. The path of that humiliation led from Bethlehem's barn to insignificant Nazareth to shameful Calvary. There is little wonder why Paul calls the incarnation the great mystery of godliness (1 Tim. 3:16). God was manifest in lowly flesh to obey humbly as a servant all the way to the death of the cross.

The Endowments of the Messiah

The term *messiah* means "the anointed one." Verse 2 delineates the Spirit's anointing of the God-man, enabling and equipping Him for the tremendous task He was commissioned to accomplish. The "spirit of the LORD" that would rest on Him is a direct reference to the Holy Spirit, the Spirit who is the Lord. Being empowered by the Holy Spirit was proof of messiahship (Isa. 61:1–3). Significantly, it was the descending and remaining of the Holy Spirit on Jesus at His baptism that was the confirming evidence for John that Jesus was the Christ, the Son of God (John 1:33–34). This spiritual anointing is admittedly a mysterious truth. At the very least it highlights the cooperation of the Godhead in the work of salvation. The Father elected the Mediator; the Son executed the mediation; the Spirit empowered the Mediator.

Isaiah mentions six consequences of the Spirit's anointing. These occur in three pairs and touch on the three spheres of Christ's mediatorial authority as Priest, King, and Prophet. First, He has the power to be Priest: "the spirit of wisdom and understanding." Discernment was a key function of the priestly office, whether in distinguishing between what was clean and unclean or determining God's will through Urim and Thummim. Unlike any other, Jesus had the ability to appraise situations and with keen insight render the right decisions. He could infallibly distinguish between the true and the false, even to man's very heart.

Second, Christ has the power to be King: "the spirit of counsel and might." "Counsel" refers to the ability to form wise plans, and "might" refers to the ability to execute those plans. Together they signify the exercise of His sovereignty and unfailing success in accomplishing His mission.

Third, Christ has the power to be a Prophet: "the spirit of knowledge and of the fear of the LORD." So often, Scripture links the knowledge of God with the fear of God. A prophet is God's representative to man, and the prophet must therefore have an intimate knowledge of the One he represents. As the eternal Son, Christ had an intimate and unique knowledge of God (Matt. 11:27). In the light of that intimate knowledge, Jesus lived in the fear of God, ever conscious of the One whom He obeyed (Ps. 40:6–7) and from whom He received daily instruction, giving Him the seasonable word for the needy (Isa. 50:4). All together, these spiritual endowments affected His intellectual, practical, and religious ministries. Christ was well equipped to be the only Mediator between God and men.

The Engagements of Messiah

In Isaiah 11:3–5, Isaiah sums up Christ's work with three thoughts.

First, *He saves His people* (v. 4a). The poor and meek are those who are helpless and weak, those who have been humbled and afflicted. In the ultimate and spiritual sense, these are people humbled by conviction before God and oppressed by the bondage of sin from which they cannot free themselves. But there is deliverance in Christ (61:1–3); these are the very kind of people He came to seek and to save.

Second, *He will destroy sinners* (vv. 4b–5). Righteousness demands justice, and those who are not saved will be smitten with the rod of His mouth and slain by the breath of His lips. The same breath that creates life will blow sinners away like wind-driven chaff. Verse 5 employs the imagery of an ancient belt wrestler who was ready to face the contest and struggle. His belt held the weapons of righteousness and faithfulness that could not be snatched away by the opponent; victory was certain. The standard by which they were defeated was inflexible and consistently executed.

Third, *He will judge infallibly* (v. 3). He makes no mistakes on the day of judgment regarding either those who are saved or those who are to be destroyed; His knowledge of the human heart is profound.

The imagery of verse 3 is suggestive. The literal translation is "His smelling is by the fear of the Lord." It is a picture of perception and discernment similar to our own expression "something doesn't smell right." The standard by which He discerns is the fear of the Lord, which in the Old Testament often designates the essence of true religion and piety. He judges on the basis of a true relationship with God, something that is knowable only by seeing the heart. Hence the judgment is not just by outward sight (appearance) or sound (profession). As the infallible Judge, He looks through every facade to the real condition of the heart. He knows what is in man (John 2:25).

So as Isaiah makes the last installment in the Immanuel Trilogy, he makes it unmistakably clear that eternal destiny is linked to this God-man. The Messiah is equipped to save; He is equipped to condemn. Thus it is imperative to follow the counsel of Psalm 2:12 to "kiss the Son, lest he be angry, and ye perish from the way.... Blessed are all they that put their trust in him."

30

Praise for Christ's Birth

ISAIAH 12

Isaiah 12 is a poem of gratitude for grace that stands alone in its beauty. But in context, it is an inspired note of thanksgiving for Christ's birth. It is the climax of the Book of Immanuel in chapters 7–12. In chapter 7, the Lord announced that in a day of chaos a virgin would conceive and bear a son whose name would be Immanuel—a most unusual, unique, but real human birth whereby the eternal Son of God became incarnate. In chapter 9, the Lord identified the authority, character, kingdom, and success of the child who was to be born. It is a text that highlights the power and irony of grace, revealing the difference Christmas would make in a dark world. The light of the gospel would dispel the darkness. In chapter 11, the mystery of the incarnation is in view. Christ's humanity is linked to David, and His spiritual endowments for ministry are delineated. It is at the end of these outstanding Christmas texts that Isaiah breaks forth in praise and thanksgiving for God's unspeakable gift and for what that gift means for those who receive it. The song can be summed up under two principal heads: the motives for praise and the manner of praise.

Motives for Praise

God's goodness and greatness are the ultimate reasons for praise. Verse 5 says that God has done "excellent things" (i.e., sublime things): this expresses His goodness. Verse 6 says explicitly that the

Holy One of Israel is great in the midst of His people. How great is the grace of the holy, transcendent God, who condescends to be with His people! This sounds like Paul's definition of the mystery of godliness that God was manifest in the flesh (1 Tim. 3:16). Thinking about this good and great Immanuel generates praise for two specific reasons.

The first reason is that *those of us who are believers have peace with God* (v. 1). Christ arrived with the angelic declaration of peace and goodwill to men (Luke 2:14). Without His coming, there would be no possibility of sinners ever being reconciled to God. Isaiah begins the song of praise by remembering the misery of his condition of alienation from God and his being the object of God's just anger: "thou wast angry with me." Literally, God was hot against him; the divine nose was red, an anthropomorphic image of intense and justified wrath. Sin is the great obstacle to peace with God; it is an insurmountable impediment to fellowship. And this divine anger is not passive. It is actively poured out against all unrighteousness. Consequently, the soul that sins will die; God is holy, just, and righteously intolerant of sin. Significantly, Isaiah personalizes the fact of his plight under God's wrath, which is directed not against sin in the abstract but against sinners personally. Until we acknowledge the depth of the misery from which we have been delivered, we will not likely express the grateful praise that we should.

But Isaiah was as conscious of his deliverance as he was of his misery: "thine anger is turned away" (v. 1). Divine anger had given way to reconciliation—what a remarkable transition! God Himself did what was necessary to resolve the tension, to bridge the immeasurable chasm, to remove the enmity. God's grace is not capricious. This reconciliation required the coming of the Curse-Reverser. Verse 1 does not specifically mention that coming, but remember that chapter 12 is the climax of those three great messianic texts that have made it explicitly clear Immanuel was on the way. This is why context is such an important component in the interpreting process. This new peace with God is, therefore, the gift of Christmas. Bethlehem was the first step to Calvary, where the blood of the cross would purchase peace (Col. 1:20–22). It is because God's anger was turned away from the believer to Christ that peace is even possible; it is when that truth is personalized that there is reason for praise. The consequence of that peace is the enjoyment and experience of God's mercy: "Thou comfortedst me" (v. 1). This refers to God's showing pity and mercy, resulting in rest for the soul. This restful peace is one of the benefits of the gospel. If there were no incarnation there would be no cross and there would be no salvation. But thanks be to God for His unspeakable gift of giving His Son in the likeness of our sinful flesh to give us peace! Peace with God is certainly reason for praise.

The second reason for praise is that *believers can claim God as a personal Savior*. God's wrath is not an abstraction, and neither is His salvation. It is personal: "Behold, God is my salvation." This is an affirmation of faith that leads to a testimony of the confidence of faith: "I will trust, and not be afraid" (v. 2). The word "trust" focuses on the objective side of faith. It expresses the confidence, the sense of safety and security, that results from resting in a secure refuge. The legitimacy of the confidence depends on the reliability of the refuge; the object of faith always determines the value of faith. The God who is the salvation of His people is a worthy object of such confidence. Not being afraid is the subjective side of faith. It refers to the absence of trembling, anxiety, or dread. It is the experience of the peace of mind that is warranted because of the objective reality that is firm and unfailing.

This confession of faith leads to the experience of joy. The prophet exults that "the LORD JEHOVAH is my strength and my song; he also is become my salvation" (v. 2). The juxtaposition of the divine names Ya and Yahweh puts the whole focus on the person of God. He is the covenant-making and covenant-keeping God who is worthy of praise and who generates joy in His redeemed people. Experiencing salvific joy should produce a desire for even more experience. There is something addicting about grace. Isaiah uses the image of drawing water from a well to describe the ongoing experience of grace. The well pictures that which is refreshing, reviving, sustaining, and enlivening; it is grace that brings to life and sustains life. God's well of salvation is deep and will never run dry. So it is for every believer habitually to dip deep into that well to experience more and more of the joy of God's salvation. Christ's birth announced joy to the world. It is our salvation if we can truly say, "Joy to me."

Manner of Praise

On the human level, it is the polite and right thing to do when receiving gifts to express thanks. How much more is it the right thing to do in response to the unspeakable gift that God has given in the sending of His Son! Isaiah gives us a template for how we ought to thank the Lord for salvation.

First, we are to *give thanks*: "Praise the LORD" (v. 4). The word "praise" has the idea of giving voice to confession, praise, and gratitude. In praise, we confess or acknowledge the Lord for who He is and what He has done, and with gratitude of heart we express thanks to Him specifically for what He has done for us. Significantly, Isaiah 12 illustrates the logic of the three sections of the Heidelberg Catechism. God was angry: that's misery. God is not angry anymore: that's deliverance. Praise God: that's gratitude.

Second, we are to *pray*: "Call upon his name" (v. 4). Prayer is the means by which we express our continuing debt of dependence on Him. Not to pray is spiritual insensitivity and ingratitude. One of the great consequences of reconciliation (peace with God) is the fellowship, communion, and open access to heaven's throne. All this has been made possible by Christ, who came into this world as Immanuel to bring His people to God. Again, on the human level, there is often excitement when receiving a gift, but soon the newness wears off and the gift is ignored. How tragic it is for a professing believer to "get used to" being saved! If we keep Christ in view, the newness will not wear off, and we will take advantage of all we have in Him, not the least of which is access to the throne of grace.

Third, we are to *testify*: "Declare his doings among the people, make mention that his name is exalted" (v. 4). Part of the excitement about receiving a gift is telling others what you received. How much more should that testimony accompany the reception of the most precious gift given on that first Christmas day! The "gift of Christmas" is the gospel—the good news that God gave His Son to deal with sin. Believers should not be able to keep that to themselves but rather should make known His mighty acts of salvation and deliverance. Evangelism is praise in action. Making mention of His exalted name has the idea of bringing it to mental focus by making His high and inaccessible greatness a matter of conscious thought. What we think about determines what we do. With a mind fixed on the Lord, we should live so that all who see and know us should be impressed with our God.

Fourth, we are to *sing*: "Sing unto the LORD" (v. 5). So often in Scripture singing is a synonym of praise. Singing is a way to worship and honor Him. Verse 6 makes it clear that the sentiment of the heart is more important than the melody: "Cry out and shout." So even if carrying or keeping the tune is difficult, a heart that is overwhelmed with grace will want to make a joyful noise to the Lord. There should be a genuine spiritual excitement about what God has done in the gospel of saving grace. The bottom line is simply that we should never get over the wonder of Christ's birth.

31

The Identity and Work of the Servant

ISAIAH 42:6–8

The designation "servant of the Lord" is an honorific title expressing both a special relationship between the servant and the Lord as well as a functionary subordination in which the servant performs obediently the will of the Lord. Throughout the Old Testament, specially called men of God were labeled as God's servants. Moses, more than any other saint, was identified as the servant of the Lord about forty times (e.g., Deut. 34:5; Josh. 1:1–2; 2 Kings 21:8). But several others enjoyed the honor of that designation too: Abraham (Gen. 26:24), Joshua (Josh. 24:29), Samson (Judg. 15:18), Caleb (Num. 14:24), David (2 Sam. 7:19–20), Elijah (1 Kings 18:36), Job (Job 1:8), Nehemiah (Neh. 1:6), prophets and priests generally (Jer. 7:25; Ps. 134:1, respectively), and even the nation of Israel as a whole (Jer. 30:10; 46:27–28). Sometimes even the unexpected received the title: Nebuchadnezzar, the pagan Babylonian king, unknowingly was raised up and used by God to accomplish the Lord's will (Jer. 27:6; 43:10).

Uniting this whole list is that the servant was especially chosen by God to stand at the head of a people to perform a special mission for God on behalf of the people. It was a position of great privilege and grave responsibility. Consequently, the title Servant of the Lord, when referring to Christ, is like the title Messiah in that there are many lesser referents that in one way or another point to the ideal Servant. The failures of all the other servants heighten the need and desire for the One who will not fail. Christ stands in a unique relationship to the Lord and performs the divine will to absolute perfection.

It was the prophet Isaiah who, under divine inspiration, began to make the connection between the title Servant of the Lord and the promised Messiah. Referring to the Servant theme over thirty times in his prophecy, Isaiah points to the failures of lesser servants to establish the need for the ideal Servant who faithfully and obediently does whatever is necessary to accomplish God's purpose of saving His people. Isaiah's Servant theology reaches its climax in four great messages: 42:1–9; 49:1–12; 50:4–11; and 52:13–53:12. In these Servant Songs, Isaiah, with Pauline precision, declares the identity and saving work of God's only Redeemer for sinners.

I confess that as I come to these Servant Songs I have mixed feelings. On the one hand, there is so much here that finding something to say about the text is easy. On the other hand, so much is here that reaching the depths and height of meaning is impossible. When I come to these songs, I am in over my head and out of my league. But I think that is how we should always feel when we come to look full in the face of the Savior. That is exactly where Isaiah is making us look. In this series of meditations, I will give a synopsis of these remarkable messianic passages and will at least point out some of the great messianic elements that you should focus on as you meditate and work your way through these passages. Read the passages and just take your time; don't be in a hurry to leave.

Isaiah 42:1–9

In this text the Servant is a special person who successfully executes a special mission. Verse 1 focuses attention on the unique relationship between the Servant and the Lord. He is the elect of God, the eternally chosen Mediator set apart to do a work that no one else could possibly do. This takes us to that Trinitarian council of redemption, in which the eternal Son of God, the eternal object of the Father's delight, received His commission to be the Savior of sinners. You see what I mean about this subject's depth! Verse 8 suggests something else about the uniqueness of this special person:

although a servant, He is also the glory of God. God gives His glory to none other, but as we know also from the New Testament, Christ is the brightness of God's glory, and it is in the face of Christ that God's glory shines (Heb. 1:3; Col. 1:15; 2 Cor. 4:6, respectively). The logic is conclusive: the Servant is God.

Most of this passage details aspects of the Servant's mission with a primary emphasis on the prophetic ministry, one of the essential mediatorial operations. His prophetic ministry is unlike that of any lesser prophet because He is both the Messenger and the message (Isa. 42:6). As the ideal Prophet, He reveals truth (vv. 1, 3), enlightens blind eyes, and liberates from spiritual bondage (v. 7). He conducts His prophetic mission without ostentation and with meekness (vv. 2–3). Relate that to the number of times during Christ's earthly ministry that He, having performed some act of mercy or miracle, instructed the beneficiary of that act to keep it quiet (e.g., Mark 5:43). Any lesser prophet would have put those accomplishments in bold print on his résumé. Finally, His mission would be successful because of His own faithful resolve (v. 4), the empowerment by the Holy Spirit (v. 1), and the will and sustaining help of God (vv. 1, 6, 9).

Isaiah 49:1–12

This text also develops the prophetic ministry of the Servant, calling specific attention to the Servant's divine commission and assurance of divine aid in achieving every detail of His mission. The theme of worldwide success runs through the entire song. It begins with the Servant Himself addressing His message to the world (v. 1). The middle then declares that He is not only the Savior of Israel but "a light to the Gentiles" as well, that salvation may extend to "the end of the earth" (v. 6). The song ends with people from the entire world coming by means of the way created by the Servant (vv. 11–12).

Reading this is almost like reading Romans 11 and Ephesians 2, which describe so wondrously the Gentile inclusion in the body of Christ. We don't have to wait until the New Testament to learn that God intended to save Gentiles as well as Jews, all through the same

Christ. The promise of Christ in the Old Testament was never a uniquely Jewish promise. What a blessing it is, whether as Gentiles or Jews, to know that our salvation was not a divine afterthought; the bringing together of every race and nation to be one in Christ has been God's purpose from the beginning. Check out Revelation 7:9 for a peek into the final fulfillment of that purpose.

In this song, the Servant testifies to His consciousness of divine calling and commission as the Prophet whose message was sharp as a sword (v. 2). This imagery parallels and perhaps prefigures John's sight of the exalted Christ with the sharp sword, which is the Word of God, proceeding from His mouth (Rev. 19:15, 21). It is a certain reminder as to how vitally important it is to hear and heed the words of this ideal Prophet.

This text also highlights one of the mysterious aspects of the Servant's ministry: His absolute trust and dependence on God. It is mysterious because it boggles the mind. Although the Servant is the eternal God, in the faithful performance of His humiliation work He submitted Himself to the will of His God. This is deep theology. On the one hand, there is an ontological equality in the Trinity. This refers to the essential essence of being of the Godhead. As the eternal Son of God, the second person of the Trinity is very God of very God. On the other hand, there is an economical aspect of the Trinity, by which each of the coequal and coeternal persons of the Trinity have distinct functions. As the Christ, the Mediator between God and men, the second person of the Trinity fulfills His work of mediation in dependence on the Father. Both are true and should not be confused. Isaiah did not employ those terms, but that was his theology. Deep!

During the years of Christ's humiliation, more people rejected Him than accepted Him, giving the appearance that the whole work was in vain (v. 4). Yet in unrelenting resolve and faith, He claimed the Lord was His strength (v. 5). The Lord proved to be a reliable object of messianic trust in that He preserved the Servant and guaranteed His success. He is the covenant head of a people, He establishes a kingdom, He liberates prisoners, He gives sight to the blind, He feeds the hungry, and He opens the way to glory (vv. 8–12). This second of the Servant Songs gives us boldness in preaching the gospel and confidence in believing the gospel. The gospel really works because the Servant was absolutely successful in what He came to do.

There is more to come.

32

The Servant as the Ideal Prophet

ISAIAH 50:4–11

Throughout his ministry, Isaiah cried out against sin. He preached people's great need of salvation and God's gracious provision of that salvation in the person of God's Christ. He preached Christ as the virgin-born Immanuel, the given Son who is Wonderful, Counselor, the Mighty God, the Everlasting Father, the Prince of Peace. He made it clear that God's chosen Redeemer is both very God and very man; the perfect Mediator; the ideal Prophet, Priest, and King. It would take more space than I have in this meditation simply to list Isaiah's descriptions and titles of Messiah, humankind's only hope of salvation.

But of all of his messianic sermons, Isaiah's identification of Christ as the Servant of the Lord is perhaps the most far-reaching. In the first two songs, Isaiah focused on the Servant as the elect Redeemer first as able to deliver those held in sin's bondage (42:1–9) and then as the covenant head of redemption (49:1–12). In this third sermon song, Isaiah declares Him to be the ideal Prophet, the perfect representative of the Lord. In his typical theological precision, Isaiah surrounds his declaration of Christ with a denunciation of humanity's sin and an admonition to trust Christ, making it clear that every person's eternal destiny is linked to his or her relationship to the Servant of the Lord. In this meditation we will reflect on four observations about Christ as the confident, true, and unique representative of God, the ideal Prophet who is God's way and will for salvation.

Dedication

The prophet, by simple definition, was God's representative to people—God's mouthpiece. The authority of the prophet was only as he would speak what God had spoken to him. No one represented God perfectly except for the Servant, and no one conformed to the prophetic pattern more than the Servant. He was dedicated to both receiving and delivering the word from the Lord. God gave Him the words daily (morning by morning) and gave Him the ears to hear (v. 4). There was constant communication between the Servant and the Lord; receiving the fresh word was the first priority of the day. His ears were perpetually opened to receive the instruction (see the same image in Ps. 40:6–9). The Servant was the perfect learner. Significantly, in His earthly ministry, Jesus often affirmed that He spoke only what the Father had instructed Him to speak (Matt. 11:27; John 5:30–37; 8:28–29). That was evidence of being a true prophet.

Not only would the Servant have ears to hear, He would have "the tongue of the learned, that I should know how to speak a word in season" (Isa. 50:4). He knew how to sustain the weary with a word, bringing good news to the afflicted, liberty to captives, comfort to mourners, and light to the blind (60:1–3). What words Jesus spoke! No man ever spoke like He did. With heavenly affirmation, the Father said, "This is my beloved Son.... Hear ye him" (Matt. 17:5).

Determination

The Servant's dedication to the word resulted not only in His faithful proclamation of it to others but also in His own determined, resolute obedience. Many lesser prophets were often reluctant to accept their prophetic orders, but not so with the ideal Prophet. He never resisted, rebelled, or retreated from the path of duty no matter where it led. His mission was preeminent, and He voluntarily and willingly gave Himself to the work. As predicted in Genesis 3:15, there would be outward hindrances to the mission, but there was no inward resistance: He was "not rebellious, neither turned away back" (Isa. 50:5).

The path of His determined obedience led to suffering, but He did not flinch (vv. 6–7). Amazingly, the sufferings predicted some seven hundred years before the fact found explicit fulfillment in the circumstances of the cross (v. 6). Even a cursory knowledge of the life of Christ puts this prophetic word in historic perspective. He was scourged, yielding Himself to the floggers who barbarically whipped His exposed skin. His beard was plucked, inflicting not only pain but insult, as the beard was a symbol of manhood and dignity. He was humiliated with both verbal insults and spittle as an expression of contempt and disdain. And He endured it all without turning His face away. Only He who was without sin could endure such torment without rebellion. Such suffering speaks to both the depths of sin for man to so afflict God's Son and the heights of grace that God's Son voluntarily endured it all for His people.

Defense

The Servant's exaltation and vindication follow His obedience (see Phil. 2:7–11). The Servant declared His confidence that God would come to His defense with a threefold affirmation of faith. Twice He affirmed that God would help Him (Isa. 50:7, 9), and once that the Lord was near (v. 8). Although it appeared that all were against Him, the reality is that God was for Him. Sinners accused, blasphemed, and misunderstood Him, but God was on His side. Therefore, no accusation could stand. What Paul summed up in 1 Timothy 3:16 proved true over and again throughout Christ's life and climactically in His resurrection: the God who was manifested in the flesh was vindicated by the Spirit. What the Father declared concerning Christ's sonship at His baptism and His transfiguration, He declared with power at His resurrection (Rom. 1:4). Although He was despised by man, the Servant was beloved of God.

One of the things I love most about this part of the text is that what is said about Christ in verses 8 and 9 is applied to believers in union with Christ in Romans 8. None can condemn Christ, and none can condemn those in Christ. His people share in His success and exaltation.

Confident that God would be His defense, the Servant would set His face like a flint to fulfill His mission. He knew that nothing could frustrate God's redemptive purpose. He knew that failure was impossible. His path of obedient suffering that led to vindication and victory achieved a certain gospel.

Declaration

The Servant Song technically ends at verse 9, but Isaiah's declaration in verses 10 and 11 is a fitting conclusion. He offers an admonition to trust the Servant (v. 10) and a warning against rejecting Him (v. 11). There is hope for those who walk in darkness when they believe and repent. To trust the name of the Lord is to find security and safety, placing confidence in His person and work. To "stay upon" God is to lean or rely on Him in rest and dependence. This faith sets aside all self-help and self-reliance and rests solely on the Lord. To fear the Lord is equated with obeying the Servant. This fear and obedience describe the kind of repentance necessary to turn away from natural reasoning to follow Him in a new way of life. The Servant is the only way out of darkness.

Since the Servant is the only way, the only hope, and the only Savior, it is imperative to hear and heed the warning against rejecting Him. Isaiah cautions those who try to light their own way out of darkness that they are in jeopardy of lying down in sorrow. The word "sorrow" in Hebrew is more ominous, referring to a place of torment and pain. The fire of self-help, a false religion, leads only to failure, disappointment, and ultimate destruction. Eternal destiny is linked to the Servant. The bottom line is that the Servant is God's ideal Prophet who reveals God's way and will for salvation. Hear Him.

The Suffering Servant

ISAIAH 52:13–53:12

If the book of Isaiah is the Mount Everest of prophetic literature, then this text is the pinnacle of the mountain. This is the climax of Isaiah's songs about the Servant of the Lord. He has already identified the ideal Servant as the Savior of sinners who is Himself the Word of life. Finally, he brings our attention to the Servant as the suffering Lamb of God, who gave Himself as the supreme sacrifice for the sins of His people.

If this final song were all we knew of the gospel, we would still know it well since its message includes all the essential truths of the death, burial, and resurrection of Christ and the saving implications of those essential facts. This was all that Philip needed; in his witness to the Ethiopian, he "began at the same scripture, and preached unto him Jesus" (Acts 8:35). There is no way in the limited framework of this study that I can come close to doing justice to the fullness and beauty of this depiction of the Suffering Servant. No exposition can ever plumb its depth, yet just reading it lifts the heart to spiritual heights. Not only is the theology profound but the poetic arrangement of stanzas shines with clear symmetry. Stanzas 1 and 5, the beginning and the end, sound forth the theme of the Lamb's total success and victory. The middle stanzas ironically describe the Lamb's humiliation and death—the reason for the exaltation.

In this song we look fully at the Savior. I will limit my analysis to a synopsis of the principal message of each stanza. I encourage you to spend some prayerful time meditating and rejoicing over the message of this song that encompasses so much messianic theology.

The Success of the Servant

Stanza 1 (Isa. 52:13–15) gives an overview of most of the specific themes developed in the rest of the song, but its main focus is on the success and exaltation of the Servant. Isaiah highlights the fact, consequences, and path to success. Every step in the path to glory was calculated for success. The Servant will be exalted and extolled, but the path to that success takes Him through the throes of humiliation and suffering. The prophet's logic here parallels Paul's hymn of Christ, who became obedient unto death, by which He earned the exaltation of heaven and the subjugation of every creature (Phil. 2:5–11). The suffering would be so intense that He would be disfigured beyond recognition. So battered, buffeted, smitten, and scourged would He be that people would look on Him with para-lyzing astonishment. Yet this path of suffering was the means of purifying many nations. The fact of His suffering was horrific; the why of His suffering was the salvation of His people.

The Spurning of the Servant

Stanza 2 (Isa. 53:1–3) describes the humiliation and rejection of the Servant. He was rejected because nothing identified Him as the expected king. Born and bred in humble surroundings and unpretentious in appearance, there was nothing to identify Him as royalty. He grew up like a tender plant, or suckling, an image describing that which was useless, pruned, and cast away. He was a root in a dry and barren ground, pointing to His birth in a stable in an obscure village and His life of poverty. His being without form or comeliness was not a description of His physical features but rather recognized there was nothing outwardly majestic about Him—no pomp or splendor or royal attire. Consequently, He was treated with contempt (regarded as worthless), shunned, and ignored. His whole life was filled with misery ("acquainted with grief," v. 3), earn-ing Him the title Man of Sorrows. His whole life was characterized by misery, pains, and anguish of body and soul. Natural sight could reveal nothing attractive about Him. Sinners turned their faces from Him, not giving Him a second thought, refusing to consider Him at all. Tragically, that is as true for sinners today as it was for those who were contemporary with Him. Now, like then, the eye of faith alone beholds His beauty.

The Sufferings of the Servant

Stanza 3 (Isa. 53:4–6) vividly pictures His suffering. Four thoughts stand out.

First, the sufferings were vicarious, or substitutionary. He took on Himself the sorrows and grief that depict the awful consequences of sin. These consequences of sin were not His own but ours: our griefs, our sorrows, our transgressions, our iniquities. These sufferings in both body and soul were necessary because of our sins, and the sorrow and grief He bore testified to the terrible consequences of those sins.

Second, the sufferings were real. His sufferings reached a climax when God violently pierced Him in order to achieve our peace and forgiveness. He was wounded, violently pierced through; He was bruised, crushed, and shattered in pieces. The language of suffering is intense and graphic. There are no stronger expressions to denote the severity of His suffering unto death.

Third, the sufferings were redemptive. The purpose of His sufferings was to procure our peace and to provide healing. This peace refers to reconciliation with God, and this healing refers to the spiritual forgiveness of sins.

Fourth, the sufferings were essential. They were necessary for the sinner's salvation because people left to themselves are hopelessly lost. We are like foolish sheep that wander aimlessly and yet somehow always away from God. The Lord took the initiative in this vicarious execution, and the Servant took the blow that we deserved, thereby bringing us to God (see 1 Peter 2:24–25). We must wait until the New Testament to learn that He made the atonement on a Roman cross, but we don't have to wait to see the vicarious atonement.

The Submission of the Servant

Stanza 4 (Isa. 53:7–9) underscores the voluntary nature of the Servant's suffering obedience. Note the explicitly minute prophecies concerning His arrest, trial, death, and burial—the events of His passion. He submitted to suffering. He humbly allowed Himself to be afflicted without attempting to flee or offering self-defense. He was silent. In Pilate's hall He answered not a word; "When he was reviled, reviled not again; when he suffered, he threatened not" (1 Peter 2:23). He submitted to death. After His arrest and unjust trial, He was violently, brutally, and vicariously cut off from the land of the living. He became obedient to the violent death of the cross (Phil. 2:8).

There were few among His contemporaries who considered the significance of His death. They thought He deserved it (Isa. 53:4) when in reality it was "for the transgression of my people was he stricken" (v. 8; literally, "because of my people the stroke to Him"). Then He was buried. The burial was evidence of a real death. The prophetic description of His burial reads as though it were history. Here is a literal translation of verse 9: "One made His grave [i.e., His grave was assigned] to be with wicked men, but He was with a rich man in His death." He was not buried in the public plot of criminals as expected but rather in the private tomb of Joseph. It was a grave that had not yet seen corruption, and it was returned no worse for the wear. Essentially, the only details the New Testament adds to Isaiah's account of Christ's passion and burial are the names of Judas, Pilate, Herod, and Joseph of Arimathea.

The Satisfaction of the Servant

Stanza 5 (Isa. 53:10–12) is the grand climax, coming full circle again to the Servant's success and exaltation. He did not suffer and die in vain. The Servant accomplished God's eternal purpose by offering Himself as the guilt offering, paying the price and making full recompense for sin. *God was satisfied with the work of Christ.* What the Servant would do was the will of God. Verse 10 says, "It pleased the LORD to bruise him." The word "pleased" does not suggest delight but rather decree or purpose. It was the will of God to grind

Him. Christ was delivered into the hands of wicked men for sure, but ultimately He was "delivered by the determinate counsel and foreknowledge of God" (Acts 2:23). Christ was satisfied with His own work.

That all of this follows His atoning death points to His victorious resurrection and earned exaltation. In reward for His full obedience, the Servant would see the promised seed, enjoy prolonged days, and know the pleasure of the Lord. Hebrews 12:2 says that Jesus "endured the cross" "for the joy that was set before him." In a real sense, a key component of that joy was the people who the Father had given to Him as His inheritance for fulfilling all the demands of the plan of redemption. What a thought that is! When Jesus suffered and died, He had all of His people in view. His prolonging days point to His never-ending life, for since He was raised from the dead, He cannot die again, for death no longer has mastery (see Rom. 6:9). His knowing the pleasure of the Lord points to His accomplishing the purpose of His mission, the happy results of His sacrifice. *Believers are satisfied with Christ.* Sinners are justified by knowing Him. His seed receives the salvation He accomplished for them. Indeed, all that He achieved in His substitutionary work is applied to those for whom He lived and died. They also share in His inheritance, becoming joint heirs with Christ.

In verse 12 the chapter ends with a rich restatement that sums up the work of the Servant. He died willingly ("poured out his soul unto death"); He suffered submissively (allowing Himself to be "numbered with the transgressors"); He suffered and died vicariously ("he bare the sin of many"); He lives and continues to serve victoriously ("made intercession for the transgressors"). It is not surprising that we often refer to the Gospel according to Isaiah, and what a gospel it is!

34

Keeping the Sabbath

ISAIAH 58:13–14

Keeping the Sabbath is foreign to most Christians today whether they are Reformed or dispensational. Opinions differ both in terms of its legitimate relevance for Christians and regarding its specific practices if relevant. The bottom line is that keeping the Sabbath is a requirement of God's moral law, and as such Christians should endeavor to keep the law—not in order to gain divine favor or salvation (that would be legalism) but because they have received divine grace (that would be sanctification). Those in Christ are free from the law as a means of life, but they are not free from the law as a way of life. Grace always puts the law in its proper place, and this certainly applies to the practice of worship. If we are to worship in the beauty of holiness, we must worship according to what God defines as holiness. Grace gives us the desire and the ability to do it. Nothing is more "anti-grace" than disregarding God's law. The closing verses of Isaiah 58 are perhaps the most explicit biblical instructions for a spiritual keeping of the Sabbath that chart the course away from a merely legalistic duty. The Sabbath is cause for delight.

This fourth commandment, recorded on stone in Exodus 20 and expounded by Moses in Deuteronomy 5, requires keeping the Sabbath. The inspired inscription of Exodus together with the inspired interpretation and application of Deuteronomy give clear direction for using the Sabbath as an aid to worship.

Definition of Terms

A proper definition of terms is crucial to any discussion, and this is certainly the case for any discussion of the Sabbath since so much of the misunderstanding stems from improper definitions. Let's start at the beginning. The verb "remember" in the Exodus statement (20:8) suggests that the people were aware of the Sabbath before God gave the law at Sinai. This is illustrated in the narrative in Exodus 16, where the Lord sets down the rules for gathering manna. Remembering does denote a mental recall, but it involves much more. Too often remembering and its counterpart forgetting are mental operations over which we have little control. It is a common human malady to forget what we should remember and to remember what we would like to forget. But the Hebrew terms for these mental maneuvers express willful, voluntary acts rather than uncontrollable, involuntary processes. In other words, to remember is to think about something on purpose; to forget is to refuse to think about something on purpose. Consequently, the Exodus statement requires conscious reflection and equates to Deuteronomy's command to observe the Sabbath day, which in turn requires attentive and careful obedience.

Perhaps the biggest misconception involving the fourth commandment concerns the meaning of the term *sabbath*, which is basically a transliteration of the Hebrew term. In spite of the association of the word in this context with the seventh day, the term does not inherently refer to the seventh day nor does it have any connection to the number 7 at all. The Sabbath designates the seventh day of the week only when the context specifies it as the seventh day. The word comes from a verbal root meaning "to cease." Simply, the Sabbath is a day that stops or a day that marks or sets a limit. It is a day of cessation, regardless of what day of the week it is. In fact, in the Old Testament's calendar, there were any number of days designated sabbath that would not have fallen on the last day of the week. The undeniable fact that the term *sabbath* does not uniquely designate the seventh day of the week ought to remove any objections to referring to the first day of the week as the Christian Sabbath. It is crucial to note that the law's imperative required keeping the Sabbath day holy without specifying what that day was. The principle was that one day in seven was to be a Sabbath day, a day of rest. Inherent in the statement was a built-in provision for a dispensational shift of days but not for a dispensational subtraction from the Ten Commandments.

The infinitive expression "to keep it holy" or "to sanctify it" (the Hebrew text is the same in both Exodus and Deuteronomy) explains what remembering or keeping the Sabbath entails. This form of the verb "to be holy" grammatically means putting something in a given state or condition, which tells us simply that the Sabbath day is to be put into a state of holiness. Since the basic idea of holiness is separation, the idea is that the Sabbath must be made separate or distinct. Sanctifying the Sabbath requires setting it apart, making it different from all the other days of the week. Clear enough!

Logic of the Sabbath

If the Exodus and Deuteronomy passages are considered together, there are two significant and related reasons why the Sabbath is required. According to Exodus, the Sabbath day is to be free from all labor because of the example God established at creation: He rested. God rested, and we must rest as well in imitation of Him. His holiness is the perfect standard of ours; we must be holy because He is holy. Imitating His rest is tantamount to experiencing His presence. Throughout the Scriptures, the Sabbath principle is a key component of a theology of rest. Theologically or spiritually, to be in the place of rest is to be where God is. Being in the presence of God is an objective in worship, and remembering the Sabbath helps to accomplish that objective. According to Deuteronomy, the Sabbath is to be observed because God delivered His people from bondage. Resting in His presence and remembering His grace go hand in hand. Relief from the mundane affairs of life allows time for proper reflection and worship of the Lord for who He is and what He has done. It takes time and a proper frame of mind to worship, and the Sabbath provides for both.

This is good logic. A scriptural keeping of the Sabbath is a means of shelving legitimate but mundane concerns and blocking out distractions that compete with spiritual matters for attention. Christians must set themselves apart from the labors and happenings of everyday existence in order to worship the Lord effectively. By setting aside those things that are lawful and necessary on other days and making it the delight of the heart to spend time in public and private worship and in performing works of necessity and mercy with a true heart, the Christian will enjoy God and find the necessary impetus to serve Him with fervent zeal. Suffice it to say that God deserves constant worship and praise. In His providence, however, He has given us other things to do that demand our time and attention. He has given us six days to accomplish all that we must legitimately accomplish. In His law, He has set aside a time when we can and must give our full attention to Him. Without such a day, that kind of worship is impossible, but He has set aside a time when giving full time and full attention to Him is possible. That is a demonstration of His goodness to us to aid us in both our work and our worship. I like the way one theologian summed it up when he called the Sabbath "a gift of divine grace for the sanctification of the people." And it is even better to put it in the words of Christ—"The sabbath was made for man" (Mark 2:27).

Even apart from the biblical mandate for keeping the Sabbath, it just plain makes sense. Worship takes time and requires attentive concentration, both of which the Sabbath facilitates. Too often Christians enter the sanctuary with a million things on their mind; it is not surprising, therefore, that so many churches today experience shallow worship. By setting aside the ordinary business of life, it is possible to enjoy a frame of mind that allows unhindered thoughts of God. Keeping the Sabbath is not just a code of dos and don'ts; it must be a spiritual issue, a matter of the heart. Isaiah 58:13–14 sums up the way to observe the Sabbath: it is a day to be observed with a spirit of self-denunciation, a spirit of devotion, and a spirit of joy. The Sabbath is not a dull day to get through; it will not be a holy day unless it is a happy day. It is God's gift to us.

35

Good News

ISAIAH 61:1–3

When Adam fell, all mankind sinned in him and fell with him in that first transgression. The fall brought the curse and plunged mankind into a state of sin, misery, and death. All people are burdened with the guilt of that original sin, have lost any and every hint of righteousness, are absolutely corrupt in their whole nature, and live in a way that exposes the stink of their spiritual death. Consequently, every person has lost communion with God and is under divine wrath, condemned, and liable to all the miseries of this life, to death, and to the prospect of the pains of hell forever. The news could not be worse.

But God, who is rich in mercy, has made a way for people to escape the state of sin and to enter a state of eternal salvation. Immediately after man fell, God announced the Redeemer, the Seed of the woman, who would and could reverse the curse for His people. That Redeemer is the Lord Jesus Christ, who in the fullness of time came into the world as the second Adam to restore what the first Adam had lost. The news could not be better. This good news message, the gospel, is the grand theme of all Scripture. The coming of Christ was the central event of all history, and there is no more important message for mankind than the simple yet profound truth that Jesus saves.

In Isaiah 61:1–3, this good news comes from the mouth of Christ Himself. This text is a climax to the many predictions of Messiah in Isaiah's prophecy. Isaiah has taken us from Christ's virgin birth, to

His vicarious suffering and death, to His triumphant resurrection
and exaltation, to His return in glory. But here are words that no
merely human prophet could claim; they are grand and wonderful words from the Savior. Jesus confirmed this at the synagogue in
Nazareth. Having read the opening verses of Isaiah 61, He forthrightly declared, "This day is this scripture fulfilled in your ears"
(Luke 4:21). Since no man ever spoke like Him, it is imperative to
listen well to His words. These are words of life and hope. This declaration highlights three thoughts about the work of Christ that sum
up the good news: His mandate, message, and mission.

Messiah's Mandate

Jesus's public ministry was marked by bold claims and wondrous
deeds. It was necessary at the beginning of His preaching to establish His credentials, and His first sermon in the Nazareth synagogue
was the opportunity. His prerecorded message in Isaiah explained
His right, authority, power, and ability; it was the ideal text to prove
who He was. Verse 1 reveals two thoughts that authenticate His
ministry.

First, His mandate is based on a divine commission: "The LORD
hath anointed me." The word "anointed" means "to smear with a
liquid" (usually olive oil) and is the verbal form of the noun *messiah*.
Those anointed—typically prophets, priests, and kings—were set
apart and consecrated for a particular purpose. Every component of
service associated with those messianic offices reached ideal manifestation in the person of Jesus. God in eternity had set His Son
apart to be the Mediator between God and men, the ideal Prophet,
Priest, and King. Thus, His mandate was founded on the eternal
purpose of the Trinity that the Son of God would become the Son
of Man to be the only Redeemer of God's elect. The good news He
would declare was in reality the eternal purpose of the Godhead.

Second, His mandate was exercised by divine power: "The Spirit
of the Lord GOD is upon me." The spiritual empowering of the
Messiah for service was a frequent, though mysterious, messianic
theme (see Isa. 11:2). Any and all who do the work and will of God

require this special infusion of power by the Holy Spirit. Although Jesus was the God-man, in His messianic office He experienced this enabling and empowering by the Spirit. In fact, the Spirit's descending and remaining on Him was irrefutable evidence of His messianic identity. The dove descended on Jesus at His baptism to portray symbolically and vividly that He was God's beloved Son and would conduct His ministry in heaven's might. No mere man would ever experience such spiritual empowering, "for God giveth not the Spirit by measure unto him" (John 3:34).

Messiah's Message

As the ideal Prophet, Christ declared God's will and way of salvation. His message was always in season, appropriate to the needs of people. This summary text highlights four themes that marked His preaching.

First was evangelization: "to preach good tidings unto the meek" (Isa. 61:1). "The meek" refers specifically to those who are afflicted, oppressed, and burdened by sin and death. They are poor in the sense that they do not have the resources to deal with their affliction; they are helpless and hopeless. The term describes the condition of every sinner. But the good news is that there is hope. Christ preached the full pardon and deliverance of sin by His own atoning death and victorious resurrection. Significantly, when John the Baptist was in prison and wondered if Jesus was really the Christ after all, Christ simply said to tell John that the poor were having the gospel preached to them (Matt. 11:5). That settled it. It is not surprising that when Jesus linked Himself to this text at Nazareth, they "wondered at the gracious words which proceeded out of his mouth" (Luke 4:22). These good tidings were the best news that people could ever hear.

Second was consolation: "to bind up the brokenhearted" (v. 1). This is the very thing the Lord does for His people (Ps. 147:3). Christ has a message of peace and comfort for those with broken and contrite hearts who are weighed down with the sense of guilt and shame. Every sinner who grieves over the state of his or her soul can take heart because Christ has the cure for the wounded heart; He is rest for those who labor and are heavy laden.

Third is liberation: "to proclaim liberty…and the opening of the prison" (v. 1). Here the reference is spiritual, not literal, and points to a new exodus for those captive in sin, bound by the fetters of iniquity, in a prison of spiritual darkness. Christ's message is light in the darkness (John 8:12) and deliverance for those in captivity (Eph. 4:8). Deliverance from the bondage of corruption and liberty in Christ are common gospel themes—rightly so, for "if the Son therefore shall make you free, ye shall be free indeed" (John 8:36).

Fourth is admonition: "to proclaim the acceptable year of the LORD, and the day of vengeance of our God" (v. 2). The warning is twofold. The acceptable year is literally "the year of favor or goodwill." The language is that of the Jubilee, when slaves were freed and land was restored. It was a great and glorious year, but it was just a year. The opportunity for deliverance was magnificent but temporary. Christ declares that the year of favor will transition to a day of vengeance. Messiah is judge as well as Savior; He will conquer by either grace or the rod of iron. There is a time when God's Spirit strives with a person and a time when He will not. So sinners must heed Christ's warning to seek the Lord while He permits Himself to be found (Isa. 55:6). The good news is urgent.

Messiah's Mission

Verse 3 states three objectives that Christ will accomplish in His mission. First, *His mission is to justify sinners.* Those who receive His message are "trees of righteousness, the planting of the LORD." They are planted on the solid ground of His righteousness and cannot be uprooted (Matt. 15:13). Second, *His mission is to transform lives.* Life is different for those who "mourn in Zion." Salvation transforms sinners to new creatures. They receive a crown of beauty to replace the ashes of penance, the oil of gladness to replace sorrow, a garment of praise to replace the burdens. All these are figures that speak of transformation; grace never leaves people where they were or what they were. Third, *His mission is to glorify God.* Salvation is good news for the sinner, but it is ultimately to the praise of the glory of His grace (Eph. 1:6). Christ was able to say as His earthly mission was coming to a close, "I have glorified thee on the earth: I have finished the work which thou gavest me to do" (John 17:4).

This passage has summarized the whole work of Christ for God's glory and our good. Recorded first in the Old Testament and then declared at the beginning of Christ's public ministry to affirm His identity as the Messiah, it still declares the good news. May we hear and heed.

36

A Warning from Jeremiah

JEREMIAH 7:1–15

Religion can be most deceptive. Exposing falsehood was an oft-occurring theme in Jeremiah's preaching. He mocked the absurdity of false gods, which were nothing but broken cisterns (Jer. 2:13). He was in constant conflict with false prophets, who without divine authority or authorization preached peace without peace (see Jer. 8:9–11). He also condemned the false security that characterized his day. Ironically, the very generation that was on the eve of national disaster felt lightheartedly confident that religion would exempt them from judgment. External religion breeds a sense of safety. This meditation will reflect on the theme of religious hypocrisy from one of Jeremiah's great sermons. Often designated as the "Temple Sermon," the message in Jeremiah 7 cuts to the quick as it issues God's warning against this serious danger of worship.

The Existence of Hypocrisy

Perhaps one of the most salient and sobering lessons from this sermon is that hypocrisy can exist in the best places. The Lord instructed Jeremiah to "stand in the gate of the LORD's house" (Jer. 7:2). The point is sobering. This was not a message directed either to pagans or to the rabble of the backstreets and alleys of Jerusalem or even to religious renegades. On the contrary, it was directed to the most outwardly religious segment of society. If I may put it in these terms, it was directed to respectable churchgoers who were members of the most conservative and orthodox church in town. Not only were these people going to the right place but they were going for the right reason too: "to worship the LORD" (v. 2). They entered the temple gates with the pretense of bowing down before the Lord, giving God His due. From the outside everything looked right: they were in the right place doing the right things. That Jeremiah exhorted these worshipers to repent (v. 3) makes it all too clear that worship ritual does not guarantee that the worshiper is right with God. Mechanical worship is but a thin disguise for the hypocrite, and no church is exempt, no matter how right the rituals.

The Expression of Hypocrisy

With prophetic precision and inspired insight, Jeremiah identified two expressions of hypocrisy among his parishioners. First, the hypocritical worshipers affirmed a false creed. The threefold repetition of the phrase "the temple of the LORD" expresses the unorthodox confession of faith of the seemingly orthodox worshipers (Jer. 7:4). The repetition of this "temple theology" may have had some superstitious significance, as though by their saying it over and over it would come true and ward off danger; or it may simply have signified the zeal and fervor with which they affirmed the creed. Regardless, it evidences a misplaced confidence in the structure rather than the spiritual substance of the temple. The temple was the sign of God's presence, and there was a long history of God's protecting His dwelling place against every enemy. The "temple theology" attributed something magical to the place where the Lord had chosen to dwell. They apparently assumed that if they could keep God happy by giving Him what they thought He wanted in the temple ceremonies, He would stay and all would be well. They expressed confidence in tradition, in location, and in practice but not in the Lord Himself.

Second, the false creed gave expression to a false trust. Jeremiah declared that they were trusting "lying words, that cannot profit" (v. 8; see also v. 4). The word "trust" implies a feeling of strong confidence and safety in its object. But regardless of how safe they felt, they were not safe at all because they were trusting, literally, "the words of the lie" (vv. 4, 8). Referring to something that is empty, worthless, and consequently futile, the word for "lie" underscores a vital lesson about faith and trust: the object of faith determines the value of faith. It is not the fact of faith that saves; it is the object of faith that saves. These people trusted the temple with its external rituals without internalizing the divinely intended message of the rituals. Religion can be dangerously deceptive.

The Exhibition of Hypocrisy

Disconnect between "religious life" and "real life" is a common mark of hypocrisy. Hypocrites tend to assume that religious activity earns them the freedom to live without restraint and with impunity. Jeremiah's temple congregation annunciated that assumption in these terms: "We are delivered to do all these abominations" (Jer. 7:10). Notwithstanding their consistent worship in the temple, their lifestyle exhibited a disregard for God's law and a light regard for God's holiness. The list of crimes of which they were guilty violated both divisions of the Decalogue (v. 9: stealing, murder, adultery, false oaths, idolatry, and polytheism). True religion produces a desire in the heart to walk in holiness; life must correspond to profession. How a person views the law of God is always an index to the genuineness of his or her religion. Obedience will never be perfect, but it is always the outgrowth of true trust.

How a person regards the law of God is a reflection of how he or she regards the Lord Himself. Coming to stand before the Lord in His holy temple and claiming deliverance or sanction to sin (v. 10) exhibited a spiritual callousness and insensitivity to the holiness of God. That the people went through the motions of worship while at the same time blatantly transgressing God's law betrays a low estimation of who the Lord really is. Worshiping in the fear of God fosters daily living in the fear of God. True worship always connects with life.

The Exposure of Hypocrisy

"The LORD is in his holy temple, the LORD's throne is in heaven: his eyes behold, his eyelids try, the children of men" (Ps. 11:4). Heartless, external, and hypocritical worship may satisfy the worshiper and impress the observer, but the Lord sees it for what it is and will deal with it according to His infallible knowledge and inflexible judgment.

Jeremiah 7:11 records some of the most sobering words of the passage: "Is this house, which is called by my name, become a den of robbers in your eyes? Behold, even I have seen it, saith the LORD." Although the temple should have been a most sacred place because it was hallowed by God's name, it had become a cave of thieves, a hideout for bandits. This is the analogy of the text. Israel would commit every conceivable crime on the outside (v. 9) and then retreat to the temple, claiming to be delivered (v. 10). The temple was their hideout, where they would be exempt from the demands and penalty of the law. But the Lord declared, "I have seen it" (v. 11). He knew right where they were, and the temple was no place of safety for them. Sadly, Israel's notion persists. Many have made church to be a hideout, assuming that no matter what they do everything will be okay if they can just get to church or say sorry at bedtime prayer. But God is still incapable of being fooled; He still sees. Religion provides no refuge for hypocrites.

Not only does God know all about hypocritical worship but He constantly warned against it and consistently judged it. The Lord reminded the people that He had spoken to them "rising up early and speaking" and that He had called to them without their hearing or answering (v. 13). "Rising up early" is a Hebrew idiom that refers not to the time of action but rather to the zeal and fervency with which an action occurs. The divine warning against heartless religion was a high priority and a common component of inspired preaching from the days of Moses right through to the days of Jeremiah.

To illustrate His consistency in judging hypocrisy, the Lord gave a history lesson. The Lord told the temple worshipers in Jerusalem to remember what had happened to the tabernacle worshipers at Shiloh (vv. 12, 14). The tabernacle, like the temple, was a place of worship, sacrifice, and revelation. But when the previous generation turned it into a hideout for all their wickedness, God did not spare it. Shiloh was not a safe place just because the tabernacle was there (1 Samuel 4). The demise of Shiloh was concrete evidence of God's intolerance of talismanic religion. God asked the temple hypocrites of Jeremiah's day, "Where is the tabernacle?" God asks the church hypocrites of today, "Where is the tabernacle? Where is the temple?" History makes it clear that God is not satisfied with religion.

The Excision of Hypocrisy

The only hope for hypocrites is to quit their hypocrisy. The introduction to Jeremiah's temple sermon was the command to repent: "Amend your ways and your doings" (Jer. 7:3). Amending ways required making good (the literal rendering of "amend") the whole course of life, including the inclinations, propensities, and desires of the heart as well as the habits of living. Making good the doings required the alteration of the specific deeds that were generated by the inner character. This was not a call for reformation or for resolution to do better, but a call for the transformation of the heart. In verses 5 and 6, Jeremiah set down some specific guidelines for applying repentance to life. Interestingly, the specifics covered both divisions of the law, evidencing love for neighbor as well as love for God (kindness to orphans and widows, preservation of life, and ethical monotheism). It is always true that a person's behavior toward others is an index of the extent of his or her devotion to God. Regardless of the specific applications he made to the temple worshipers, Jeremiah's point is timeless: true religion always connects with behavior.

It is also invariably true that God accepts true repentance: "The sacrifices of God are a broken spirit: a broken and a contrite heart, O God, thou wilt not despise" (Ps. 51:17). If the people repented, God promised to keep them in the land of promise (Jer. 7:3, 7). There was a way to escape judgment. Although there are inherent dangers in religion, true religion in the heart is the sinner's only hope. The heart is always the key.

37

A Warning from Ezekiel

EZEKIEL 8

In one of His frequent exchanges with the Pharisees, the Lord Jesus said, "In vain they do worship me" (Matt. 15:9; see also Mark 7:7). The sad danger is that vain worship is possible. Worshiping in vain is worshiping without purpose or result, in emptiness and deception. Two factors mark this worthless worship. First, it abandons God's directives in favor of human traditions: "Thus have ye made the commandment of God of none effect by your tradition…teaching for doctrines the commandments of men" (Matt. 15:6, 9; see also Mark 7:7–8). Second, vain worship is talk without heart: "This people draweth nigh unto me with their mouth, and honoureth me with their lips; but their heart is far from me" (Matt. 15:8; see also Mark 7:6). Heartless religion was possible in the Old Testament era. It was rampant in the days of Christ's earthly incarnation. Unhappily, it pervades even the best of churches today. God has never been and never will be satisfied with heartless worship.

Beyond doubt, one of the most pathetically poignant scenes in Scripture is that of Christ standing outside the door of the church in Laodicea knocking to enter (Rev. 3:20). Here was a prosperous church going through the motions of worship, all the while unconscious that Christ was absent. I wonder how often this biblical scene is repeated in what appear to be the very best churches in our time. The place of public worship should be a holy place sanctified by the presence of the Lord. It is tragic when worship activity occurs without the divine presence.

If it is tragic when worship occurs without the presence of God, it is even more tragic when worship drives God away. Ezekiel 8 pictures such a sad state of affairs in the temple of Ezekiel's time. Filled with mysterious visions, confusing symbols, and seemingly irrelevant details, the book of Ezekiel is one of the most difficult Old Testament books to understand. But Ezekiel provides almost unparalleled insight into the nature of God. The book throughout reveals God's gloriously holy presence with its corollary implications and demands. In the particular vision recorded in chapters 8–10, God's glorious presence is contrasted with Israel's perverse sinfulness. The vision progresses downward until "the glory of the LORD departed" from the threshold of the temple (10:18). The Lord's departure from the place of worship is one of the dangers associated with worship. When Ichabod ("no glory") is written over the church entrance, it would be best to close the doors altogether. Ultimately, that is what God did to the temple.

In the part of the vision I want to consider, the Lord enabled Ezekiel to see worship in the temple as He saw it. Anyone else would have seen the rituals performed precisely as Moses had prescribed. But what would have been impressive to natural sight was an absolute abomination from God's perspective. The application extends to modern worship in the church as well. How the Lord sees the church is infinitely more important than what appears on the surface. What goes on in the heart is always more crucial than what goes on in the pew. Let me sum up the vision in Ezekiel 8 by noting why and when God's presence departs from the place of worship. It is a sobering message.

God Leaves When His Glory Is Shared

Although Ezekiel remained bodily in Babylon, in this divinely revealed vision the Spirit snatched him up by his hair and flew him to the temple in Jerusalem (8:3). He immediately saw two mutually exclusive things, and this was the problem. On the one hand, he saw the Lord: "And behold, the glory of the God of Israel was there" (v. 4); it was the same manifestation of divine glory that previously had caused him to fall on his face (1:28). Falling on his face was the right thing to do. Seeing the majestically holy, glorious, and sovereign Lord as He graciously reveals Himself should generate that submissive and humble response. The Lord is the only legitimate object of worship, and His glory belonged in the temple.

But sadly, Ezekiel saw something else in the temple, something that did not belong there: "the seat of the image of jealousy, which provoketh to jealousy" (8:3; see also v. 5). The exact identity of this image that incited carnal passion and provoked divine wrath is disputed. But its presence, not its precise identity, is the crucial issue. It is noteworthy, however, that during the wicked reign of Manasseh, such images were actually in the temple (2 Kings 21:3–7), and this may be an allusion to the pagan goddess Asherah (translated "grove" in the King James Version). During the righteous reign of Josiah, however, the images were removed (2 Kings 23:6). If this is the allusion, then Ezekiel's seeing the image there is all the more significant. God enabled the prophet to see through the religious sham. Although the material image was not there, the *spirit* of the image was there in the hearts of the worshipers. Josiah could reform the fashion of worship, but he could not transform the hearts of the idolaters.

Human beings are such natural idolaters that an image does not have to be materially in place for them to violate the first commandment: "Thou shalt have no other gods before me" (Ex. 20:3). The Lord demands total allegiance and will not tolerate divided worship or permit competition with Himself: "I am the LORD: that is my name: and my glory will I not give to another, neither my praise to graven images" (Isa. 42:8). Whether images rest on pedestals or reside in hearts, God is infinitely jealous for His name and His glory, and He will leave a place before He shares His place with anything else. Ezekiel's X-ray vision exposed what was really happening in the minds and hearts of those going through the motions of worshiping Jehovah. The time had come for the Lord to "go far off" from the sanctuary (Ezek. 8:6). He had to leave. Years earlier the Philistines had stolen the ark, and the name Ichabod told the tale (1 Sam. 4:21–22). It was deplorable when the enemy held the ark hostage; it is far more calamitous when a people professedly worshiping the Lord actually drive Him away. The sad fact is that it happens.

God Leaves When His Gospel Is Replaced

The principal lesson about true worship, pictured and prophesied by the temple ritual, is that God is approachable only through the blood of atonement. Without the shedding of blood there can be no forgiveness (see Lev. 17:11; Heb. 9:22), and without forgiveness there can be no fellowship with God (see Ps. 65:3–4). Therefore, any worship or religious routine that minimizes, denies, or distracts from the central truth of the atonement—the foundation of the gospel—is in jeopardy of missing the Lord. Of course, the ultimate reality is that Jesus Christ *is* the gospel. Apart from Christ and His atoning work, true worship is impossible. Any worship bypassing Christ is false worship.

Although the Old Testament revealed the person and work of Christ in many ways, the rituals of the tabernacle and temple vividly portrayed in particular His atoning work. Understanding this truth explains the shameful severity of what Ezekiel witnessed in his temple vision. The first thing he saw was the image of jealousy erected at the north entrance of the temple (8:3, 5). The mere presence of the image was bad enough, but the placement of the image exposed the depths of the people's ungodly folly. The northern gate was the altar gate, the place where sacrifices were offered (see Lev. 1:11). By setting aside the sacrifice and finding a substitution for the blood, they assumed that God was different from what He is, that people are different from what they are, and that sin is less severe than it is.

When God's way of worship is set aside, people are left to their own devices and imaginations in their vain efforts to approach God. What Ezekiel saw was nothing more than "Cain worship," worship that never works. Once the blood is rejected, hell is the only limit to what a base and unregenerate heart can contrive as worship (see Rom. 1:18–32). As Ezekiel pushed forward through the temple (8:8), he saw the worship of animals (v. 10), of Tammuz (v. 14), and of the sun (vv. 16–18).

The images of the creeping things and abominable beasts plastered all over the walls vividly violated the second commandment (Ex. 20:4). The worship of Tammuz revealed a God-for-profit motive. Tammuz was a fertility god who in times of drought and famine was confined to the underworld. His escape from the underworld resulted in crops and prosperity. Since prosperity depended on the welfare of Tammuz, worship was a means of keeping him around. Even today many seek to worship God with "Tammuz theology." To use worship as a means of manipulating God for personal interest or gain is a violation of the third commandment (v. 7). God will not be used. The sun worshipers represent the violation of the first commandment itself (Ezek. 8:3). That they faced the rising sun with their backs to the temple is a graphic demonstration that true worship and false worship are mutually exclusive (v. 16).

It is not surprising that the word "abomination" occurs repeatedly in this temple vision (8: 6, 9, 10, 13, 15, 17). Referring to something disgusting, detestable, and unacceptable, this word often designates idolatry and false worship. It is not surprising that God's presence would leave such a place. The Lord promised to meet His people at the place of sacrifice (Ex. 29:42–43); there is, therefore, no hope of His presence apart from atonement. To replace the gospel with anything else will mean being left alone.

False worship always betrays a blindly ignorant misinterpretation and misrepresentation of the Lord. When people don't see the Lord for who He is, they convince themselves that God does not see them either. Those committing the abominations convinced themselves in their supposedly dark and secret places that the "LORD seeth us not" (8:12). Ironically, while they were professing God's blindness to them and their behavior, the Lord was looking right at them or, more precisely, right through them. And in view of what God saw, there was nothing He could do but leave (10:18) and declare His necessary judgment: "Therefore will I also deal in fury: mine eye shall not spare, neither will I have pity: and though they cry in mine ears with a loud voice, yet will I not hear them" (8:18). If the presence of God is fullness of joy (Ps. 16:11), then His absence is judgment. Ezekiel's warning is clear enough: people must worship God alone in His way alone—or else.

38

Efficacious Grace

EZEKIEL 36:22–32

It is always good to remember that salvation is all of grace and that the salvation of every genuine believer should be to the praise of the glory of that grace. There are any number of texts in Scripture that highlight God's grace to sinners—both in the Old and New Testaments. Ezekiel 36 is one of those texts and brings us to the heart of Ezekiel's salvation theology. This passage is a comprehensive enunciation of God's plan of salvation and very likely was the passage Christ had in mind when He spoke to Nicodemus about the new birth and was amazed when that teacher in Israel did not know these things (John 3). No one can come to this text without being confronted with people's desperate need. Both Ezekiel and Christ make it clear that unless there is a radical transformation of heart there can be no spiritual life. That is an impossible demand if people are left to themselves. But the beauty of the gospel is that God does not leave people to themselves; He does for sinners what sinners cannot do for themselves. That the same truth is expressed in both Old and New Testaments teaches us that there is a grand unity in God's dealing with people in salvation. It is an everlasting gospel.

The verses for our consideration draw attention to the source of salvation and to some essential components of salvation. The proposition of the passage is clear: God's grace is successfully effective to save sinners. Ezekiel makes two principal points about this efficacious grace.

Salvation Is All of Grace

God's grace is a glorious truth, but one that is hard for sinners to grasp. There is something about grace that is unattractive to natural man. It makes man terribly small and God incomprehensibly big. Grace is contrary to all natural reasoning since it is freely given to those who do not deserve it—indeed, to those who deserve damnation instead. Ezekiel addresses this by focusing first on the source rather than the recipients of grace.

The Lord's Glory: The Goal of Grace

Salvation surely results in the sinner's good, but salvation is ultimately about God's glory. Throughout this passage, the Lord declares that His gracious work is not for the sake of the people but for the sake of His own holy name (Ezek. 36:22–23). God's name refers to the totality of His person, including all of His infinite perfections. Saving grace magnifies the Lord. He was going to act in such a way that even the heathen would "know that I am the LORD" (v. 23). Isaiah declares the same holy motive: "For mine own sake, even for mine own sake, will I do it.... I will not give my glory unto another" (Isa. 48:11). The salvation of sinners is a way by which God sanctifies (sets apart, makes distinct, exalts) His great name (Ezek. 36:23). The prophet Micah also caught the truth of this with his question, "Who is a God like unto thee, that pardoneth iniquity?" (Mic. 7:18). Similarly, in that "Grand Canyon" text in Ephesians 1, Paul repeats three times that salvation is all to the praise of the glory of His grace (vv. 6, 12, 14). Even though sinners are the beneficiaries of salvation grace, salvation is ultimately about God.

The Lord's Work: The Means of Grace

God purposes grace, and God always accomplishes His purposes. Grace is not abstract theory; it is a reality that operates through divine initiative. Salvation is not some vague plan that is revealed just for human evaluation or consideration. People are totally incapable of responding to the gospel message without first being enabled to do so. God makes the first move, or there would be and could be no movement to Him. Ezekiel underscores this truth repeatedly in this passage with all the Hebrew first-person verbs designating what the Lord does (36:22–27, 29, 30). God is the author and finisher of salvation. Salvation, indeed, is of the Lord. Therefore, the sinner's positive response is the consequence of God's gracious work. Reception of grace is evidence of grace. There is an old hymn that sums it up nicely:

> I sought the Lord, and afterward I knew
> He moved my soul to seek Him, seeking me.
> It was not I that found, O Savior true,
> no, I was found of thee.

That salvation is all of grace has significant implications. First, sinners can never hope to earn salvation. To attempt to work for salvation or even to make a contribution is a denial of grace and an affront to divine glory. This rebukes all pride. Second, sinners need never despair of salvation. If salvation depended on a person's merit or works, there would be constant torture in the soul. A person's nagging doubt as to whether she had done enough or if sufficient merit existed would rob her soul of the peace that the gospel affords. But grace shifts the ground of salvation away from self to God. Grace is greater than sin, and resting in what grace has done leads to the third implication. Sinners saved by grace have cause for joy. The application of grace never fails its purpose. Let us stand in wonder of God's amazing and wonderful grace.

Saving Grace Is Efficacious

The gospel of saving grace really and truly works. Grace does what is necessary to fit a sinner for heaven. Ezekiel summarizes the effectiveness of grace in three ways.

Grace Reconciles Exiled Sinners

Sin separates from God. The first Adam was expelled from Paradise because of his sin, and all the sons of Adam have been exiled and banished ever since. By nature, man is alienated from God. If reconciliation is possible, it is because God in Christ has removed the impediments to restored fellowship. Ezekiel uses the symbolism of ceremonial cleansing to describe this reconciliation (36:25, 29). To be ceremonially unclean was to be outside the sphere of fellowship, to be separated from God and all the spiritual benefits of life. But regardless of the nature of the uncleanness (leprosy, birth, contact with death), there was always an appropriate sacrifice to address the problem. Ezekiel utilizes the Levitical imagery to describe this work of grace.

"Then will I sprinkle clean water upon you" (v. 25). The sprinkling was a rite of purification to remove symbolically the impediments to fellowship. This sprinkling was typical (a picture prophecy) of Christ, who is the cleansing fountain (see Zech. 13:1). It points directly to the application of the blood of Christ, the only means of cleansing the soul from the guilt and power of sin. Happily, what God cleanses is clean: "Ye shall be clean" (Ezek. 36:25): "I will also save you from all your uncleanness" (v. 29). Reconciliation results in covenant fellowship: "Ye shall be my people, and I will be your God" (v. 28).

Grace Regenerates Dead Sinners

In verse 26, the Lord gives a new heart (mind, will, affections) and a new spirit (the impulses that drive and regulate desires, thoughts, and conduct). The old heart is a stone. It is lifeless, hard, and unfeeling. This is a vivid image of the helplessness and hopelessness of the human heart that is dead in sin. The heart, the most vital of organs, is petrified in utter death, incapable of responding to the good of the gospel. You would wait forever before you could find a spark of life in a stone, but here is the grace of the gospel: the Lord takes away the lifeless heart and gives a new one that is capable of new and spiritual impulses, feelings, and desires—a heart that now is capable of answering to God. This is the new birth. It is a change in the very nature of a person's being as spiritual life is implanted into that which had no life. Without this new heart that makes a person a new creature, there is no hope. This is why Christ said, "Ye must be born again" (John 3:7). Without grace, the new birth is impossible.

Grace Empowers Saved Saints

"And I will put my spirit within you" (Ezek. 36:27). By means of God's indwelling Spirit, the renewed person enjoys God's abiding presence. In true regeneration, God the Spirit enters the very soul, enabling fellowship and companionship (v. 28). This indwelling Spirit also provides enabling grace to do the things that please the Lord: walk in His statutes, keep His judgments, and obey Him. A changed life is evidence of grace. Grace never leaves sinners where it finds them. God's gracious salvation works not only to bring sinners to spiritual life but also to lead them in the way of life. The inner change that occurs in regeneration leads to the life of sanctification. Being renewed in the whole man after God's image enables the progressive dying to sin and living in righteousness.

God's gracious salvation is complete, and Ezekiel's brief synopsis of it is to the point and most instructive. We could almost paraphrase Christ's question to Nicodemus in that night class in this way: "Art thou a master of Israel and you've never read Ezekiel 36?" But surely, as we meditate on this text, let us echo Paul's assessment of all we have in Christ by praising the glory of His grace.

〜 39 〜

Dry Bones: From Death to Life

EZEKIEL 37:1–10

The mysterious and often strange visions of Ezekiel make the prophecy difficult to understand. But those who take the time and effort to grapple with the book always are benefited; after all, it is inspired by God and thus profitable for instruction. Ezekiel provides insight into the nature of God that is almost without parallel in the Scriptures. Unfortunately, far too many people have bemused themselves with Ezekiel and concocted interpretations more strange than the visions themselves, including spaceships and extraterrestrial beings as part of his opening vision of the four-faced living creatures and wheels within wheels by the river Chebar. Undeniably, the Lord showed Ezekiel some strange sights and instructed him to do some odd things in chapters 4–5 such as building models of the city, lying on his left and right sides for 430 successive days, and cutting and disposing of his hair in various ways. But every vision or symbolic act was packed with spiritual lessons.

I want to draw attention to perhaps the strangest of all the visions and instructions God gave to the prophet: his vision of the valley of dry bones and the command to preach to them in chapter 37. Interpreters argue about the time of fulfillment and what it may or may not mean in terms of a national conversion of Israel. But as is so often the case, arguments of this nature obscure the principal message for every day—that is, the message of everlasting gospel.

In His conversation with Nicodemus in John 3, Jesus is absolutely clear that no one enters the kingdom of God without being born again. The first birth, which determines race and nationality, is never sufficient for citizenship in the kingdom of God, so regardless of whatever national implications this vision may suggest, the primary message is the gospel with application for all sinners in every age and of every race. The dead must be brought to life by supernatural, divine intervention, or there is no hope. Ezekiel's vision of the valley of dry bones is a picture of spiritual conversion and transformation. It pictures the power of the gospel to bring life to death; by grace and divine power, believers who were dead sinners are made alive together with Christ (Eph. 2:5). What Paul declared in express theological proposition, Ezekiel proclaimed with prophetic symbol. They both preached that the gospel is a message of life from death and that God is the solution to the sinner's need. Ezekiel pictures this message with two main points.

Sinners Are Spiritually Dead

Verses 1–3 picture a horrific scene. The vision begins with the Spirit of the Lord transporting Ezekiel to a "valley which was full of bones." Two thoughts are apparent. First, *death is a desperate condition.* The picture of death could not be more vivid; it was a sight of silent desolation. Not even a corpse was in sight. All the prophet could see was a scattering of dry bones, picked clean by vultures and bleached by the sun. It was a scene of utter deadness not even giving the appearance of a formed skeleton—skulls here and there with ribs, leg bones, and arm bones strewn around the valley. The scene was an obvious picture of the absence of life: inactivity, insensitivity, inability to act or react to external stimuli. It is a picture of lifeless hopelessness.

The spiritual lesson is obvious as well. The valley of the dry, scattered bones pictures sin-deadened humanity as it appears before God. In Pauline terms, man in his natural state is "dead in trespasses and sins" (Eph. 2:1). Being dead in sin suggests that sin is both the cause of death and the sphere of corruption. But certainly death is a graphic image to describe how desperately hopeless man's condition is. Life flows from the Lord who is the fountain of life, and sin separates man from Him (Isa. 59:2) and therefore from life itself. Separated from God, man cannot live. The effect of that spiritual death is spiritual coldness, blindness, and insensitivity. Just as dry bones are oblivious to the sphere of life, so sinners are oblivious to spiritual life. This is why Paul would say, "The natural man receiveth not the things of the Spirit of God: for they are foolishness unto him: neither can he know them, because they are spiritually discerned" (1 Cor. 2:14).

Second, *death presents a hopeless prospect.* At least for now, prior to resurrection day, death is irreversible. That is why the Lord's question to Ezekiel seems so out of the bounds of logic: "Son of man, can these bones live?" (v. 3). All the prophet could see were bleached and brittle bones, a scene of total and helpless inability. The prospect of life was absurd, out of the question. These bones were beyond recovery, and certainly if left alone in their present condition had no prospect of life. Human reason would have to respond with a resounding no! Dead is dead. Yet the prophet's response to God's question is equally astounding: "O Lord GOD, thou knowest" (v. 3). What an answer this was! Ezekiel knew God well enough not to restrict Him to human limitations. The prophet knew that what was humanly impossible was not divinely impossible. Ezekiel's response was an affirmation of faith and marked the transition from miserable despair to hope. Ezekiel's declaration that God knows parallels Paul's amazing "but God" statement in Ephesians 2:4–5: "But God, who is rich in mercy, for his great love wherewith he loved us, even when we were dead in sins, hath quickened us together with Christ, (by grace ye are saved)." The only hope for dead sinners is the Lord.

God Imparts Spiritual Life

The second principal point of the vision focuses on the means and the end of God's grace to dry bones. It is a message of hope. The gospel is good news: God imparts spiritual life to dead sinners. Verses 4–10 underscore two key thoughts about how God gives life to the lifeless.

First, the application of the gospel is *preceded by evangelism.* God commanded Ezekiel, "Prophesy upon these bones" (v. 4). This odd scene of the prophet preaching to scattered bones is a vivid illustration of Paul's explanation of how the gospel works: "So then faith cometh by hearing, and hearing by the word of God" (Rom. 10:17) and then the question "How shall they hear without a preacher?" (v. 14). Again, human reason would say preaching to dead people is a futile exercise since they are incapable of any response. It is wonderfully true that all of salvation is of the Lord, and part of that all is that He has defined the means to accomplish the end. God's command to call dead sinners to life is His declared will, and declaring the gospel is the privileged duty of His servants.

Ezekiel is not left to himself to determine what to preach. God had instructed him at the commencement of his ministry that all he had to do was to proclaim, "Thus saith the Lord GOD" (2:4). And now to this lifeless congregation, he proclaims the good news of what God will do in imparting life. God is the source and restorer of life (37:5–6). All the "I wills" make it clear that God is the initiator and agent of life. The message to dead sinners is that God alone can save, or there can be no salvation.

As Ezekiel begins to preach, things begin to happen (vv. 7–8). The bones begin to shake; they fit themselves together; flesh, muscle, and skin appear. It seems that his preaching is having amazing effects. Yet notwithstanding the more attractive appearance of the congregation, they were still nothing but lifeless corpses. This is sobering for the messenger of the gospel to realize that preaching is capable of outward reforms, of making someone look better on the outside, but preaching cannot generate life. Life comes from God alone. On the other hand, it is encouraging to realize that the results of preaching are the prerogative of God. The evangelist is to evangelize and leave the results to God.

This leads to the second key thought that life is *accomplished by the Spirit* (vv. 9–10). Preachers can issue the general call of the gospel, but only God's Spirit can apply the grace of life with the effectual and irresistible call. The Holy Spirit enables conversion (faith and repentance) by the implantation of the principle of life in the spiritual corpse. To make the point, God commands Ezekiel to prophesy to the wind. The word "wind" is the word *spirit* and pictures the necessary involvement and work of the Spirit of God to breathe life into dead sinners. Just as the first Adam was a lifeless form until the special divine breath brought him to life, so every saved sinner is alive by virtue of that regenerating breath of the Spirit of God. This is the new birth that Jesus expounded to Nicodemus in John 3. The blowing of the wind is invisible and mysterious, but it is always known by its effects. So it is with the Holy Spirit's work in salvation. By the blowing of the divine breath, the dead live. When the Holy Spirit breathes life, there is and must be life.

Salvation of dead sinners is a miraculous and irresistible work of creation. Verse 10 explicitly pictures the successful transformation. What were brittle bones became a great and powerful army, evidencing the vigor of life. So the vision of the valley of dry bones gives hope to the dead that there is a way to life. Sinners need not despair that they cannot do enough to earn life because they cannot. But what people cannot do for themselves, God has done. That is grace. That is good news. Saints should rejoice that they live because of life-giving grace and should pray earnestly that the Spirit of God would so blow in the valley of dry bones to transform it to a valley of life.

40

A Story of Courage

DANIEL 3

Daniel 3 is a story of courage. Set in a world system that was both ignorant of and hostile to truth, the story of the fiery furnace teaches us that we must stand firm and faithful regardless of the external pressures to compromise. Shadrach, Meshach, and Abednego teach us that the courage to do so comes from faith in God and His word. Knowing that whatever happened was God's will enabled them to face their situation with confidence. It is that kind of total dependence on God that empowers believers to stand on the promises. Although the trial of Shadrach, Meshach, and Abednego was unique, it nonetheless illustrates the kind of problem faced by every generation of saints and guides us to the solution. Their absolute commitment to the Lord enabled them to resist the world's pressure and to rest on the Lord.

The World's Pressures

This world is no friend of grace. Yet this hostile world is where God has placed His people, where they must live to serve and glorify Him. This incident in the life of Shadrach, Meshach, and Abednego outlines the ageless tactics used by the world to seduce believers to worldliness and worldly thinking.

First, *conformity to the world is made attractive.* The issue confronting the expatriated Hebrews centered on the grand statue of gold that Nebuchadnezzar had erected of himself (Dan. 3:1).

Resting on a nine-foot base and extending ninety feet into the air, this huge image very likely only approximated how much larger than life Nebuchadnezzar saw himself.

The unveiling of the statue provided an occasion for celebration and great pomp. The crowd consisted of a "who's who" of Babylon: celebrities were invited (v. 2), and they were to lead the masses gathered from every part of the empire (v. 4). There was even a great orchestra to provide music for the official ceremony (v. 5). This was a national happening; just being there was an honor. The only price of admission was bowing to the image at the sound of the musical cue. The entire scene shows how acceptance and being a part of something can prove almost irresistibly attractive. Nobody wants to be left out.

Second, *nonconformity is made dangerous.* A furnace of burning fire situated for all to see (v. 6) supplied a powerful motive to comply with the state's demand. The smoke billowing from the furnace threatened everyone to listen carefully for the music that signaled the appropriate time to pay homage to the image. The smoke was enough to force the crowd to bow down in unison.

Without doubt, many bowed down thoughtlessly. More than likely, some bowed with less than reverential thoughts toward Nebuchadnezzar. It is always safe and easy to follow the crowd, whether we do it thoughtlessly, hypocritically, or sincerely. The crowd can tolerate insincerity but not independence, particularly when motivated by religious conviction based on biblical truth. The world tends to be intolerant of any who defy society's norms because of adherence to biblical principles. Today's consequence for nonconformity to the world may not be death in an oven, but separation from the world always entails repercussions.

Third, *nonconformity is made conspicuous.* When the note sounded, everybody there bowed except Shadrach, Meshach, and Abednego (vv. 7–8, 12). Standing alone was probably the greatest pressure of all to bend the knee like everybody else; the smoke from the furnace had to be plainly visible with no heads in the way to obscure the view. But the text gives no hint that the three had even a moment's

doubt about their decision to stand. It would have been easy to ratio-
nalize in their conspicuous solitude that they could bow down and
still please God. "If we burn in the furnace, there will be no other
witness left in Babylon. Where is Daniel, anyway?" "We probably
should bow down. After all, God has ordained human government,
and He expects us to obey those in authority over us." "Nobody
knows us here. What would it hurt?" It's not hard to imagine the
possible excuses justifying a compromise of convictions. The point is
clear enough: it is hard to stand alone.

The Believer's Courageous Faith

Courage is not a uniquely spiritual virtue, but when that courage
flows from an unwavering conviction of the unchangeable truth of
God's word and from a personal resolve to take God at His word, it
becomes a virtue that is spiritual indeed. It is an expression of faith.
This story suggests some important lessons for every Christian concerning how to walk with courageous faith.

First, *courageous faith is based on God's word.* This principle is crucial if we are going to stand well in crisis. Shadrach, Meshach, and
Abednego had enough spiritual discernment to interpret the king's
demand for what it really was. This ecumenical celebration was more
than a political rally expressing allegiance to Nebuchadnezzar. They
rightly understood the command to bow down and worship the image
to have religious overtones. Connecting it to Babylonian paganism,
they interpreted the commanded gesture as forbidden idolatry (v. 12).
Obedience to God was not optional (Ex. 20:3). Obedience is always
the necessary corollary to faith.

Second, *courageous faith operates regardless of the consequences.* The
first consequence was malicious anger. Although the entire crowd
was supposed to bow when the music sounded, somebody in the
crowd must have seen the three standing because the Chaldeans
knew what had happened. When they found out, they "accused the
Jews" (Dan. 3:8). A more literal translation of the Aramaic of verse 8
expresses something of the spiteful vehemence of the Chaldeans:
"they ate the pieces of the Jews." The ungodly hate what they do not

understand. The Babylonians could not comprehend why the Jews stood defiantly against the crowd. All they could do was interpret the behavior as strange, antisocial, and unBabylonian. Nobody enjoys being misunderstood, ridiculed, or hated. But the three Hebrews knew that God's cause was more important than personal feelings.

When Nebuchadnezzar heard, he gave the Jews the benefit of the doubt (vv. 13–18), assuming they had misunderstood. What appeared to be the king's patience was just another avenue of testing. It is a common ploy of Satan to bring into question the results of faithful obedience. So far, the only thing achieved by standing was to incite anger. Upon reevaluation, maybe defying the command was not the best course of behavior. The visible results of trusting and obeying God must not be factors. We are to trust and obey for the sake of trusting and obeying; there is no other way.

Third, *courageous faith is neither obnoxious nor presumptuous*. The three faced the consequences of their decision without arrogance toward the king and without presumption before the Lord. When confronted by Nebuchadnezzar, they respectfully acknowledged that the indictment against them was accurate and that there was no need to offer any defense (v. 16). Too often, Christians, while taking the right stand on issues, do so in such a self-righteous and arrogant manner that even other Christians who agree with them want to disassociate themselves. Being cantankerous only harms the cause. Even more outstanding was their sure confidence in God's will, even though they did not know how the divine will would come together for them. God's ability to deliver them from the king's furnace was not in doubt; they knew He could. But they did not know if He would (vv. 17–18). They were willing to risk their lives, certain that whatever happened would be the good and perfect will of God. That kind of commitment is not natural; it is the operation of faith.

God's Unfailing Purpose

One way or another, God achieves His glory and His people's good, but He doesn't always do it the way we might expect. The accomplishing of that purpose for Shadrach, Meshach, and Abednego did not mean preventing adversity: they were thrown alive into the fire (vv. 19–23). Nebuchadnezzar had become so enraged against the three that he gave orders to stoke the flames, intensifying the heat as much as possible. So hot was the furnace that the heat fatally scorched the would-be executioners. No doubt that as the three were being cast into the fire, they thought that their time was up and that they would soon be in the presence of their Lord. This bit of irony highlights the amazing nature of the rest of the story.

Although it was the will of God to place His servants in the furnace, it was not His will to leave them alone. Shadrach, Meshach, and Abednego were wrong about their time being up, but they were right about their being soon in the presence of their Lord. Although the now-dead executioners had tossed three bound men into the flames, the astonished king saw four men walking around, giving no sign of fear or pain. The fourth man really caught the king's attention, and he exclaimed, "The form of the fourth is like the Son of God" (v. 25). This statement raises two questions: Whom did Nebuchadnezzar see? Whom did Nebuchadnezzar think he saw?

Let me answer the second question first. The Aramaic expression translates literally "a son of gods." Semitic language often uses the word *son* to designate members of a class. This would mean that Nebuchadnezzar recognized the fourth individual as belonging to the class of supernatural beings, a designation that fits with his referring to the individual as an "angel" in verse 28. As a pagan, Nebuchadnezzar would not have known about the second person of the Trinity, but the sight was so glorious that even a pagan could recognize that this was someone supernatural.

Now to the first question: I believe that Nebuchadnezzar saw the second person of the Trinity in Christophany, a preincarnate appearance of the Lord Jesus Christ. Although Nebuchadnezzar saw Him, the Lord did not appear for his benefit; He was there for the comfort and encouragement of the three who had been faithful to Him in what they perceived to be their death. The Lord's presence may not always be—and usually is not—evident to the natural sight, but it is always the reality of faith. Whereas the Lord's presence with

His people is a guaranteed promise, physical deliverance from danger is not (see Heb. 11:36–38). In this incident, however, it was the Lord's will to deliver.

The Lord's deliverance was remarkable and complete. When all was done, those rescued from the fire did not even smell of smoke (Dan. 3:27). God loosed them from their bonds (v. 25), comforted them in their trial (vv. 24–25, 28), protected them from harm (v. 27), and honored them before their previous accusers, causing them to prosper (v. 30). In this instance, spectacular deliverance was the best way for God to receive glory. Proud Nebuchadnezzar was forced to admit that "there is no other God that can deliver after this sort," and he made it a crime throughout his kingdom to blaspheme this God (v. 29). What started as a solitary witness to the one true and living God by three seemingly insignificant young men in the plain of Dura spread by the decree of a pagan king to the whole realm. This is an undisputed example of God's using the wrath of man to get praise for Himself (Ps. 76:10).

41

A Story of Conversion

DANIEL 4

Daniel 4 records a striking transformation in the personal life of Nebuchadnezzar. Nebuchadnezzar was a head of state and therefore a public man. But even public figures are private souls who are individually accountable before God. I would argue that Nebuchadnezzar's transformation was more than a mere behavioral reformation or attitude adjustment; it was, rather, a spiritual conversion of his soul.

The conversion of sinners is always up close and personal; God saves sinners individually, not corporately. Even though every conversion is unique, a common pattern does operate. Nothing is of more eternal consequence than personal conversion. Nebuchadnezzar's unique testimony suggests three things common to every genuine conversion: need, divine intervention, and profession.

Before highlighting some of the truths from this story, an explanation about the order of events in chapter 4 will be helpful. The sequence is potentially confusing unless we recognize that almost the whole chapter is Nebuchadnezzar's testimony after his conversion. The chapter begins with a doxology in retrospect of what God has done (vv. 1–3). This is followed by a detailed account of the dream and Daniel's interpretation and warning to the king (vv. 4–27), which preceded his conversion. Daniel then interrupts to record the actualization of what was dreamed (vv. 28–33), and the chapter ends with Nebuchadnezzar's first-person profession of faith (vv. 34–37). With this in mind, we can discover the key lessons about conversion.

Preconversion Pride

King Nebuchadnezzar spoke: "Is not this great Babylon, that I have built for the house of the kingdom by the might of my power, and for the honour of my majesty?" (Dan. 4:30). The greatness of Babylon was undeniable. Modern archaeologists still marvel over the architectural genius and magnificence of the Babylon that Nebuchadnezzar had built. How much more its ancient residents and visitors would have been impressed with this queen of all cities. With its seemingly impregnable walls, the imposing Ishtar Gate, the grand temples, the lavish palace, and the wonder of the hanging gardens, Babylon's splendor was unrivaled. From the perspective of natural sight, Nebuchadnezzar had every reason to be proud of his accomplishments.

Nothing, however, can be concluded from natural sight alone. Daniel had made it explicitly clear to Nebuchadnezzar at the beginning of his reign that "the God of heaven hath given thee a kingdom, power, and strength, and glory" (2:37). In his conceit, Nebuchadnezzar took credit for it all.

Although Nebuchadnezzar's manifestation of pride was unique, his self-absorbing pride is the common and fatal malady of all sinners, whether prosperous or poor, achievers or nonachievers. The unchanging spiritual law is that God "resisteth the proud, and giveth grace to the humble" (1 Peter 5:5). Nebuchadnezzar stood in need of grace. Unless the Lord intervened and changed his heart, Nebuchadnezzar was headed to a tragic eternity. So it is for every sinner: divine intervention is necessary to change the otherwise certain destination.

Divine Intervention

Conversion is marked by faith toward God and repentance from sin: it is the first conscious response to the grace of God that irresistibly invades the heart, implanting spiritual life and enabling spiritual perception. The story of Nebuchadnezzar's conversion puts a face on Paul's theological propositions that "faith cometh by hearing, and hearing by the word of God" (Rom. 10:17) and that "there is no difference between the Jew and the Greek: for the same Lord over all is rich unto all that call upon him" (v. 12). The Lord graciously gave the word and governed the circumstances that led the pagan king to salvation.

First, the Lord gave the word through a dream, a common means of God's communication to sinners in that dispensation. Without spiritual life or perception, however, Nebuchadnezzar had no idea what the dream meant, only that it was troubling (Dan. 4:5). God intended grace for Nebuchadnezzar, and He insured that everything would be in place for the temporal execution of that grace. Among the reasons God had sovereignly brought Daniel to Babylon was to position the necessary preacher for the conversion of the proud king. Again Paul's inspired theology explains the means God uses to save sinners: "How then shall they call on him in whom they have not believed? and how shall they believe in him of whom they have not heard? and how shall they hear without a preacher? And how shall they preach, except they be sent?" (Rom. 10:14–15). Since God is both the author and the finisher of faith (Heb. 12:2), there is never any chance that some essential component of the means of grace will fail to achieve the purpose of grace. God controls and governs time with a view to His eternal purpose, including His purpose to save individuals, whose salvation is always to the praise of the glory of His grace (see Eph. 1:4–12).

Since God resists the proud and gives grace to the humble, He had to humble proud Nebuchadnezzar to awaken within him his need for grace. Only as sinners are brought to the end of themselves are they moved to recognize the Lord. In the dream, the Lord revealed to the king the path of humiliation, and Daniel interpreted and applied the word. Here are the salient points of the dream and their relevance. The king saw a flourishing tree, large and fruitful enough to provide sustenance for all the creatures of earth (Dan. 4:10). But then the tree was chopped down to a stump (vv. 14–15). Strangely, the stump was fettered and abandoned to the elements of nature (v. 15). And even more strangely, the stump was changed into a beast, destined to live off the grass of the field for a period of seven times (vv. 15–16).

When Daniel learned the details of the dream, he knew it was going to be a hard message to deliver, but he faithfully delivered it. He told Nebuchadnezzar that the tree represented the rise of his empire and his personal majesty (v. 22). The chopping down of the tree and the remaining stump represented God's intent to remove the exercise of sovereignty from Nebuchadnezzar personally, forcing him to live like an ox for a period of seven times, most likely seven years (vv. 23–25). Daniel made it clear that God was lowering him in order to bring him to his spiritual senses (vv. 24–26). Like any good preacher, Daniel gave the word and pressed his one-man congregation to repent while there was time: "Wherefore, O king, let my counsel be acceptable unto thee, and break off thy sins by righteousness, and thine iniquities by shewing mercy to the poor; if it may be a lengthening of thy tranquillity" (v. 27).

Second, God governed the circumstances to achieve His purpose. A year passed after the dream with no evidence of repentance. But in His own time, the Lord in mercy intervened, and Daniel 4:28 effectively sums it up: "All this came upon the king Nebuchadnezzar." At the very moment the king was bragging, a voice from heaven interrupted, and the humiliation process began. To put it simply, Nebuchadnezzar lost his mind. God drove him crazy. It seems as though the once-glorious monarch thought he was a cow, and all that his royal herdsmen could do was to tie him up in the backyard of the palace and let him do what cows do. We can only wonder how the court's "spin doctors" handled this situation for seven years. While the administration undoubtedly kept this a secret from the public, God secured the kingdom for the insane king (v. 26), but more significantly He was having His way in Nebuchadnezzar's heart. At the appropriate moment, the king lifted his "cow" eyes to heaven and realized what he never had realized before in his previously rational state: *God rules* (v. 34). The only feasible explanation for this transition from irrationality to spiritually rational understanding is the gracious intervention of God. Without such divine interference, every sinner is doomed; with it sinners are wondrously converted.

In chapter 7, Daniel represents Nebuchadnezzar and his kingdom as a winged lion whose wings were plucked and who received the heart of a man (v. 4). What Daniel visualized occurred in the event described in chapter 4. The irony is noteworthy. In vision, Daniel saw the beast humanized. In fact, the humanizing of the beast was accomplished by the bestializing of the human. The point to learn is this: when God has purposed to save a sinner, He does all that is necessary to save that sinner. In one way or another, He always works through conviction and circumstance to bring the sinner to his sense of spiritual need. His purpose never fails; God's plans always come together.

Postconversion Profession

Daniel 4 is the last record we have of Nebuchadnezzar. Exactly when his conversion occurred is impossible to date, but very probably it was toward the end of his career. Scripture does not preserve for us the details of how his life changed. It does, however, record for us his profession of faith. One of the evidences of saving grace is the ability to comprehend spiritual truth (1 Cor. 2:10–14). Again, according to Paul in Romans 10:9, one of the conditions of salvation is confessing with the mouth that Jesus is Lord. After his humiliation and spiritual awakening, Nebuchadnezzar uttered a mouth confession of unquestionable orthodoxy concerning the absolute lordship of the God of heaven (Dan. 4:34–35, 37). Daniel had expressed this truth to Nebuchadnezzar at the beginning in chapter 2, but the truth was without effect in an unresponsive heart. As a pagan and polytheist, Nebuchadnezzar was at times willing to salute Daniel's God for revealing secrets (2:47) or the God of Shadrach, Meshach, and Abednego for rescuing the young men from fire (3:29). Polytheists were quite happy to say "uncle" when somebody else's god showed some superiority. But the confession in chapter 4 goes beyond saying uncle. When God changed the heart, the truth took hold and the mouth opened in humble praise and willing submission. Nebuchadnezzar acknowledged the Most High God as the one true and living God whose sovereign authority both in heaven and on earth is eternal, incontestable, and irresistible and whose works are always right and just. That is quite a creed.

Nebuchadnezzar's conversion illustrates another dimension of God's sovereign control over men, their circumstances, and their times. On one level God used Nebuchadnezzar and his empire as an instrument in His own hand to accomplish His own purpose. Nebuchadnezzar was a key player in the big picture. On another level, God dealt with Nebuchadnezzar as an ordinary sinner in need of saving grace. God took one who was His servant in time and made him His child for eternity.

42

A Story of Condemnation

DANIEL 5

Daniel 5 chronicles the last few hours of the time allotted to Belshazzar. Its instruction regarding sin and its consequences illustrates the folly of not learning the lessons taught by God in time. Although designated "the king of the Chaldeans" (v. 30), Belshazzar was not a particularly significant figure from either the secular or the sacred perspective. For hundreds of centuries after his death, the book of Daniel was the only known record that he even existed. Archaeology has unearthed a few references that explain his coregency with Nabonidus, but even the secular records make plain his minor political status as a secondary figure who administered the affairs of the city during the frequent absences of Nabonidus. He had position without ultimate power. Living in luxury, he probably had more time on his hands than he knew what to do with. Daniel 5, however, makes it gravely clear that he didn't have as much time as he thought. But then nobody does.

The transition from the Babylonian kingdom to the Medo-Persian kingdom was an integral component in the big picture of God's redemptive plan, revealing His kingdom and leading to His Christ. This up-close-and-personal glimpse of the last moments of Belshazzar's life reveals how minutely and complexly God has orchestrated the affairs of time to accomplish all of His purposes. If I can use a familiar adage, God is well able "to kill two birds with one stone." His execution of the big plan leading to Christ included the execution of Belshazzar. Just as God's distribution of saving grace is always individually personal, so is the dispersing of His justice. If Nebuchadnezzar's personal story gives hope to sinners, Belshazzar's issues a warning—it is a story of condemnation.

A Momentary Pleasure

Belshazzar's legacy is tragic. Although Daniel uses him on two occasions simply as a calendar to date visions (7:1 and 8:1), the only information giving any insight into his character or contributions concerns a drunken celebration that ends in death. He planned a banquet and invited a thousand state officials, along with his wives and concubines (5:1–4). Since official state affairs did not normally include women, their presence indicates that this was not a time for business; it was party time. It wasn't long before the wine started flowing freely, and one thing began to lead to another. Soon the crowd was drunk, and we can only imagine the sensuous abandonment that occurred. From a worldly assessment, they were really having fun.

As so often occurs in sinful abandonment, the sins of the flesh express themselves in sacrilege against God. In his stupor, Belshazzar ordered his servants to bring in the holy vessels from the temple in Jerusalem to be used as goblets for the continued profligacy of his drunken guests. Years earlier Nebuchadnezzar had transported these gold and silver vessels from Jerusalem to Babylon as part of his spoils of victory. Archiving these religious artifacts and displaying them as the evidence of Marduk's superiority over the gods of conquered peoples were normal procedure. But profaning them was not the norm. And particularly the profaning of those items that had been consecrated to the one true and living God was a blasphemous and serious mistake. Belshazzar was so taken up by the thrill of the moment that he gave no thought to the eternal consequences of his temporal transgression. That is invariably one of the real dangers of sin. Sin serves the moment, but its pleasures are only "for a season" (Heb. 11:25). Belshazzar was having the time of his life.

A Monumental Pronouncement

Unexpectedly, the God whom Belshazzar mocked contributed to the celebration. Out of nowhere, fingers appeared, writing a cryptic message on the wall (Dan. 5:5). Although he was drunk and drunken people sometimes see things that aren't really there, Belshazzar knew all too certainly that what he saw was real. He sobered up quickly (v. 6) and brought in his advisors to decipher the handwriting on the wall (v. 7). For whatever reason, none of the wise men were able to read the message, let alone tell what it meant (v. 8). When the queen heard about the quandary, she told Belshazzar about Daniel and recounted his extraordinary display of wisdom back in the days of Nebuchadnezzar (vv. 10–12). So Belshazzar sent for Daniel and offered him a significant reward for reading and interpreting the message, including promotion to the third rank in the kingdom (v. 16). That would place Daniel right after Belshazzar, who was second after Nabonidus. Daniel most likely had already read the message and was therefore quick to turn down the offer (v. 17). Being third in line that night was not a particularly attractive place to be.

He did agree, however, to read and interpret the message to the distraught king, but not before preaching a little sermon. Daniel always insisted that the Lord's word be accompanied by application. He took as the "text" for this sermon God's sovereign and gracious dealings with Nebuchadnezzar (vv. 18–21). He recounted how God at first had given the kingdom and glory to Nebuchadnezzar and how He humiliated the king in order to bring him to the personal knowledge of truth. Nebuchadnezzar had gotten the point, but Belshazzar did not, even though he knew the story (v. 22). In spite of what he knew, he lifted up himself against the Lord, refusing to glorify "the God in whose hand" his breath was (v. 23). Belshazzar failed to learn this vital lesson from history: his times were in God's hand.

Having directed Belshazzar's attention to the absolute sovereignty of God, Daniel turned to the handwriting on the wall. Ironically, even the location of the writing may have served to emphasize the message. We know from excavations of various ancient palaces that the walls were often decorated with reliefs depicting the exploits and conquests of the regime. That the Lord wrote the message of doom over the record of triumph revealed that those temporal achievements were nothing in comparison to the more weighty issues of eternity. God's works always override man's.

The word of condemnation was brief but powerful: "MENE, MENE, TEKEL, UPHARSIN" (v. 25). I've often wondered why the wise men of Babylon could not read this when even my beginning Aramaic students have little trouble parsing and crudely translating the text: "Having been counted, having been counted, having been weighed, and having been divided." That's crude, but that's essentially what it says. After he read it, Daniel did not translate it, but he did give the grim interpretation (vv. 26–28). He interpreted the "MENE" to mean that God had numbered the days of Belshazzar's reign, and the number was up. "TEKEL" meant that God had weighed the king, and he failed to balance the scales. "PERES" (the singular form of UPHARSIN) meant that the Medes and Persians would take the kingdom. It is interesting that "MENE" and "TEKEL" are both singular forms, whereas "UPHARSIN" is plural. I think the significance of this is that the first two are directed to Belshazzar personally, whereas the last refers to the empire corporately. Once the personal words were fulfilled, what happened to the kingdom would be of no consequence to the king, but the phrasing emphasizes how all at once God addressed both the big and the little pictures of His purpose. The big picture would continue according to plan; there was still the fullness of time to come. But unhappily, in regard to Belshazzar's little place in the picture, time was about to end.

An Immediate Punishment

No time was wasted in fulfilling the wall's portent. Verse 30 ominously says it all: "In that night was Belshazzar the king of the Chaldeans slain." There is not a word here that is difficult to understand, and I can add nothing to it.

A night that started with a king's party ended with the king's departure from this world. I don't know how old Belshazzar was when he was slain, but I'm almost certain that when that night began, he had no idea it would be his last. He no doubt thought he had plenty of time left—if he thought about it at all. That is the way natural men tend to think. The psalmist described the thinking of the wicked like this: "Their inward thought is, that their houses shall continue for ever, and their dwelling places to all generations" (Ps. 49:11). Death is always something that happens to others, and somehow people can easily convince themselves that they will be the grand exception to what they see happening to others. But the Bible is explicit that it is a human thing to die (Heb. 9:27). Only God knows the date, time, and place of that appointment, but notwithstanding our ignorance of those details, it will be an appointment that we will not miss.

If Belshazzar's last night on earth teaches us anything, it is that we must take advantage of the time we have to make sure that we are right with God. Since we do not know the eternally scheduled time of our death, it is imperative that we be ready for it whenever it comes. What we do in time regarding our relationship with God fixes our place in eternity. The words to a poem whose author is now anonymous convey a most pointed message:

> Life at best is very brief,
> Like the falling of a leaf,
> Like the binding of a sheaf: Be in time.
>
> Fleeting days are telling fast
> That the die will soon be cast,
> And the fatal line be passed: Be in time.

The kind of direct, divine superintendence evidenced in the story of Belshazzar remains true. His story stands as a sobering warning of the Lord's norm in dealing with sinners who live oblivious to His law. Ecclesiastes 9:1 declares "that the righteous, and the wise…are in the hand of God." That ought to be a comfort to every believer. But it is also true for the wicked. What is a source of comfort to saints should be a source of concern for sinners to repent before it is too late. But so long as there is time, there is hope even for sinners: "For to him that is joined to all the living there is hope" (v. 4). Sinners, regardless of age, occupation, or circumstance, should heed the warning of the handwriting on the wall.

43

The Message of Hosea for Today

HOSEA 1–14

Hosea, whose name means "salvation," has been called the tenderest of the prophets, the St. John of the Old Testament. He is the prophet of love. There is more talk and less understanding about God's love than almost any other divine perfection. Most people define God's love based on their own experience. Even the Christian's love for God is generated by an attraction to God: we love Him because He first loved us. God, however, does not love because He sees something attractive in the object of His love. God loves because He is love. Christians must humbly acknowledge that they do not deserve or merit divine favor. Hosea, both by his life and by his preaching, taught vital truths about the love of God.

Hosea preached during the years immediately preceding Israel's fall to the Assyrians. The list of kings in Hosea 1:1 spans over a century, but his ministry began sometime before the death of Jeroboam II in 753 BC and ended about 725 BC after Hezekiah's ascension but prior to Samaria's fall in 722 BC. He ministered to a wicked society, overripe for divine judgment. His list of Israel's sins reads like an unabridged encyclopedia article on ungodliness. The people were lawless, unjust, rebellious, evil, and completely missed the mark of God's holy standards. To these unworthy sinners on the brink of national disaster, Hosea issued the summons to repent (6:1) and declared God's continuing love for His wayward, backsliding people. Hosea's message was of sovereign grace and love. His theme highlighted the love of God that remained constant even though scorned by Israel. God's love is constant and unchanging.

Two lines of analysis sum up Hosea's message: one was symbolic and the other directly to the point. The symbolic message was Hosea's marriage to Gomer (the focus of chapters 1–3). It was not uncommon for prophets to employ object lessons or symbolic acts as part of their preaching, but Hosea was unique in that his whole life of shame and sorrow was linked to his message. Chapter 1 records his marriage to Gomer and the birth of three children. There are differences of interpretations, but most likely Gomer was pure at the beginning of the marriage but later became defiled as she surrendered to her latent propensity to adultery. The text bears this out when it says in verses 3–4 that she bore to him a son, Jezreel ("God scatters"). That statement is missing in the birth of Lo-Ruhamah ("not pitied," v. 6) and Lo-Ammi ("not my people," v. 8), which would suggest that Hosea was not the father of these two children. This is part of the picture. Hosea's marriage to Gomer parallels God's marriage to Israel: a good beginning that turned tragic (see Jer. 2:2–3). Hosea 3:1 is the key verse of the prophecy as God instructs Hosea to love Gomer "according to the love of the LORD toward the children of Israel." Humanly speaking, Hosea's love for Gomer did not make any sense. She did not deserve it, but regardless of Gomer's sin, Hosea was faithful. But that is the point. Humanly speaking, God's love for sinners makes no sense, but He is gracious and faithful. It was easy for the people to see Hosea's grief. They were to learn that what Gomer did to Hosea they were doing to God, and what Hosea did for Gomer God does for His people. As Hosea's marriage was a symbol to Israel, Israel's marriage to the Lord is a symbol to the church. The message is indeed for today.

Chapters 4–14 record Hosea's direct message to the people. His message about God's marriage to Israel can be summed up in three points. First, *it is initiated by divine love*. In human love relationships somebody always makes the first move. So it is spiritually, and the initiator is always God. We love Him because He first loved us. The fact of God's love is expressly stated (3:1; 11:1; 14:4), and it is a love motivated totally by grace. God gave evidence of His love in three ways. First, He entered into a covenant, a pledge of everlasting loyalty (2:18–20). Second, He gave them a law, communicating to them how to please Him (8:12). Third, He gave them a land, a picture of rest and fellowship in His presence (2:8–12). What God did for Israel is typical of what He does for individuals. Believers must recognize that in Christ they are the object of God's love, entirely of grace. Every good is a token of His love.

Second, *God's love was spurned by sin.* The response to God's love should have been humble gratitude and loving obedience. Hosea 6:6 declares what God desired: mercy and knowledge of Himself rather than religious offerings. But contrary to His desire, the nation "transgressed" and "dealt treacherously" (a word often used for the violation of marriage vows, 6:7). Hosea 4:1 sums up God's accusations against the people with three charges. *There was no truth.* They were unreliable and untrustworthy in fulfilling their obligations to God. *There was no mercy.* The covenant loyalty that should have been constant was temporary and unsubstantial. *There was no knowledge.* There was no apprehension of the truth about God and no experience of a personal relationship with Him. The many references throughout the book to their breaking the law and their preference for Baal testify to the widespread ignorance of God and His law. They rebelled against authority (8:1) and regarded God's law as loathsome and repugnant (v. 12). Their spiritual adultery was linked to ignorance of God (5:4), and that ignorance earned judgment (4:6). The lesson is obvious. If ignorance of God was the essence of the problem, knowing God is the solution to spiritual problems. That was true then and is true now.

The third point in Hosea's sermon is that *God's love was maintained by loyalty.* Israel was bent on backsliding (11:7), but God remained faithful (v. 8). Three thoughts sum up this point. First, discipline is the evidence of loyalty. Sin had inescapable consequences (8:7; 9:7, 9; 10:13), but the purpose of discipline was not destruction but to awaken spiritual concerns and pursuits (5:15). Second, restoration is the goal of loyalty. God's plan to restore had three steps. He would isolate them, putting a hedge around them until they recognized God's superiority over Baal (2:6–7). He impoverished them in order for them to learn to depend on Him completely (vv. 9–12). He enticed them, alluring and persuading them irresistibly with love (vv. 14–23). Third, repentance is the proper response to loyalty. There were no shortcuts to repentance, but there was a way back home (6:1–3; 14:1–3). There is hope for the backslider that God has left open the door to home. Other prophets admonished sinners to turn because certain judgment was ahead. Hosea admonished sinners to turn because God was behind them.

The closing verse of Hosea settles the issue of the book's relevance for today (14:9). It is wise to understand what Hosea says. It is instructive and encouraging to know that there is a way to God open to those so undeserving. This is the gospel.

44

The Message of Joel for Today

JOEL 1–3

Although Joel did not directly date his prophecy, the circumstantial evidence points to the ninth century BC—during either the illegal renegade rule of Queen Athaliah or the early days of the boy-king Joash, who had providentially escaped Athaliah's deadly plot against the royal seed (2 Kings 11–12). The days were dark, both politically and spiritually. There seemed to be little prospect for hope, but not even wicked Athaliah could frustrate God's purpose and plan. The Lord raised up the prophet Joel to provide the theological interpretation of all the tragic events of the day and to announce details of God's fixed plans for the future. Joel 1 describes an invasion of an innumerable army of ravenous locusts that devastated the country with severe economic and religious consequences. It was the cause of consternation, deprivation, and perplexity. Although the particular circumstances are not the same now as then, the situation of our day is not much different from Joel's. Our day is marked by darkness, chaos, and uncertainty—politically, religiously, economically, socially, environmentally. Joel's message to his generation is equally relevant to ours. Just substitute "coronavirus" for "locusts."

Joel made it clear that what to the natural eye seemed to be a natural disaster—the locust plague—was in reality a manifestation of the day of the Lord. Disasters happen regularly according to the laws of nature and direction of providence, and they were particularly common and predictable in Palestine. But this locust plague was different: as a day of the Lord, it was literally a shattering from Shaddai (1:15). Shaddai, normally the title of God associated with provision, was now revealed as the God who purposefully took all provisions away. God had directly, supernaturally, unmistakably intervened in human affairs to accomplish His purpose of judgment against the nation's sin. Eternity had broken into time. The locusts, palmerworms, cankerworms, and caterpillars were dedicated and obedient soldiers under the command of the Lord Himself. Joel declared that God had not only punished but that He would punish again with even greater severity and devastation unless the people repented. Using both the past (chapter 1) and future day of the Lord (chapter 2) as the incentive, the prophet issued two great calls for repentance (1:13–14; 2:12–17). Turning to the Lord was the only hope, but it was a real hope because God does not turn away those who turn to Him.

The invitations in Joel 1 focused on the external manifestations of repentance: putting on sackcloth and fasting. Sackcloth was coarse material from either goat or camel hair that would be extremely uncomfortable. Fasting was an occasion to put aside physical concerns and pursuits to devote attention to spiritual matters. The focus of fasting was not to deprive or punish the body but to afflict the soul (Lev. 16:29). Sadly, without heart devotion to the Lord, man can turn the best of religious practices to nothing more than outward acts. The call to repentance in Joel 2 does not exclude the appropriate outward displays, but it does underscore the importance of inward reality: "Turn ye even to me with all your heart, and with fasting, and with weeping, and with mourning: and rend your heart, and not your garments, and turn unto the LORD your God" (2:12–13). *Turning* is the key word in the Old Testament for evangelical repentance, picturing a complete reversal of direction. It is a turning away from sin to God, resulting in new attitudes and a change of perspective. True repentance is a matter of the *heart*, the principal word for the inner being: mind, emotion, and will. Intellectually, heart repentance requires a change in thought about God, acknowledging sin's offense against His holiness. Emotionally, it expresses itself in contrition over sin, and volitionally, it involves the resolution to flee to God in apprehension of His mercy. God does not despise this kind of broken and contrite heart. The external evidences of repentance will accompany (weeping, mourning, fasting), but it is imperative to "rend" the heart and not just the garments.

Not only does Joel expose sin, declare judgment, and call to repentance, he gives assurance of God's mercy that guarantees acceptance. Joel 2:13 is a remarkable catalog of divine perfections that give hope to the hopeless. He is gracious—that objective and sovereign display of divine favor to those undeserving. He is merciful—that subjective display of compassion to those in a pitiable state along with the necessary action to alleviate the condition. He is slow to anger—literally, "long of nostrils," a figure picturing His patience and long-suffering, without which none would be saved. He is of great kindness—His faithful loyalty to His covenant oath that guarantees His word to receive all those who come to Him. He relents concerning judgment—His pledge to deal in mercy and not in wrath to those who repent. If God were not who He is, there would be no hope. Joel preached a God of hope to a people who seemed to be too far gone for hope.

After Joel described the locust judgment, predicted a more severe one to come, and issued a call to repentance, he detailed the blessings that God purposed for His people. The blessing was threefold: an immediate temporal restoration of what the locust had eaten (2:21–27), a later spiritual blessing fulfilled on the day of Pentecost (vv. 28–32; see Acts 2:16–21), a yet later blessing involving judgment on every enemy and special favor on God's people (chapter 3). The unifying principle of each is that the experience of restoration and blessing is available to God's people whenever they repent and seek Him. God has a purpose to advance His kingdom that cannot be frustrated. The immediate blessing of restoration was marked by prosperity, praise, and experience of God's presence (2:26–27). The prospect of such a revival should incite the church today to seek the Lord. God was able to reverse the devastation caused by the locusts;

He is able to reverse the darkness of our day as well. Joel teaches us that it is not a vain thing to seek the Lord in genuine repentance.

The two later blessings are reminders that God has a purpose for His kingdom that is unconditionally certain. Pentecost commenced a key epoch in the progression of redemption with the massive effusion of spiritual power available to all in the church to serve in kingdom work. Whereas in the Old Testament spiritual empowering was limited to the leadership, in the New Testament era every believer has access to the empowering of the Holy Spirit. Joel's prophecy regarding Pentecost makes his message especially relevant to the ministry of the church today.

Joel's final prophecy in chapter 3 remains future for the church and thus most relevant. It is a solemn reminder to sinners that they must repent before it is too late. Those multitudes in the valley of decision (v. 14) are in the place of no return; the judgment has been decreed. But the day of judgment on the wicked is also a day of deliverance for God's people (vv. 18–21). It is a timeless and universal truth that there is safety, security, and salvation with the Lord and doom without Him. That is what Joel preached, and it is a message for the church today.

45

The Requirements of True Religion

MICAH 6:8

Micah 6:8 records one of Scripture's classic declarations of God's definition of true religion: "He hath shewed thee, O man, what is good; and what doth the LORD require of thee, but to do justly, and to love mercy, and to walk humbly with thy God?" A contemporary with Isaiah, Micah preached both when apostasy was at its nadir under King Ahaz and when religious reform was at its peak under King Hezekiah. During both extremes, religion in one form or another dominated life and in many ways blinded people to the problem of sin. Religious people are often the hardest to convict of sin because they assume that what they are doing is what God wants. In order to prove that these religious people were not right with God, the inspired prophet summoned them to court. With irrefutable evidence, he proved that their religion did not satisfy God's spiritual demands and that rather than appeasing or distracting God with their ritual, they merited His just punishment. Though this court session concerned ancient Israel, the issues are universal and timeless.

Verse 8 is the heart of God's refutation of Israel's religious self-defense. With penetrating precision, the Lord makes it clear that they had no excuse because what He regarded as acceptable and what He demanded was a matter of record: "He hath shewed thee, O man." The word translated "shewed" means to report or announce by putting something conspicuously in front of someone. Not only had God told them what He wanted but He had told them clearly in unmistakable terms. They had no excuse for not knowing, and neither do we.

Three summary expressions demonstrate the elements of true religion by showing that genuine piety encompasses all of human life and duty, both to God and to man. Although salvation begins on the inside and shows itself on the outside, this statement reverses the order: outward, inward, and upward. The logic is clear: failure to behave properly toward other people destroys the legitimacy of any profession of being right with God. Outward behavior is an index to the heart.

Outward

The first requirement is *doing justice*. Although this term occurs in judicial contexts referring to a legal decision, claim, or suit, it also has a social or ethical sense, focusing on the fulfilling of or conformity to legal requirements. Moses set clear demands concerning responsibilities and obligations to others (e.g., Deut. 24:17–22). The prophets clearly identified justice as fulfilling these legal and social demands "between a man and his neighbour" (Jer. 7:5). Isaiah 1:17 defined "justice" as relieving the oppressed, defending the orphans, and pleading for widows. Christ confirmed this unchanging demand when He summarized the law and prophets by saying "all things whatsoever ye would that men should do to you, do ye even so to them" (Matt. 7:12).

Similarly, the Savior's synopsis of the two greatest commandments affirms the necessary link between a right relationship with God and people: love God totally and love neighbor as self (Mark 12:29–31). The apostolic definition of pure religion in terms of caring for orphans and widows (James 1:27) further reveals that this divine requirement is something that continues to be conspicuously set before people. Social justice is not the essence of saving faith, but it is an evidence of it. The gospel cannot be defined in terms of social welfare, but disregard for and mistreatment of our fellow human beings is incongruous to true spiritual religion.

Inward

The second requirement is *loving mercy*. More than an emotional expression of affection, the verb "love" means to set or incline the will toward the chosen object. God demands that genuine religion be marked by a will bent to mercy. Any exercise of the will involves the heart; thus, this second requirement moves away from outward displays to inner motives. Best rendered "loyalty," the word "mercy" is uniquely associated with the covenant and often involves reciprocity. That God faithfully demonstrates His everlasting loyalty to His people is a constant and frequent theme of the Old Testament (e.g., Psalm 136). The focus here, however, is on the loyalty that the Lord expects from the heart of His people. Though this word may find expression in acts of kindness to others, it includes much more. An attitude that produces appropriate action, "mercy" sums up the motive and duty of true religion. In simple terms, the only loyalty that a person can render God is obedience. Comparing 1 Samuel 15:22 and Hosea 6:6 justifies this conclusion. Whereas Samuel's pointed rebuke to Saul was "to obey is better than sacrifice," Hosea conveyed God's statement "I desired mercy, and not sacrifice."

On the one hand, loyalty to God, expressed by obedience, takes precedence over mere acts of religion. Religion without heart is idolatry, an abomination. Obeying God's commandments, on the other hand, is evidence of true love for Him: "If ye love me, keep my commandments" (John 14:15). A sincere heart that is bent to observe loyalty will gladly perform every duty God specifies, whether social or religious. It would do well for us to remember Christ's words to the Pharisees: "Go ye and learn what that meaneth, I will have mercy" (Matt. 9:13).

Upward

The third requirement is *walking humbly with God*. Walking is a frequent image that refers to customs, habits, or way of life. The word "humbly" occurs only here in the Old Testament and has the idea of living cautiously or carefully. This cautious lifestyle is in the presence of the Lord (cf. Eph. 5:15, 17—"walk circumspectly...understanding what the will of the Lord is"). The message is clear. True religion is not a historic decision without consequent effect on life nor an occasional act of goodness performed with faith. True religion consists in a whole life lived in awareness of God. To walk aware of God, who is unseen, is to walk by faith. It is this submissive faith that is required of any and all who would please Him (Heb. 11:6). This demand is foundational. If this requirement is satisfied, the other two will inevitably follow. It is this submissive faith that yields the evidences of grace. It is not surprising and not without significance that Christ exposed the hypocrisy of the Pharisees by accusing them of omitting the most important matters of the law: "judgment, mercy, and faith" (Matt. 23:23). In essence, Christ referred to Micah 6:8. What condemned the Jews of Micah's day condemned the Pharisees of Christ's day. Indeed, the requirements of true religion never change.

Scripture is explicitly clear that God has never been nor will ever be satisfied with external religion or empty profession without a true heart of faith on the inside that authenticates itself by true holiness on the outside. True religion links belief and behavior. We must remember that what happened to Israel happened for our example and for our admonition. The New Testament's repetition of the same divine requirements for true heart religion highlights the need for constant application to the church. That Micah uses the court scene as the literary means to make his point to Israel reminds us of the coming day of judgment when all hearts will be open and naked before the eyes of Him to whom we have to give account. The judgment on that day will be infallible, and the verdict will be eternal. It behooves us all "to do justly, and to love mercy, and to walk humbly with [our] God."

The Song of Majesty

NAHUM 1:2–7

Nahum, a much-ignored prophet, records one of the grandest descriptions of God in all Scripture. Nahum, whose name means "compassion" or "consolation," reveals God in terms of His justice, power, and goodness, artfully and theologically intertwining the message of judgment and grace. His message of consolation to Israel was that God would judge Nineveh, a great and bloody city, a city full of lies and robberies, a city whose savagery was proverbial both in Scripture and in its own records. A century earlier, the city was spared because the people had repented at the preaching of Jonah, but now judgment would fall on a new generation whose gross iniquities would find no pardon. It was inevitable.

Nahum's oracle against Nineveh is timeless because God always deals with sinners and saints the same way. Sinners of every age and place must learn not to trifle with God, and saints of every age and place must learn to rest secure in divine grace and goodness. Nahum's warning to sinners in the seventh century BC of the terrible vengeance of God points every sinner to repent and to find God's infinite goodness that secures every saint. This song of majesty highlights three truths about God that are compelling reasons for repentance and rejoicing.

God's Justice Is Inflexible
Without partiality, God gives to all sinners their due. His character

demands it, and sinners deserve it. In verse 2, Nahum underscores four aspects of God's character that render the sinner's punishment necessary. First, God is jealous. This does not imply that God is given to petty suspicions, but that He demands total loyalty and exclusive allegiance and worship. Divine jealousy refers to the Lord's fervent and hot zeal for His own glory, for truth, and for His people. He will not share His glory with another and is intolerant of any competing allegiance (see Ex. 34:14; Deut. 4:24).

Second, God is an avenger. The word "revenge" (also translated "take vengeance") occurs three times, binding the verse together. God's wrath is the consequence of and demonstration of His jealousy. The verbal forms express the habitual consistency of this divine behavior. Ironically, the word for vengeance differs in only one letter from Nahum's name meaning "comfort." Comfort gives way to condemnation. This vengeance is not capricious or whimsical; it flows not out of temper but out of nature. It is not vindictiveness or malice but His righteous demand of justice.

Third, God is furious, literally, "master of wrath." The idiom means that God is good at executing wrath. Just and terrible are His judgments. There is no wrath like divine wrath; there is no fury like divine fury. It stands as a warning not to take God lightly or dismiss His law.

Fourth, God is a watcher (translated "he reserveth"). He observes or keeps watch over; nothing escapes His omniscience. He sees all; He knows all. Consequently, His judgments are infallible (see Heb. 4:13). Sinners must be warned that it is a fearful thing to fall into the hands of such a fearful and justly angry God.

Inflexible justice is served as sinners get what they deserve. Nahum describes the objects of God's wrath as enemies (literally, "haters") and adversaries, those who are His foes. The terms speak of both the objective state of alienation from God and the subjective display of hostility toward God. By nature they are children of wrath; by behavior they are children of disobedience. Significantly, the terms express a mutual hostility. Neither side is passive, but one side is helpless, as God will put all His enemies under His feet. This is a sobering word that God will not in any way "acquit the wicked" (Nahum 1:3). His justice is inflexible, and there is nothing more fearful than to get from God exactly what is deserved.

God's Power Is Irresistible

God's power is in focus in verses 3–6 and is summed up declaratively in the explicit statement that He is "great in power." Nahum explains this divine power from three perspectives. First, God's power is tempered by patience. Verse 3 begins with the statement that "the LORD is slow to anger," or more literally, "long of nostrils." This is a frequent image for patience and longsuffering, the idea being that it takes a long time for the Lord's nose to become red or hot. This bold and graphic anthropomorphism suggests that the Lord's anger does not flare up unreasonably or uncontrollably. Most significant is its link to God's power. Human vengeance always reckons from the vantage of potential weakness; it must be swift so that the opposition does not somehow get the upper hand. But divine vengeance delays not out of weakness but out of strength. If God were less powerful, He would be less patient. Because He is omnipotent, there is no threat or possibility that the enemy could ever gain an advantage. God can be as patient as He is because He is as powerful as He is.

Second, God's power is proven by providence. Nahum focuses on God's rule over natural creation to illustrate His control over the spiritual. The Lord governs the heavens, the air, and the sky. These are beyond human control but reveal evidence of divine movement, as even the clouds are the dust of His feet. He controls the seas and rivers, setting their shores and altering their course at will. Things that are uncontrollable by human beings are the servants of God. Most likely, this alludes to the Red Sea and the Jordan, which dried up according to His word. The Lord also governs the earth. The prophet mentions Bashan, Carmel, and Lebanon, places noted for their fertility, as evidence that God can remove their prosperity as easily as He gave it. The mountains, symbolic of what is most stable, must quake at God's presence. Certainly if God has power and authority to govern all creation, there is no person who can withstand Him. That's the next point.

Third, God's power is executed in His judgment. The questions of verse 6 answer themselves: "Who can stand before his indignation? and who can abide in the fierceness of his anger?" If the majestic mountains melt before Him, how can puny man stand? Psalm 1:5 explicitly declares that the ungodly will not be able to stand in the day of judgment. Sinners will have no defense, no excuse, no ground on which to stand. God's judgment will issue forth like the fire and brimstone that fell on Sodom and Gomorrah and like molten lava flowing irresistibly from an erupting volcano, destroying everything in its path. Sinners must be warned to flee the wrath to come. But that raises the question: Where can sinners go?

God's Goodness Is Immense

Ironically, hope for salvation is found in the source of the wrath. It is impossible to outrun God's wrath, so the alternative is to run to Him. He is as powerful in grace as He is in justice. Nahum's assertion, "The LORD is good" (v. 7) echoes the psalmist: "For thou, Lord, art good, and ready to forgive; and plenteous in mercy unto all them that call upon thee" (Ps. 86:5). That says it all!

Two specific thoughts in Nahum 1:7 expound on God's gracious benevolence to His people. First, it is effective. The Lord is the place of safety for His people. He is a refuge or stronghold that is accessible to those in trouble and a secure fortress that is impregnable from any threat of calamity. To be safe in the arms of Jesus, who is the security for salvation, is to be out of the reach of hostile danger and most significantly to be out of reach of the wrath of God that will be let loose against sinners outside of Christ.

Second, God's gracious goodness is infallible: "He knoweth them that trust in him" (v. 7). The word "trust" has the idea of finding refuge and security. It is one of the principal words for faith in the Old Testament and is most fitting to describe the confident sense of security belonging to those who seek and find their refuge in the Lord Himself, the only sure stronghold. Nahum parallels Paul, who said,

"Nevertheless the foundation of God standeth sure, having this seal, The Lord knoweth them that are his" (2 Tim. 2:19). He knows His people collectively and individually, evidenced in His thorough, efficient care, concern, and special interest. Indeed, how immeasurably great is the goodness of God!

Nahum's song in praise of God's majesty serves an evangelistic purpose by warning sinners to see the terror of divine justice and to flee to Christ. There will be no mistakes on the day of judgment, a day that is certain to come. Zephaniah offers a fitting conclusion and application to Nahum's song: "Seek ye the LORD.... It may be ye shall be hid in the day of the LORD's anger" (Zeph. 2:3).

47

The God of Then Is the God of Now

ZECHARIAH 2:1–5

The transition from one year to the next is a time for special reflection about where we are, where we have been, and where we are going. There are always reasons for praise and thanksgiving in remembrance of what the Lord has done; there are usually regrets for personal failures. There is always the resolve not to fail again and the expectancy that the Lord will do even greater things in the days ahead. But too often in our assessment, we tend to be discouraged when things are not what we think they should be.

Though not at the threshold of a new year, the population of Judah that returned to Jerusalem after the Babylonian exile was at the threshold of a new day. They had returned to the land in obedience. They were where they were supposed to be, but nothing was right. The city was in ruins and the temple lay in shambles. They were not experiencing the expected blessing they assumed would accompany their return to the promised land. Ezra records some of the discouragements and oppositions faced by the people. In His goodness, God raised up Zechariah, the prophet of hope, to address the discouragement factor. Significantly, Zechariah's name means "Jehovah remembers"; that is something God's people should never forget. Zechariah encouraged the people and motivated them to kingdom service by directing their attention to God's unfailing purpose and plan for them. Aspects of the plan involved the distant future, but the timing of the promise was irrelevant to the fact of it.

The hope was certain. God transcends time, whether past or future, so what we can learn about the God of then is always applicable to now because He changes not.

We need to learn from Zechariah's word of hope to the post-exilic inhabitants of Jerusalem that God's purpose for His people is greater than their expectations. That was true then; it is true now.

Zechariah 2 is the third in a series of eight night visions that the Lord gave the prophet addressing the whole glorious scope and sequence of His purpose and plan. In this vision, Zechariah sees a man with a measuring line who is about to measure Jerusalem and teaches three wonderful truths for consideration: first, God's purpose for His people is greater than expectations (vv. 1–5); second, God's protection of His people gives confidence for duty (vv. 6–9); and third, God's presence with His people is reason for joy (vv. 10–13). In this meditation, we are going to think especially on the first truth for encouragement as we learn the principal lesson of the vision that Paul sums up in the amazing words of Ephesians 3:20: God is "able to do exceeding abundantly above all that we ask or think."

Faith's Expectations Are Great

The mission of the man with the measuring line was to mark the borders of Jerusalem to identify the "city limits." The mission itself was no small demonstration of faith, for in a very real sense there was nothing to measure. As far as the eye could see, the city was in total ruin. The rubble of walls demolished in the Babylonian destruction cluttered the ground, and the once-glorious temple lay in ruins. The evidences of past sins and failures were overwhelmingly obvious. Sight saw nothing but devastation, but faith was able to look beyond the debris to envision a restored city. This was not just wishful thinking but an expression of faith in God's promise. Jeremiah had recorded God's hopeful words prior to the exile: "I know the thoughts that I think toward you, saith the LORD, thoughts of peace, and not of evil, to give you an expected end" (Jer. 29:11). Part of those divinely peaceful thoughts was God's good word that the Jews would return to this place (vv. 10–14). Measuring the city limits was in essence claiming the promise that God would again be jealous for His people and return to them in mercy (Zech. 1:14–16). It is always good and proper to act according to God's promises.

Yet to measure is to mark borders, to set limits. Faith expresses the confidence that God will keep His word, but sometimes sight interferes and interjects a bit of caution lest we believe too much. So often the weakness of faith is evident in its exercise. There is always a risk of believing too much lest we become disappointed when what we perceive to be the way God should work does not look like our notions. This is where the man with the measuring line was, and it is where so many Christians today tend to be as well. We know and believe what God has said, yet sometimes our reason is clouded by perception and experience that somehow prevent us from claiming all the riches we have in Christ or praying for things "too big." We believe; it should be our prayer that God will help our unbelief.

God's Purpose Is Greater

In his vision Zechariah sees an angel that approaches the man with the measuring line and essentially instructs him to stop measuring the city. Measuring the city then was premature because "Jerusalem shall be inhabited as towns without walls" (v. 4). To mark the city limits was impossible because in God's plan there would be no walls to mark the borders. Here is the remarkable lesson: God's purpose transcends our limitations to grasp it, and measuring the fullness of God's blessing is impossible. That was true in Zechariah's day; it is true in our day as well.

The text gives two reasons for the prohibition to stop trying to measure the city walls. In the ancient world, walls served two purposes: to mark territory and to provide defense. The two explanations address both of these purposes. First, there will be no walls to measure because the population of the city cannot be contained ("the multitude of men and cattle therein," v. 4). Years earlier, Isaiah gave the same instruction: "Enlarge the place of thy tent…for thou shalt break forth on the right hand and on the left; and thy seed shall inherit the Gentiles" (Isa. 54:2–3). In the same passage, the

Lord says, "For a small moment have I forsaken thee; but with great mercies will I gather thee" (v. 7). In God's purpose of grace, citizenship in His kingdom extends to and includes people from every race on earth (see Rev. 7:9). With this explanation, the Lord directs attention away from the physical city to that spiritual city and kingdom of far greater importance than brick and mortar. It points to the unrelenting advance of Christ's church.

Second, there will be no wall to measure because God's presence provides inviolable security: "I…will be unto her a wall of fire round about, and will be the glory in the midst of her" (Zech. 2:5). Later on, Zechariah describes a scene of peace where those who are most susceptible to danger (the young and the old) are in the most dangerous places (the city streets) but are safe and secure because the Lord is "returned unto Zion, and will dwell in the midst of Jerusalem" (8:2–5). It appears to be a peace that is too marvelous for human comprehension, but it is not anything extraordinary to God (v. 6). His presence makes the difference, and if God be for His people then none can be against them (Rom. 8:31)—at least, not in a way that really matters.

So as we anticipate what the next while is going to bring our way, we should be encouraged by Zechariah's vision, which is as relevant to us in the twenty-first century AD as it was to those in the sixth century BC. The God of then is the God of now. It is good to know that God's people in every age are part of His unfailing plan of grace. Let us be bold to ask of Him great things regarding our work in His kingdom, knowing and believing that He is able to do far more than we can ask or even think. Let us put away the measuring line.

48

A Picture Worth a Soul

ZECHARIAH 3

Three months after his call to be a prophet, Zechariah received a comprehensive revelation concerning the people and kingdom of God. It came in a series of visions that seemed to occur in uninterrupted procession in a single night. In these visions, God overviewed His redemptive plan and purpose from the immediate temporal context to the distant future. The first three visions specifically set before the people the hope of national deliverance and prosperity, a hope that was certain and authenticated by the word of the Lord. Yet the spiritually minded, particularly, would have been conscious that their personal holiness did not merit such grandiose promises. And they would have been correct. The basis of favor was not in their merits; the basis was God's grace. So the fourth vision narrows from national to individual focus and addresses the very personal issue of salvation from sin.

The principal scene of this fourth vision centers on Joshua the high priest. Since the high priest was the paramount representative of the people of God, we must see him here not only in terms of the individual but also in terms of his office. Therefore, what is true of Joshua is true for every justified sinner. That is the ultimate point of the vision as it symbolically pictures the gospel truth of free and gracious justification.

As we meditate on this vision, keep in mind the classic Reformed and biblically precise definition of justification in the Westminster

Shorter Catechism 33: "Justification is an act of God's free grace, wherein he pardoneth all our sins, and accepteth us as righteous in his sight, only for the righteousness of Christ imputed to us, and received by faith alone." This vision is instructive to teach sinners what must be done if they are to be plucked from the burning (Zech. 3:2); it is instructive to saints to remind them that none can lay anything to the charge of God's elect because it is God who justifies (Rom. 8:33). Four essential components of justification are pictured in the vision. They say that a picture is worth a thousand words; whom may or may not be true, but here is a picture that is worth a soul.

The Need for Justification

The need for justification is great. The passage begins with a judicial scene in which Joshua, the accused, is standing before the Angel of the Lord (a reference to Christ), the judge, and is being accused by Satan, the prosecutor. "Satan" literally means the accuser or adversary and is a noun form of the verb translated here "to resist." In other words, Satan was being Satan, or the accuser was accusing. He is the great adversary who accuses God to us (Gen. 3:1–5) and us to God (see Job 1:6–12; 2:1–7).

The specific accusation against Joshua is not recorded but can be inferred from how Joshua is dressed (Zech. 3:3). It is an accurate picture of how all people on their own stand before God. He stands silently before the judge, dressed in detestably filthy garments with no self-defense. The language is graphic in describing the garments as heinously detestable and disgusting, fouled by excrement and vomit. The sight is not pretty, but it vividly pictures how people appear before God in all the filthy rags of their own righteousness; it is a true and accurate picture of the sinner's moral pollution.

Because of unrighteousness, all human beings are guilty before the just God. That part of Satan's accusation was true because people have no inherent right to stand before God and to be accepted on their own merit. Joshua's vile condition cries for something to be done. It requires a free justification just as Paul argues: because all have sinned, God must justify freely or there could be no justification (see the logic of Rom. 3:23–24).

The Act of Justification

The act of justification is gracious. Joshua was silent; he offered no self-defense; he was guilty as charged. But the vision highlights the beauty of the gospel in that God does for people what they cannot do for themselves. Seemingly out of the blue, God rebukes Satan and rescues Joshua as a brand plucked from the burning. Joshua was fit for destruction but delivered by grace and was accepted before the Lord and allowed to stand in His presence. The accuser was swept away; he had no power to condemn the one that God accepts (see Rom. 8:31–39).

The text highlights two essential elements of that acceptance. First, the Lord graciously pardoned sin. This is pictured by the removal of the filthy garments and explained directly: "I have caused thine iniquity to pass from thee" (Zech. 3:4). The guilt and therefore the liability for punishment and penalty were removed. But taking away the filthy garments alone would result only in nakedness before God and the susceptibility to foul things up again. Something positive had to be done.

Second, the Lord provided righteousness. Not only were the filthy garments removed but they were replaced with costly and glorious clothes. The "fair mitre" (v. 5) refers to the headdress of the high priest inscribed with the engraving, "HOLINESS TO THE LORD" (Ex. 28:36). The filth was replaced by radiating holiness, without which no person can see God. This represents that robe of righteousness, the garment of salvation (Isa. 61:10), which renders the wearer presentable before the Lord.

In justification God both pardons sin and imputes the righteousness of Christ. Significantly, as this transaction was taking place, "the angel of the LORD stood by" (Zech. 3:5). This is part of the vivid picture and suggests the important role Christ has in sinners' legal defense. His constant "standing by" as the representative and the advocate for His people provides assurance of continuing acceptance before the Lord. What Zechariah saw in vision is not much different from what John forthrightly declared: "And if any man sin, we have an advocate with the Father, Jesus Christ the righteous: and he is the propitiation for our sins" (1 John 2:1–2).

The Ground of Justification

The ground of justification is solid. God's pardoning of sinners is gracious, but it is not capricious. This brings us to the Branch (Zech. 3:8). By Zechariah's time (sixth century BC), "branch" was part of official and inspired messianic vocabulary. Given the antecedent revelation through Isaiah and Jeremiah, Zechariah knew well that the Branch was the God-man who is so vital in the context of this picture of justification. It is the Lord's sending the Branch that would be the meritorious grounds by which He justifies sinners. That the Branch is called the Servant, charged particularly with all Isaiah's Servant theology, speaks of His humble obedience in life and to death. I would suggest the reference to iniquity's being removed in one day (v. 9) points to His cross, the only place where iniquity was effectively removed. Christ's perfect life (His active obedience) and His effectual death (His passive obedience) are the only meritorious ground for salvation.

The Demand of Justification

The demand of justification is logical. Zechariah makes it clear that a change in legal standing demands a change in moral behavior. A change in standing demands a change in walking. Justification always issues in sanctification; position always affects experience. Grace never leaves anyone where it finds them. Those justified are to persevere in godliness by walking in God's ways (a manner of life conforming to God's law), keeping His charge (obedience and fidelity to God's ordinances), and maintaining justice (Zech. 3:7). They are to be like Christ; they are to imitate and represent Him. Zechariah described Joshua and his fellows as "men wondered at" (v. 8). Literally, they were "men of a sign" who were to be types of something else; they were to signify the Branch. So it is that every justified sinner is to be like Christ, to be conformed to His image.

The vision begins with a picture of despair coming from a condemning heart that too often hears the accusations of the accuser, and it ends with the assurance and hope that God will remove every obstacle to blessing for His people, even the sin that separates them from Him (Isa. 59:2). The vision illustrates John's declaration that "if our heart condemn us, God is greater than our heart" (1 John 3:20). Rather than being abandoned to the fire (Zech. 3:2), God's people are as a stone on which are seven eyes (v. 9). Opinions differ as to what this means, but I would suggest that the stone represents the Lord's people, His kingdom, on or toward which He directs His seven eyes, a symbol of His omniscience and consequent protecting care.

They will also enjoy, because of the work of the Branch, peace and prosperity. This is the point of the symbolism in verse 10 of calling every man neighbor (peace) and residing under the vine and fig tree (prosperity). God has the answers to all our concerns, both corporate and individual. What He has promised that seems to be too good to be true is not. His providing the means for salvation from sin by the Branch assures that everything else He has promised is sure. Paul put it this way: "He that spared not his own Son, but delivered him up for us all, how shall he not with him also freely give us all things?" (Rom. 8:32).

In symbolic vision, Zechariah has painted a picture with words vividly portraying the wonder of the gospel truth of justification. The theology is profound, yet the picture is simple and clear. Indeed, it is a picture worth a soul. As you look at the picture, be sure to get the point.

49

What's in a Name?

ZECHARIAH 10:4

The names of God are more than simply labels; they are means by which God reveals something about His person, His perfections, and His work. They both identify and describe. And what is true about the names of God generally is true about the names of Christ specifically. The Old Testament contains many names and titles of Christ that draw attention to a particular aspect of His person or His work. The use of these special titles for Messiah was an effective way for advancing knowledge about Him in the Old Testament dispensation and for teaching us about Christ in this dispensation because He is the same yesterday, today, and forever. So if we can find the titles of Christ in the Old Testament, we have found Him and we will learn important lessons about Him.

The book of Zechariah is one of the most intensely and explicitly messianic of all the prophets. We could indeed well refer to the book as the Gospel according to Zechariah. There is hardly an essential truth about Christ's person or work not addressed in this little prophecy. Zechariah 10:4 is one of those key messianic texts that identifies Christ, and it does so with a series of descriptive terms. These are common nouns or expressions used for personal designation. The technical term for this is an *appellative*, a common noun used as a descriptive name, like referring to your minister as pastor. Because they are common nouns, they may not always be immediately recognizable, but they are always instructive.

"Out of him came forth the corner, out of him the nail, out of him the battle bow, out of him every oppressor together." The person described in Zechariah 10:4 is God's answer to the bad shepherds (rulers) who had troubled the flock of His people (vv. 2–3). The Lord of hosts would visit His people and reverse their fortunes. The agent by whom the bad shepherds would be punished and the flock blessed is the corner, the nail, the battle bow, and the absolute ruler. The statement "out of him" or, more literally, "from him" (the Lord) precedes each of these four titles, suggesting the divine anointing and commission of the Messiah to conduct His ministry.

Corner

That Christ is the Corner testifies to His being the sure and stable foundation. This same word occurs in Isaiah's more extensive description: "Behold, I lay in Zion for a foundation a stone, a tried stone, a precious *corner* stone, a sure foundation: he that believeth shall not make haste" (Isa. 28:16, emphasis added). Likewise, it is the word in Psalm 118:22: "The stone which the builders refused is become the head stone of the *corner*" (emphasis added). The New Testament demands the Christological interpretation (see Matt. 21:42; Acts 4:11; 1 Peter 2:4–8). In contrast to the vain and worthless objects of trust mentioned in Zechariah 10:2 (idols, diviners, dreamers), from the Lord would come the Corner, the only trustworthy object for faith. That was true then, and it is true now. The object of faith determines the value of faith, and the only object of saving faith is Christ.

Nail

That Christ is the Nail testifies to His ability to bear the load in supporting His people. This nail is a peg in the wall for hanging items. Unless the peg is solid, it will be useless for hanging anything. Ezekiel plays on this thought when he says that the "wood" of a vine would be a worthless pin for hanging vessels (Ezek. 15:3). Isaiah's report of Eliakim's promotion to administer the keys to David's house illustrates this function of the nail: "And I will fasten him as a nail in a sure place…. And they shall hang upon him all the glory [weight] of his father's house" (Isa. 22:23–24). Sadly, Eliakim's nail loosened and the burden hanging on it fell off (v. 25). This failure of what seemed to be a sure support points to the fact that there is only one Nail that is strong enough and sure enough to hold any burden. That unfailing Nail is Christ. In contrast to the bad shepherds who took advantage of and increased the burden of the people, the Lord would fix an immovable Nail that would hold up under any weight and load. It is good to know that not only did Christ bear the load of our guilt and sin but that He is ever able to bear the load of our troubles and cares. We can hang it all on Him.

Battle Bow

That Christ is the Battle Bow testifies to His being the active champion and warrior for His people. This highlights that aspect of His mediatorial kingship in which He subdues and conquers all of His and our enemies. The psalmist speaks of the same activity in that great royal and messianic Psalm 45: "Thine arrows are sharp in the heart of the king's enemies; whereby the people fall under thee" (v. 5). This kingly behavior is on the surface of the Zechariah text. It is this divinely sent Battle Bow who will execute God's anger against the bad shepherds and punish the goats. Certainly the final manifestation of this warrior King will come when He rides in on that white horse with a sharp sword in His mouth to smite the nations (Rev. 19:12–15). In the meantime, Christ is the able and unfailing defender of His people.

Absolute Ruler

That Christ is the Absolute Ruler testifies to His certain sovereignty. The translation of this last line is notoriously difficult. The word the King James Version translates as "oppressor" is the word I am focusing on when I say that Christ is the Absolute Ruler. There is no question that the word designates a ruler, and many occurrences of the word in the Old Testament refer to hard taskmasters or slave drivers who would use any means to force their subjects into compliance. This explains the translation "oppressor." But I would suggest that the word itself simply defines one who has ultimate authority over another. The character of the ruler determines whether his rule is cruel and oppressive. The parallelism with the other three expressions demands that this title refer to the same person. Therefore, the Ruler with absolute authority over His subjects is Christ. His rule is not oppressive, but it is absolute nonetheless. This is a most fitting designation of Christ in the immediate context. The people knew well the oppression of the bad shepherds (rulers). What a relief it would be to know the kind despotism of the Messiah King. Submitting to the absolute authority of Christ is always a relief; moreover, it is the wise thing to do. He will rule either by grace or by the rod of iron. The advice of Psalm 2 is appropriate in view of this absolute rule of Christ: "Kiss the Son, lest he be angry, and ye perish from the way, when his wrath is kindled but a little. Blessed are all they that put their trust in him" (v. 12). If He is the Absolute Ruler, it is best to be a citizen rather than an enemy of His kingdom. That was true then; it is true now.

So what's in a name? When the name belongs to Jesus, it is what we need to know for life. It is the only name "whereby we must be saved" (Acts 4:12) and before which every knee will bow (Phil. 2:10).

50

The Branch

ZECHARIAH 3:8; 6:12

The Old Testament prophets, in whom was the Spirit of Christ, "testified beforehand the sufferings of Christ, and the glory that should follow" (1 Peter 1:11). Christ Himself said, "Search the scriptures.... They are they which testify of me" (John 5:39). In another place the Lord declared that Moses, the Prophets, and the Psalms all spoke concerning Him (Luke 24:44). These passages highlight Jesus Christ as the great theme of the Bible. Both the Old and the New Testaments reveal God's Anointed One as the only Redeemer of sinners. Both Testaments reveal this Christ to be very God, possessing the divine nature and all of its perfections. Both Testaments reveal the Messiah to be truly man, derived by generation from the stock of Adam and the root of David. What people know about Jesus Christ they know from the Word of God. To miss the message of Christ in the Scriptures is to miss the most important revelation God has made to humanity.

True to Christ's stated purpose of Scripture, the prophet Zechariah contributes to God's unfolding revelation of the Savior. Zechariah, the great prophet of hope, ministered to Israel after the years of Babylonian exile. He directed attention to messianic times, marking aspects of both the first and second advents. Most significant are the titles that Zechariah used to highlight truths concerning the person and the work of the Christ. Each of these titles in one way or another unveils some facet of Christ's work of salvation and

His mediatory work as prophet, priest, and king. Because "Jesus Christ [is] the same yesterday, and to day, and for ever" (Heb. 13:8), these Old Testament revelations are just as relevant today as when first given. It is as true in the twenty-first century AD as in the sixth to fifth centuries BC that Jesus Christ is the sinner's only hope. In this study I want to focus on Christ as the ideal Priest.

In Zechariah 3:8 and 6:12, the prophet used the term "branch" to designate the Messiah. The messianic significance of this title had been established long before Zechariah, first by Isaiah (Isa. 4:2) and then by Jeremiah (Jer. 23:5; 33:15). Whereas Isaiah associated the term with Messiah's deity and Jeremiah with His sovereignty, Zechariah underscored an aspect of the title that was latent in his predecessors' messages as well. He used the title to stress Messiah's humanity. The imagery pictured by the word "branch" readily suggests the Messiah's human nature. Referring to a sprig or a new growth rather than a large bough, the word implies the Messiah's human lineage from the family of David. Although the Davidic throne was at that time empty and seemingly defunct, a new sprout would one day appear, fulfilling God's unconditional promise that "David shall never want a man to sit upon the throne of the house of Israel" (Jer. 33:17; see 2 Sam. 7:16). Zechariah took this term inherently connected to the Davidic promise of an ideal King and linked it to the priesthood. This linking of kingship with priesthood testified to Zechariah's understanding of the term's messianic significance. In both chapters 3 and 6, the prophet used the title Branch in the context of Joshua the high priest.

The Serving Priest

In Zechariah 3:8 God declared, "Behold, I will bring forth my servant the BRANCH." Significantly, this messianic proclamation immediately followed Zechariah's vision of Joshua's symbolic justification. Joshua in his official role as high priest stood as the people's representative before the Lord. Although the description of his filthy condition applied to his own status, it was illustrative of the condition of all God's people. The divinely ordered removal of the foul garments and their replacement with costly, royal attire graphically depicts God's gracious forgiveness of His people's sins and His clothing them with the garments of salvation, the robes of righteousness (vv. 4–5). God's declaration of forgiveness and gracious provision of a righteous standing is the only way that sinners can hope to stand accepted before the Lord. Zechariah's vision of Joshua's transformation makes it clear that people do nothing to earn or merit their acceptance before God. Throughout the whole transaction, Joshua remained silent. He offered no self-defense against the accusations of Satan. Apart from God's gracious pronouncement, human beings would remain filthy and unacceptable. Justification is indeed an act of God's free grace.

Free justification does not mean, however, that God deals capriciously with people's sin. Paul makes it explicitly clear that this justification is "through the redemption that is in Christ Jesus: whom God hath set forth to be a propitiation through faith in his blood" (Rom. 3:24–25). Zechariah 3 parallels Romans 3:26 in teaching that God is both "just" and the "justifier" on the basis of the person and work of Jesus Christ. Zechariah's revelation of God's servant, the Branch, sums up this vital message. Throughout the Old Testament the term "servant" is an honorific title attributed to those who enjoyed an intimate relationship with God. Isaiah, Zechariah's predecessor, raised this title to ideal messianic significance, demonstrating the elect Servant's unique association with the Lord and His faithful obedience in life and death (see Isaiah 42; 49; 50; 52–53). It is imperative to understand the continuity in God's revelation of Messiah. So theologically significant was Isaiah's revelation of the Servant that it becomes impossible to interpret later instances of the term without reference to that definition. Even the classic New Testament passage identifying Christ as servant links the concepts of exalted status with humble and absolute obedience (Phil. 2:5–11).

Though not expressly detailed, these ideas of honor and humble obedience are not far from the surface in Zechariah's revelation of the servant Branch. It is the righteous work of the Branch that constitutes the basis for God's justifying the guilty Joshua. By His obedience in life, the Branch earned the righteousness that was symbolized by the rich garments. By His obedience in death, the Branch merited the ground for forgiveness. The reference in Zechariah 3:9 to the removal of iniquity in one day can refer prophetically only to the atoning work of Christ. If anything is crystal clear in Scripture, it is that "without shedding of blood is no remission" (Heb. 9:22; see also Lev. 17:11). Although Zechariah does not provide the details of the Branch's life and death that only the incarnation could provide, he applies the theology of it with Pauline precision. He makes it perfectly clear that this servant Priest is the sinner's only hope.

The Ruling Priest

After the final of Zechariah's eight visions, he conducted a divinely directed object lesson involving Joshua. At the prophet's command, representatives from the captivity took silver and gold, formed a magnificent crown (note the plural of excellence, "crowns"), and placed it on Joshua's head (Zech. 6:10–11). That this coronation had significance beyond Joshua is clear from the declaration, "Behold the man whose name is The BRANCH" (v. 12). The accomplishments of this Man-Branch exceed anything that the contemporary Joshua could possibly or legitimately do. This one would be a King-Priest sitting and ruling from His throne (v. 13). Since the founding of the Aaronic priesthood and Davidic kingship, the union of these two offices was reserved for the coming Messiah, and no merely human officer from either division could usurp the authority of the other. It was part of messianic theology that David's Lord would be "a priest for ever after the order of Melchizedek," that mysterious king of righteousness and peace who was a "priest of the most high God" (Ps. 110:1, 4; Gen. 14:18, respectively). Joshua's symbolic crowning was an encouraging reminder that God's unconditional promise of a King-Priest was certain, although the ruins of a fallen temple and empty throne suggested otherwise. Even after the token ceremony was finished, the splendid crown was to remain in the soon-to-be-finished temple as a continuing memorial that the rightful King-Priest would be this temple's consummate glory (Zech. 6:13–14; see Hag. 2:7).

The theological implications of the ruling Priest are far-reaching. The day will come when the serving Priest who removed iniquity in a day will "appear the second time without sin unto salvation" (Heb. 9:28). In that day Messiah will wear the royal crown for all to see; however, that public crowning day is not the commencement of His priestly reign. He now ever lives and sits on the throne at the Father's right hand exercising His ruling and interceding priesthood in His heavenly mediation for His people. Whereas the serving Priest of Zechariah 3 concerns the humiliation of Christ, this ruling Priest focuses on Christ's exaltation. The deep humiliation was the way to earned glory (see Heb. 2:9). In His exalted session at God's right hand, the Man-Branch, knowing the infirmities of His brethren, sympathizes and effectively intercedes for them without failure. If the serving Priest was the sinner's only hope, the ruling Priest is the saint's certain hope.

51

Zechariah's Revelation of Christ

ZECHARIAH 9:9

In His office as the Christ, the anointed and only Mediator between God and men, Jesus fulfills His commission as prophet, priest, and king. Each of these office functions is essential to His saving work in behalf of His people. It is not surprising that these operations are constant themes throughout both the Old and New Testaments. In our last meditation, we gave attention to how the prophet Zechariah described the priestly work. In this study, our attention is on the kingly work of Christ.

Zechariah 9:9 stands as one of the most famous of the messianic prophecies in this book, rich in messianic revelations. In this oracle Zechariah encourages hope by pointing to the coming ideal King. The theology of mediatory kingship is profound. As king, Christ subdues His people to Himself, rules and defends them, and restrains and finally conquers every enemy. The authority of any human king is limited by the boundaries of his kingdom and the duration of his life. But unlike human kings, there are no geographical or temporal boundaries of Christ's mediatory rule. His kingdom is universal and everlasting, including the days of His earthly life.

Both the context of Zechariah 9 and the New Testament application of verse 9 place this revelation during the temporal framework of the Messiah's first advent. Zechariah sets the promise against the backdrop of a prophecy concerning Greece's world conquests and God's defeat of Greece. Significantly, in this prophetic revelation about Greece, Zechariah announces the coming King. The contribution that Greece made culturally and linguistically to the fullness of time has received much deserved attention. Though the details of those contributions are not enumerated in this prophecy, it is nonetheless impressive that Zechariah places Messiah's coming in this general time frame. The New Testament specifically identifies the fulfillment of Zechariah 9:9 as the triumphal entry of Christ into Jerusalem at the beginning of what became the week of His passion (see Matt. 21:5; John 12:15). No place is the absolute sovereignty of Christ more evident than in His victorious death and resurrection. Indeed, it is King Jesus who will rule with the iron rod from David's throne; it is King Jesus who came to conquer His people's chief enemies, sin and death. Zechariah's description of this ideal King justifies his command to Zion to rejoice and shout.

The Promised King

Zechariah's announcement "Behold, thy King cometh unto thee" went to the heart of the divine promise to David. Israel had long expected the promised, ideal King from David's royal line. There had been many kings, some good and some bad, but even the best had fallen short of the anticipated ideal. When Zechariah preached, there was no king at all. To the physical eye, being without a king meant there was no hope for a king. The prophet of hope, however, aimed the spiritual eye of faith beyond the empty throne to the sure promise. In the original language, the suffix on "king" removes any doubt that this sovereign was the anticipated fulfillment of God's oath. Although Christ's coming would have national—indeed worldwide—relevance, it had personal significance to each believer. This is the One for whom they had been waiting. For their advantage and good, their King was coming to them. The prospect of seeing the King well warranted the prophet's admonition for Zion and Jerusalem to rejoice. Although both of the imperatives have the idea of shrieking loudly, one with joy and the other in triumphant victory, they express the inner celebration as well as any outward evidence. Nothing can bring greater joy to a saint's heart than the personal

Christ. Whether in the postexilic then or in the present now, the believing sight of Christ satisfies the most discouraged of hearts. "For all the promises of God in him are yea, and in him Amen, unto the glory of God by us" (2 Cor. 1:20).

The Righteous King

Zechariah marked as one of the characteristics of the promised King that "he is just." Not only is Christ eternally and perfectly righteous by virtue of His deity, He was animated with righteousness throughout the days of His incarnation and will forever execute righteousness in His royal authority. It was part of the messianic hope that the Davidic king would judge the people with righteousness and that righteousness would flourish in his days (see Ps. 72:2, 7). Righteousness will mark the kingdom reign of Christ, but since this verse applies directly to Messiah's first advent, this perfection designates that positive and active obedience that Christ fulfilled during His earthly life. He came to fulfill all righteousness (Matt. 3:15). He did no violence, there was no deceit in His mouth, and He loved uprightness and hated iniquity. In every way He satisfied the expectations and demands of the ideal King. This sovereign did not nor could He ever fail.

The Victorious King

The coming King is "having salvation." The significance of this statement is disputed. The Masoretic text uses a form of the verb "to save" that has either a passive idea of "being saved or delivered" or a sense of "being victorious." The Septuagint and other ancient versions suggest the active sense of "one who saves"—a Savior. Although either the active or passive accurately applies to the messianic king, the Masoretic reading is preferable, that He will be *delivered*. That God's King is the object of divine help and deliverance is a recurring theme both in messianic prophecy and in the earthly experience of Christ. Psalm 18:50 explicitly declared, "Great deliverance giveth he to his king; and sheweth mercy to his anointed" (literally, Messiah; see also Pss. 20:6; 21:1, 4–5; 22:8). Throughout His incarnation

Christ realized the protecting hand of God. From His deliverance as an infant from the treacherous plot of Herod to His preservation in Gethsemane from Satan's last attempt to prevent the cross, God saved the King from premature death. The greatest deliverance of all was that demonstration of divine power that raised Christ from the death into which He had entered voluntarily and sacrificially. His deliverance marked His victory over every enemy and His ability and right to subdue every foe. His deliverance guarantees the salvation of all His people. Because He lives, His people live. Because He has been delivered, He is victorious, and He delivers and saves His people.

The Humble King

Zechariah finally describes the coming King as being "lowly." The pattern of the Hebrew noun translated "lowly" often has a passive significance. Consequently, this term meaning "afflicted" or "oppressed" encompasses not only the Messiah's poverty and meekness of spirit but the whole of His suffering life. Zechariah's use of this word closely parallels Isaiah's revelation of the Suffering Servant as being void of majesty, despised, rejected, laden with griefs and sorrows, and wounded because of the sins of His people (Isa. 53:2–5). Although He was the King, in His first earthly appearance only the eye of faith could discern His royalty. That the eyes of unbelief failed to see His kingship condemns the blindness of sinners' hearts; it does not alter the truth that Christ came as the King of kings.

Messiah's "riding upon an ass, and upon a colt the foal of an ass" further defines His humble obedience (note that in the Hebrew, the second phrase is explanatory, further describing the ass, and does not mean there were two animals). The significance of this statement is not that the donkey was a lowly creature in contrast to the stately horse. Indeed, both the Old Testament and documents from the ancient Near East demonstrate that donkeys were often mounts for royalty and rulers (see Judg. 5:10; 10:4; 12:14; 2 Sam. 16:1–2). The significance rests, rather, in the fact that the Old Testament associated horses, war machines, with self-reliance and distrust of

God (see Pss. 20:7; 33:16–17; Isa. 33:1). If anything characterized Messiah's first coming, it was His faithful, unwavering dependence on God. Furthermore, God's initial instructions concerning kings prohibited them from multiplying horses (Deut. 17:16). It would be aberrant for the ideal King, who was righteous in every other way, to associate Himself with that which marked disobedience. Even in the detail of the donkey, Christ fulfilled all righteousness.

52

The Sacrifice of the Shepherd

ZECHARIAH 13:7

In many ways, Zechariah ranks as one of the most specific and explicit of messianic prophecies in all the Old Testament. As he directs attention to the coming Christ, most remarkable is his focus on the mediatorial functions of Christ as the ideal Prophet, Priest, and King. Focusing on God's redemptive purpose to reverse the curse in and through Christ was the key to fostering and rekindling hope in a people who in so many ways had given up hope in the face of the discouragements of the day. To see Christ is to see the heart of God's promise and to be assured of every other word, for all the promises of God are yea and amen in Christ (2 Cor. 1:20).

Westminster Shorter Catechism 24 succinctly defines how Christ carries out the prophetic office: "Christ executeth the office of a prophet, in revealing to us, by His word and Spirit, the will of God for our salvation." Speaking of the Lord Jesus in prophetic terms, Hebrews declares that God spoke in various ways through the prophets but has now revealed His final word to man by His Son, "whom he hath appointed heir of all things" (1:1–2). That sums up the message of hope, for without that ultimate word, salvation would be impossible. The New Testament makes this truth clear, and so does Zechariah. In this meditation I will look at a text that among other truths explicitly declares the deity of the Messiah, the essential requirement of His ideal, mediatorial prophethood.

Zechariah 13:7 marks a transition from the deception of false
prophets to the person and work of the true Prophet. It is an important text because of both its identification of the Messiah and its
statement of His sacrificial death: "Awake, O sword, against my
shepherd, and against the man that is my fellow, saith the LORD
of hosts: smite the shepherd, and the sheep shall be scattered." In
particular, this verse makes two great statements that highlight the
deity of Messiah.

But before I address those statements, I should comment on why
the transition from false to true occurs at verse 7 and not at verse 6.
It is a hermeneutical error to miss seeing Christ where He is in the
Old Testament text; it is also an error to see Him where He is not.
Unquestionably, the reference about the wounds in the hands that
were inflicted in the house of friends in verse 6 is redolent of Christ's
being nailed to the cross at the relentless urging of His own people.
But surface similarity is not the primary factor in the interpretive
process and certainly cannot override the context. In context, the
question "What are these wounds in thine hands?" is directed to a
false prophet who, along with his counterparts, had fallen into disfa-
vor and was under the threat of the death sentence if and when caught
(vv. 2–3). Even though they tried to disguise themselves (vv. 4–5),
one of them had something exposed, the wounds in his hands, which
raised suspicion, potentially giving him away as a false prophet. The
Hebrew text refers literally to wounds "between the hands," not in
the hands. This is an idiom referring to the back or chest area, that
body surface often the target of self-mutilation as a pagan means of
invoking deity (see 1 Kings 18:28, where the prophets of Baal muti-
lated themselves). So it is not likely that the words of a false prophet
bearing the marks of his trade are prophetic of the nail prints in the
hands of Jesus.

Although not in verse 6, Christ is wonderfully and unmistakably
the focus of verse 7. What makes verse 7 such a remarkable statement is that the speaker is the Lord of hosts. The Lord first addresses
the Messiah as "my shepherd." The messianic significance of this title
occurs as early as Genesis 49:24. The "shepherd, the stone of Israel"

would come from the mighty God of Jacob. The use of the title "shepherd" was common in the ancient world. Based on the obvious pastoral imagery, the appellative was frequently employed even by pagan kings to designate their authoritative rule. The title refers to sovereign kingship and thus points to Christ's being the mediatorial King. But there is an aspect of the shepherd theology that affirms the deity of the ideal Shepherd, which is why I'm suggesting it communicates something about His being the ideal Prophet as well.

Zechariah expresses the deity of the Messiah when he records that the Lord of hosts identifies His shepherd as "the man that is my fellow" (v. 7). The word "man" often designates man in his strength, referring to a hero figure. The word comes from the same root in Isaiah 9:6, the classic messianic text listing titles that describe the character of Immanuel. Isaiah identified the son to be born as the mighty God. This literally says "God, the defender/guardian." The term God (*El*) applies only to deity and designates God in His power and transcendent majesty. The term "defender/guardian" (the root occurring in Zechariah 13:7) is not uniquely a divine word, but Scripture does apply it to the Lord, identifying Him as the security of His people. Isaiah uses the same expression in referring directly to Jehovah, the Holy One of Israel (Isa. 10:20–21). Years later but still antecedent to Zechariah, Jeremiah used the expression as he addressed the Lord in prayer: "the Great, the Mighty God, the LORD of hosts, is his name" (Jer. 32:18). Many years earlier Moses declared, "For the LORD your God is God of gods, and Lord of lords, a great God, a mighty" (Deut. 10:17). That this title became part of messianic vocabulary and theology is clear from Psalm 45, an unmistakably messianic psalm. Verse 3 entreats the Messiah, "Gird thy sword upon thy thigh, O most mighty." So by the time Zechariah used this term "man" (the mighty one) to refer to the Lord's shepherd, it was well charged with messianic import pointing to the Messiah's deity.

Also of consequence is the word "fellow." This word occurs only here and in Leviticus. Usually translated "neighbor" in Leviticus, it refers to those who have things in common such as laws and

privileges. It would be inappropriate for God in the context of Zechariah to apply this term to a mere mortal. This one, God's associate
or nearest one, stands not only in proximity to God but is equal with
God. He participates and shares in the divine nature; He is God.
So the Lord's referring to His shepherd as His fellow conforms to
Trinitarian theology that Christ and the Father are distinct in person yet one in essence.

Zechariah hints elsewhere that he understood this unique relationship. In 11:4–14 the rejected shepherd (against whom the sword
is summoned in 13:7) is Jehovah. In 12:10 Jehovah says, "They shall
look upon *me* whom they have pierced, and they shall mourn for
him" (emphasis added). The shift in pronouns from the first to the
third person testifies to the distinctive association.

That God would send His perfect representative, His Son, was
the great message of hope. I would not be at all surprised if Zechariah 13:7 was in Christ's mind when in the New Testament chapter
on the Good Shepherd He declared, "I and my Father are one"
(John 10:30). Christ Jesus is the ideal Prophet because He is God. I
can't say that too often, and there's no limit to how strongly we must
believe it.

The Lord Jesus qualifies as the ideal Prophet not only by virtue
of who He is but also by what He does. As the Westminster Shorter
Catechism 24 explains, the function of the prophet is to "[reveal]…
by his word and Spirit, the will of God for our salvation." Christ's
execution of this function is unique and distinct from every lesser
prophet since He Himself is the way of salvation that He reveals and
declares (John 14:6). Consequently, it is not unexpected to see united
into a single context facets of each of Christ's mediatorial works.

This certainly is the case in Zechariah 13:7. I have focused particularly on the prophetic component in terms of what is revealed
concerning Christ's divine nature. But that He is designated as
shepherd speaks directly to His kingship since this is a common
title for sovereigns. The text is also important because of its statement of the Messiah's sacrificial death—which points directly to
His mediatorial priesthood. Interestingly, Jesus not only links this

passage directly to the events of His crucifixion (Matt. 26:31), He also marks another parallel to Zechariah's prophecy when He says, "I am the good shepherd: the good shepherd giveth his life for the sheep" (John 10:11).

God's way of salvation required the sacrifice of the shepherd, the "fellow" of God. Zechariah 13:7 squelches any notion that the Messiah's death was anything other than the eternal purpose of God. The verse begins with Jehovah of hosts commanding the sword to awake and smite His shepherd. That God demanded the death of His equal (fellow) speaks volumes concerning the seriousness of sin and the immutability of divine justice. In Pauline language, it is only by and because of the death of Christ that God is both just and justifier (Rom. 3:26). In Zechariah's terms, it is only because God bade the sword awake against His shepherd that a cleansing fountain could be opened "for sin and for uncleanness" (Zech. 13:1).